Contents

CW01502015

Edward I's Regent

Edward I's Regent

Edmund of Cornwall, The Man Behind England's Greatest King

Michael Ray

PEN & SWORD
HISTORY

First published in Great Britain in 2022 by
Pen & Sword History
An imprint of
Pen & Sword Books Ltd
Yorkshire – Philadelphia

ISBN 978 1 39909 354 5

Typeset by Mac Style
Printed and bound in the UK by CPI Group (UK) Ltd,
Croydon, CR0 4YY.

Pen & Sword Books Limited incorporates the imprints of Atlas,
Archaeology, Aviation, Discovery, Family History, Fiction, History,
Maritime, Military, Military Classics, Politics, Select, Transport,
True Crime, Air World, Frontline Publishing, Leo Cooper, Remember
When, Seaforth Publishing, The Praetorian Press, Wharncliffe
Local History, Wharncliffe Transport, Wharncliffe True Crime
and White Owl.

For a complete list of Pen & Sword titles please contact

PEN & SWORD BOOKS LIMITED
47 Church Street, Barnsley, South Yorkshire, S70 2AS, England
E-mail: enquiries@pen-and-sword.co.uk
Website: www.pen-and-sword.co.uk

Or

PEN AND SWORD BOOKS
1950 Lawrence Rd, Havertown, PA 19083, USA
E-mail: Uspen-and-sword@casematepublishers.com
Website: www.penandswordbooks.com

For my grandsons, Lorcan and Torin Ray

Preface

E dmund of Almain was the son of Richard, Earl of Cornwall, the second son of King John and the brother of Henry III. Richard was a dominant figure in England during Henry's reign but he was also a player on the European stage, being elected King of the Romans. When he died in 1272, just before the accession of Edward I, Edmund succeeded him both as earl and as the richest man in the kingdom. He was such for almost the whole of the reign of his cousin, King Edward I. The position of magnates during the reign of Edward I was very different from those of Henry III. This was due to the strong character of the new King, bad memories of civil unrest, and the responsible actions of the earls including Edmund.

Earlier historians have had little interest in Edmund. It is over eighty years since a detailed study was made of the life of Edmund; this was Mary Midgley's 1930 Manchester University MA thesis, 'Edmund, Earl of Cornwall and his place in history'. To this day it remains unpublished and, from the note attached to the front of the University of London's copy, it appears to have been read by only three people in the last forty years. Midgley summarised Edmund's life in her edition of his Ministers' Accounts published by the Camden Society in 1942–45. In 1995, Mark Page's doctoral thesis, 'Royal and Comital Government and the Local Community in Thirteenth-Century Cornwall', dealt with Edmund as part of his study of Cornwall in that century. Nicholas Vincent produced an excellent summary of Edmund's life for the *Oxford Dictionary of National Biography* but the format of the dictionary constrains its length.

In 1883, Emily Holt published her *Not for Him, The Story of a Forgotten Hero*. Holt (1836–1893) was a writer of forty-five historical novels and religious tracts. She lived in Oxford but she was educated at home by a governess. Her later writings indicate that she was well-read, especially in history and literature.[1] In writing the story of Clarice le Theyn, Holt had as her real hero Earl Edmund, a kind, humorous and compassionate man who was blighted by his love for his wife, the glacial, overly-religious and spiteful Margaret de Clare. Edmund 'not only felt for the lower animals – a rare yet occasional state of mind in the thirteenth century – but went further and compassionated the villeins.' He had 'decidedly intelligent grey eyes' and his only physical defect was his bushy eyebrows. In Holt's eyes, Edmund was lifted to hero status because of his patronage of the Bonhommes whom the anti-Roman Catholic Holt saw as the bringers of the Protestant faith to England.[2] Although she made mistakes, she knew much about Edmund's life, including his divorce, and she used the divorce settlement documents which were not published until twelve years after her book.[3]

So why the lack of in,terest in a man of such potential importance? One answer is that Edmund's achievements did not match his inherited advantages. He had not expected to succeed his father and only became earl in the year after his older half-brother and the heir, Henry, was murdered. With the exception of Edmund of Lancaster, Edmund of Almain was closer in blood to the King than all the other earls including the Bigod Earl of Norfolk and the Clare Earl of Gloucester. On his mother's side, Edmund's aunts were all queens: Margaret of France, Eleanor of England and Beatrice of Naples and Sicily. His father's sister was Simon de Montfort's wife. Edmund accompanied his father on his visits to Germany where Richard was King. As the youngest known participant, Edmund survived the battle of Lewes. There followed a period of over a year in prison. Then came a journey to North Africa on the Lord Edward's crusade. Following the murder of his half-brother and the death of his father, Edmund became the richest man in the kingdom. He used his great wealth to support his cousin, Edward I, and acted loyally for him throughout his reign including a three-year term as Regent. Edmund was faced by a serious Welsh rebellion which he put down successfully.

Often at court, Edmund was in close contact with all the great men of the kingdom. He was able to lend them, and the King, large sums of money. By his marriage to the daughter of the Earl of Gloucester, Edmund was related to one of the greatest comital families of England but the marriage floundered. This brought him acrimony and trauma. Edmund had a well-deserved contemporary reputation for piety and was the most generous patron of religious houses of his time; he was a personal friend of one future saint and a promoter of the cause of others. He introduced the order of Bonhommes and brought the prestigious Holy Blood relic to England. His foundation of Rewley Abbey in Oxford, as a place of study for Cistercian monks, makes him one of the University's earliest supporters. As a patron of the arts, Edmund rebuilt the fire-damaged Hailes Abbey in Gloucestershire in the latest architectural style and commissioned the production of illuminated books, jewellery and clerical vestments. With lands spread across the country from Yorkshire to Cornwall, Edmund was in touch with men of differing local communities. His tenants represented a cross-section of English baronial, knightly and gentry families.

We are fortunate that documents associated with Edmund's life and activities have survived because, when he died in 1300, his earldom and lands went to his cousin, the King. Thus these documents were moved to, and kept with, the governmental records. This allows us to use valuable individual sources such as Edmund's cartulary and the accounts prepared for his estates, particularly those which cover most of his lands for the period 1296–7. These documents are now in The National Archives together with many of the results of extensive *Inquisitions post mortem* which were held following his death. Governmental and church records enable the gradual breakdown of Edmund's marriage to be traced.

Tables

Acknowledgements

This work would have been impossible without the generous support of a number of individuals. I hope that I have recalled them all and I apologise to any that I fail to thank below. Professor David Carpenter, who first taught me medieval history and supervised my thesis, encouraged me at the start and throughout this project. Professor Nicholas Vincent kindly shared his work on the charters of Edmund of Cornwall. Dr Mark Page gave me a copy of his 1995 Oxford D.Phil. thesis. Dr Andrew Spencer saved me hours of work on basic records relating to Edmund by passing over information that he garnered whilst working on his PhD thesis on the earls of Edward I. The late and much-missed Dr Lesley Boatwright gave me advice, especially on the Buckinghamshire Eyre of 1286, and helped with the translation of Edmund's epitaph. Professor Paul Brand answered my queries on legal matters promptly and fully. Dr Emma Cavell gave me a number of King's Bench and Common Pleas references concerning Edmund. Encouragement and assistance came from Drs Paul Dryburgh and Hazel Gray. Dr Adrian Jobson gave me a copy of the originals of Edmund's cartulary and discovered Edmund's nurse. Dr John Maddicott gave me sound advice throughout the work on the book and especially over publication. Dr Samantha Letters satisfied my curiosity about Ruislip whilst Professor Louise Wilkinson discussed Edmund's marriage to Margaret de Clare with me. Dr Marc Morris gave me his Oxford D.Phil. thesis on the Bigods and offered other helpful hints. Dr Henry Summerson filled in the details about the London Eyre of 1321 and Dr Jane Winters on the forests. Mick Thompson, Gardens and Archives Manager, Ashridge College, showed me around the magnificent nineteenth-century gothic building and provided me with books and images about Edmund of Cornwall's foundation which the present building replaced.

I am pleased to record my gratitude to Darren Baker for pointing me towards Pen and Sword and to Dr Danna Messer, Claire Hopkins and Laura Hirst of Pen and Sword for all their assistance with the publication. I am very grateful to Darren Baker for preparing the index.

Above all, I have to thank my wife, Yvonne, for her continuing support, advice and assistance. She has been helping me throughout my academic life and through three theses and a dissertation. This is the last major work for which I have needed her strength. My children, Louise and Andrew, have been constant in their encouragement. This book is dedicated to my grandsons.

Michael Ray
Patcham, Brighton, Sussex
January 2022

List of Abbreviations

Anglo-Norman Families   Loyd, L.C., *The Origins of Some Anglo-Norman Families*,
Harleian Society, ciii (Leeds, 1951)

Annals of Hailes   Blount, M.N., 'A Critical Edition of the Annals of Hailes', MA
thesis, University of Manchester (1974)

Antient Kalendars   *Antient Kalendars and Inventories of the Treasury of His Majesty's
Exchequer*, ed. F.Palgrave (1836)

Aspilogia   *Aspilogia III: Rolls of Arms of Edward I 1272–1307*, volume ii, ed.
G.J.Brault (1997)

Bolton Cartulary   'The Lost Cartulary of Bolton Priory', ed. K.J. Legg, Yorkshire
Archaeological Society, clx, 2008 (2009)

Boarstall Cartulary   'The Boarstall Cartulary', ed. H.E. Salter, Oxford Historical
Society, lxxxviii (1930)

Bronescombe Register   'The Register of Walter Bronescombe, Bishop of Exeter 1258–80', ed.
O.F.Robinson, Canterbury and York Society, lxxxii, lxxxvii and
xciv (1995–2003)

*Bronescombe Register
(H-R)*   'The Registers of Walter Bronescombe (A.D. 1257–1280), and Peter
Quivil (A.D. 1280–1291), Bishops of Exeter: With Some Records of
the Episcopate of Bishop Thomas de Bytton (A.D. 1292–1307); also
the Taxation of Pope Nicholas IV, A.D. 1291 (Diocese of Exeter)'*, ed.
Rev. F.C. Hingeston-Randolph (1889)

Byland Cartulary   'The Cartulary of Byland Abbey', ed. J. Burton, Surtees Society,
ccviii (2004)

CACW   *Calendar of Ancient Correspondence Concerning Wales*, ed. J.G.
Edwards (Cardiff, 1935)

Cam, *Hundred Rolls*   Cam, H.M, *The Hundred and the Hundred Rolls: An Outline of
Local Government Medieval England* (1930)

CChR   *Calendar of the Charter Rolls Preserved in the Public Record Office*
(1903–27)

CChW   *Calendar of Chancery Warrants 1244–1326* (1927)

CCR   *Calendar of the Close Rolls (*1892–)

CDI   *Calendar of Documents Relating to Ireland*, ed. H.S. Sweetman
(1877–86)

CDS   *Calendar of Documents Relating to Scotland*, ed. J. Bain (1881–88)

CFR   *Calendar of the Fine Rolls Preserved in the Public Record Office*
(1911–72)

Chronica Majora	*Matthaei Parisiensis Chronica Majora*, ed. H.R. Luard, ii and vii, Roll Series, lvii (1875–89)
CLB London	*Calendar of the Letter Books Preserved among the Archives of the Corporation of the City of London at the Guildhall, A to E*, ed. R.A. Sharpe (1899–1903)
Complete Peerage	GEC, *The Complete Peerage*, revised by V. Gibbs, H.E. Doubleday and Lord Howard de Walden (1910–57)
CPL	*Calendar of Entries in the Papal Registers relating to Great Britain and Ireland; Papal Letters, i–ii, 1198–1304*, ed. W.H. Bliss (1893–95)
CPR	*Calendar of the Patent Rolls* (1891–)
CPREJ	*Calendar of the Plea Rolls of the Exchequer of the Jews Preserved in the Public Record Office*, ii, iii, iv and vi, Jewish Historical Society of England (1910–2005)
Dunstable	*Annales Prioratus de Dunstaplia, Annales Monastici*, iii, Roll Series, xxxvi, ed. H.R. Luard, iii (1866)
EEA	*English Episcopal Acta* (1980–)
EHR	*English Historical Review*
Eye Cartulary	'Eye Priory Cartulary and Charters', ed. V. Brown, Suffolk Record Society, xii-iii (1992 & 1994)
Eynsham Cartulary	'The Cartulary of Eynsham Abbey', ed. H.E. Salter, Oxford Historical Society, xlix and li (1906–8)
Feudal Aids	*Inquisitions and Assessments Relating to Feudal Aids: With Other Analogous Documents Preserved in the Public Record Office, A.D. 1284–1431, Prepared under the Superintendence of the Deputy Keeper of the Records* (1899–1920)
FF	*Feet of Fines thus:*
FF Bucks	'A Calendar of the Feet of Fines for Buckinghamshire 1259–1307', ed. A Travers, Buckinghamshire Record Society, xxv (1989)
FF Cornwall	'Feet of Fines for Cornwall, i, 1195–1377', ed. J.H. Rowe, Devon and Cornwall Record Society (1914)
FF Devon	'Devon Feet of Fines, ii 1272–1369', ed. O.J. Reichel, F.B. Prideux and H. Tapley-Soper, Devon and Cornwall Record Society (1939)
FF Essex	'Feet of Fines for Essex, vol.ii, AD 1276–AD 1326', Essex Archaeological Society (1913–1928)
FF Gloucs	'Abstract of Feet of Fines Relating to Gloucestershire 1199–1299', ed. C.R. Elrington, Bristol and Gloucestershire Archaeological Society, Gloucestershire Record Series, xvi, (2003)
FF London and Middlesex	'A Calendar of the Feet of Fines for London and Middlesex*, volume i, *Richard I–Richard III', ed. W.J. Hardy and W. Page (1892)
FF Oxfordshire	'The Feet of Fines for Oxfordshire 1195–1291', ed. H.E. Salter, Oxford Record Society, xii (1930)

Ministers' Accounts	'Ministers' Accounts of the Earldom of Cornwall 1296–1297', ed. L.M. Midgley, Camden Society, third series, lxvi and lxviii (1942 and 1945)
Monasticon	Dugdale, W., *Monasticon Anglicanum*, 1–vi, ed. J. Caley, H. Ellis and B. Bandinel (1817–30)
Oseney Cartulary	'The Cartulary of Oseney Abbey', ed. H.E. Salter, i-vi, Oxford Historical Society, lxxxix-xic, xcvii-viii and ci (1929–36)
ODNB	*Oxford Dictionary of National Biography* (Oxford 2001–2004 and online)
Oxfordshire Forests	'Oxfordshire Forests 1246–1609', ed. B. Schumer, Oxfordshire Record Society, lxiv (2004)
Page	Page, M., ' Royal and Comital Government and the Local Community in Thirteenth-Century Cornwall', Oxford University, D.Phil. thesis (1995)
Parliamentary Rolls	*Parliament Rolls of Medieval England 1275–1504, i, 1275–1294*, ed. P. Brand (Woodbridge, 2005)
Patent Rolls	*Patent Rolls of the Reign of Henry III* (1901–3)
Pecham Register	'The Register of John Pecham, Archbishop of Canterbury 1279–1292', ii, ed. D. Douie and i, ed. F.N. Davies, Canterbury and York Society, lxv and lxiv (1967–8)
Percy Cartulary	'The Percy Chartulary', Surtees Society, cxvii (1911)
Placita Coram Rege 1297	*Placita coram domino rege apud Westmonasterium de termino Sancte Trinitatis anno regni regis Edwardi, filii regis Henrici, vicesimo quinto. The Pleas of the Court of King's Bench, Trinity term, 25 Edward I, 1927*, ed. W.P.W. Phillimore (1898)
Pontissara Register	'Registrum Johannis de Pontissara Diocesis Wintoniensis 1282–1304', ed. C. Deedes, Canterbury and York Society, xix and xx (1915–24)
PQW	*Placita de Quo Warranto temporibus E I, II and III in Curia Receptae Scaccarii Westm. asservata* (1818)
PW	*The Parliamentary Writs and Writs of Military Summons*, ed. F. Palgrave, i-ii (1827–34)
Quivel Register	*The Registers of Walter Bronescombe (A.D. 1257–1280), and Peter Quivil (A.D. 1280–1291), Bishops of Exeter: With some Records of the Episcopate of Bishop Thomas de Bytton (A.D. 1292–1307); also the Taxation of Pope Nicholas IV, A.D. 1291 (diocese of Exeter)*, ed. Rev. F. C. Hingeston-Randolph (1889)
Registrum Peckham	*Registrum Epistolarum Johannis Peckham, archiepiscopi cantuariensis*, ed. C.T. Martin, 3 vols. RS lxxvi (1882–5)
Rishanger	'The Chronicle of William de Rishanger of the Barons' Wars and the Miracles of Simon de Montfort', ed. J.O. Halwell, Camden Society, series, i, xv (1840)
Rotuli Gravesend	'Rotuli Ricardi Gravesend Diocesis Lincolniensis', ed. F.N. Davies, Canterbury and York Society, xxxi (1925)

RS	*Rolls Series*
RWH 1286–89	*Records of the Wardrobe and Household 1286–1289*, ed. B.F. Byerly and C.R. Byerly (1986)
Records of Antony Bek	'The Records of Antony Bek, Bishop and Patriarch', ed. C.M. Fraser, Surtees Society, clxii (1947)
Romeyn Register	'The Register of John Le Romeyn, Lord Archbishop of York, 1286–1296', Surtees Society, cxxiii and cxxviii (1913)
St Frideswide's Cartulary	'Cartulary of the Monastery of St Frideswide', ed. S.R. Wigram, Oxford Historical Society, xxviii and xxxxi (1895–6)
St John, Oxford, Cartulary	'The Cartulary of the Hospital of St John the Baptist, Oxford', ed. H.E. Salter, Oxford Historical Society, lxvi and lxviii-ix (1914–7)
St Michael's Mount Cartulary	'The Cartulary of St Michael's Mount,' ed. P.L. Hull, Devon and Cornwall Record Society, new series, v (1962)
Scutage Rolls	*Calendar of Various Chancery Rolls; Supplementary Close Rolls, Welsh Rolls and Scutage Rolls AD 1277–1316* (1912)
Select Cases Exchequer	'Select Cases in the Exchequer of Pleas', ed. H. Jenkinson and B.E.R. Formoy, Selden Society, xlviii, 1931 (1932)
Select Cases Kings Bench	'Select Cases in the Court of King's Bench', ii, ed. G.O. Sayles, Selden Society, lvv (1938)
Supplementary Close Rolls	*Calendar of Various Chancery Rolls; Supplementary Close Rolls, Welsh Rolls and Scutage Rolls AD 1277–1316* (1912)
Sutton Rolls	'The Rolls and Register of Bishop Oliver Sutton 1280–1299', ii, iii, ed. R.M.T. Hill, Lincoln Record Society, xliii, xlviii, lx, lxxvi (1950–81)
Swinfield Register	'Registrum Ricardi Swinfield Episcopi Herefordensis 1283–1317', ed. W. Capes, Canterbury and York Society, vi (1909)
TCE	*Thirteenth Century England, i-xii (Conferences Held at Newcastle-upon-Tyne, Durham and Gregynog* (1985–2009)
Thame Cartulary	'The Thame Cartulary', ed. H. E.Salter, Oxford Record Society, xxv-vi (1947)
Todd, Ashridge	Todd, H.J., *The History of the College of Bonhommes at Ashridge in the County of Buckingham, founded in the year 1286 by Edmund, Earl of Cornwall* (1823)
Tout, Chapters	Tout, T.F., *Chapters in Medieval Administrative History*, i-vi (Manchester, 1920–33)
VCH	*Victoria County History*, followed by County
Waverley	*Annales Monasterii de Waverleia* in *Annales Monastici*, ii, Rolls Series, xxxvi, ed. H.R. Luard (1866)
Welsh Rolls	*Calendar of Various Chancery Rolls; Supplementary Close Rolls, Welsh Rolls and Scutage Rolls AD 1277–1316* (1912)
White Kennett	*Parochial Antiquities attempted in the History of Ambrosden, Burcester and other adjacent parts of the Counties of Oxford and Buckingham* i, (Oxford, 1818)

Winchelsey Register	'*Registrum Roberti de Winchelsey, Cantuariensis Archiepiscopi 1294–1313*', ed. R.Graham, Canterbury and York Society, li and lii (1952 and 1956)
WL Edward I	*The Royal Charter Witness Lists of Edward I (1272–1307) from The Charter Rolls in the Public Record Office* transcribed and edited with an Introduction by Richard Huscroft : List and Index Society, no. 279 (1999)
WL Henry III	*The Royal Charter Witness Lists of Henry III (1226–1272)* edited with an introduction by Marc Morris, List and Index Society, nos. 291 and 292 (2001)
Worcester	*Annales Prioratus de Wigornia* in *Annales Monastici*, Roll Series, xxxvi, ed. H.R.Luard, iv (1869)
Wykes	*Chronicon Vulgo Dictum Chronicon Thomae Wykes* AD 1066–1289, *Annales Monasticii*, Roll Series, xxxvi, iv, ed. H.R.Luard (1869)
Year Books	*Year Books of Edward I*, ed. A.J.Horwood, Roll Series, xxxi, (1863)

Conventions

In the introduction to the index of his *Peter des Roches*, Nicholas Vincent discussed how toponymic surnames from the thirteenth century should be rendered.[1] He decided that for places in England, he should use 'of' instead of the particule 'de'. Thus, he used 'de' before French toponyms, which were to be given in their modern form but he was defeated by Hubert de Burgh and Earl Warenne. I have compromised along slightly different lines, preferring to retain 'de' as a sign that the person had, or his family might have had, some claim to ownership of an English place. I have tried to use 'of' for larger places especially towns where ownership is most unlikely. Thus Aylesbury, Northampton[2] and Winton (Winchester) are preceded by 'of'. I have modernised the more obvious spellings such as Drayton instead of Dreyton and Shottesbrooke instead of Shotebrok but I have left Pichelsthorn instead of Pitstone because it might confuse a reader who knows of the often used version in records. Latinised names have been translated to English versions; *Campo Arnulphi* becomes Champernown. For places in France and Switzerland, I have used the modern spellings so Grandison becomes Grandson and Pavelli, Pavilly but I could not bring myself to change Sackville to Sauqueville.

A reference is followed by a number, usually the page number. However, for *The Calendars of Inquisitions post mortem*, the reference number is used but for a long entry, the page is added as 'p'. With manuscripts, 'm' means membrane with 'd.' being the *dorse,* the rear side. With manuscript books, 'fo.' means *folio,* 'r' is *recto* (the right hand or facing page), and 'v.' is *verso,* the overleaf of the *recto*.

Note on currency

Edmund's accounts are set out in the contemporary currency of the day, l.s.d; pounds, shillings and pence. The penny could be divided into quarters or halves or three quarters – that is to say farthings, halfpennies and three-quarters of a penny. The halfpenny was called the obol in the Latin of England, although it derived originally from the Greek. Most transactions were conducted in silver pennies. In addition to using pounds worth 20 shillings, and shillings, worth 12 pence, another amount used for calculation was the mark. This was two thirds of a pound, i.e. 13 shillings and 4 pence with half a mark being 6 shillings and 8 pence.

Illustrations

A   Images
Arms of Edmund of Cornwall

British Museum, Genealogical Chronicle of the English Kings, MS Royal 14B V

The National Archives; seal of Edmund, Earl of Cornwall

Ashridge; statue of Edmund of Cornwall by Sir Richard Westmacott in the staircase hall

B   Places
Trifels castle, Rhineland-Palatinate, Germany; source of the Holy Blood relic

San Silvestro, now Chiesa di Gesù, Viterbo, scene of murder of Henry of Almain

C   Castles of Edmund of Cornwall
Berkhamsted, Hertfordshire
Eye, Suffolk
Haughley, Suffolk
Knaresborough, Yorkshire
Launceston, Cornwall
Restormel, Cornwall
Lydford, Devon
Mere, Wiltshire
Oakham, Rutland
Tintagel, Cornwall
Trematon, Cornwall
Wallingford, Berkshire

D   Religious foundation of Edmund of Cornwall
Hailes Abbey, Gloucestershire
Rewley Abbey, Oxfordshire

E   Objects associated with Edmund of Cornwall

Clare Chasuble (Victoria and Albert Museum)

Historica Scholastica, The British Library (BL Add Royal 3 D VI)

Part of an effigy, Hailes Abbey, Gloucestershire, said to be from tomb of
Edmund of Cornwall

Tiles from Hailes parish church, Gloucestershire

Tiles from Cleeve Abbey, Somerset

Arms in stained glass, Dorchester, Oxfordshire

Page from Cartulary of Edmund of Cornwall (TNA:PRO E 36/57)

Mappa Mundi fragment given to Ashridge College (Duchy of Cornwall
Office)

Chapter 1

Edmund: The Early Years

Cornubiae comes et dominus mundusque beatus
Dicitur Edmundus de regum germine natus.
Virtutis titulum trahit a probitate parentum

(Edmund, born of the stock of kings, is called Earl and
Lord of Cornwall, upright and blessed. He takes his
designation of virtue and integrity from his parents)

Some thirty miles from Euston, a rail traveller from Birmingham, sitting on the left-hand side of a train, can glimpse a mighty series of earth ramparts, a motte and some scant walls. This is Berkhamsted castle and it was here, on the day after Christmas 1249, that Edmund was born to Sanchia, the second wife of Richard, Earl of Cornwall, the brother of Henry III.[3] Edmund already had a half-brother, Henry, the son of Richard and his first wife, Isabel Marshal, who had died in 1240.[4] Although Sanchia had borne him another son, named Richard, he had died in August 1246.[5]

Edmund came from an impressive lineage. His maternal aunts were or would be queens. Married to Richard in 1243, Sanchia was one of four daughters of Raymond Berengar IV, Count of Provence, by his wife, Beatrice, the daughter of Thomas I, Count of Savoy. Margaret, the eldest daughter, was the wife of Louis IX of France and Eleanor was the Queen of Henry III, whilst the youngest, Beatrice, married Charles of Anjou, the brother of King Louis who later became King of Sicily and Naples. Sanchia was to become Queen of the Romans when Richard of Cornwall was elected to the German throne in 1257. Her uncles were also high achievers. The sons of Count Thomas, the so-called Eagles of Savoy, arrived in England through Countess Beatrice's influence. Here they were welcomed by Henry III and given extensive preferment and wealth.[6]

William, Bishop of Valence, made an immediate impact on the King who tried to win the bishopric of Winchester for him but William died young, soon after being elected Bishop of Liége. Peter was given the earldom, if not the title, of Richmond in 1240 as well as the Rape of Pevensey in Sussex. His London palace was to become the site of the Savoy chapel and hotel. Another brother, Boniface, who had been enthroned as Archbishop of Canterbury in the previous month, 'came right way rejoicing' to christen his relative, Edmund. Matthew Paris stated that 'because the Earl (Richard) was a lover of St Edmund, his name was called Edmund in honour of St Edmund, Archbishop of Canterbury and confessor.'[7] Edmund Rich had been canonised only two years earlier and Richard had been a strong supporter of the campaign for his canonisation. In 1247 Richard went to Pontigny Abbey, where Edmund Rich died, to visit the shrine for which he had paid a quarter of the cost. The year after the birth of his son, Edmund, Richard went again.[8] Was this visit to give thanks for Edmund's safe arrival? Nicholas Vincent believed that the English royal family must been piqued by how the French royal family had 'adopted' St Edmund, the first new English saint for two decades. As St Edmund had quarrelled with Henry III and had died in exile at Pontigny, this made it easier for Louis IX to intervene and preside over the translation of Edmund's body. Vincent saw Richard's visit to Pontigny as an attempt to make good the English neglect of the saint.[9] Thus the naming of Richard's son for Edmund could be seen as reinforcing the dedication and the identification of the English royal family with an English saint.

Very little is known of Edmund's childhood. Throughout his early years, his father must have been preoccupied with the tensions associated with the gradual build-up of opposition to Henry III's method of rule. Through a series of gifts of land from his brother, including a generous marriage portion for Countess Sanchia, Richard became the richest man in the kingdom and by 1247, Richard's political and financial support was vital to the King. He had come to his brother's assistance over his debts. The acquisition by Richard of the farm of the mint and the right to mint the national coinage from 1247 until 1259 brought Richard even more wealth. Matthew Paris estimated that Richard received the vast sum of £20,000 and Denholm-Young, having examined the Pipe Rolls and other estimates, felt that this might be 'in the right order of magnitude'.[10] In

1254, Richard was sold all the rights to the Jews in England which gave him the opportunity to tax them and to seize the estates of those who died without heirs.[11] When the King was in Gascony in 1254, Richard acted as his Regent in England. By then, Henry had been convinced that he should accept the offer from the Pope of the Crown of Sicily for his younger son, Edmund, the future Earl of Lancaster. Richard was not at all encouraging and he refused to make another loan to the King. This decision was not surprising as Richard had rejected the proposition of taking the Sicilian kingdom for himself when, soon after the birth of Edmund, Richard went to Lyon where he rejected this regal prize. Ironically when, in 1263, having lost patience with Henry III, the new Pope, Urban IV, gave the throne to Edmund's uncle, Charles of Anjou, the brother of Louis IX.

A brighter and more realistic prospect beckoned Richard. When the papal nominee to the vacant Kingdom of the Romans or Germany died in January 1256, Richard began a campaign to obtain the kingdom for himself. After months of negotiation, he was elected on 13 January 1257. A short time later, the majority of the seven electors, following another vote, elected King Alfonso X of Castile instead. Alfonso was perceived as the Hohenstaufen candidate, being the son of Elizabeth of Hohenstaufen and the cousin of the Emperor Frederick II. However, one elector wavered in his support and Alfonso was unable to journey to Germany. This left the field clear for Richard to become King of the Romans.

Children of great magnates were often sent away at around the age of 6 to be raised, trained and educated in other magnate households. Edmund's own father, Richard of Cornwall, was born in 1209 and lost his father, King John, when he was 7. Then, a year later, his mother left England to live in her county of Angoulême where she remarried. Richard had been sent away from court at 6 to live in John's mighty fortress at Corfe and be educated under the supervision of Peter de Maulay.[12] Richard was to live as a young orphan and this pattern was repeated a generation later. Richard's eldest son and Edmund's half-brother, Henry, was left in the care of the King when Richard left on crusade in 1240. In December 1240, young Henry of Almain was recorded at Windsor in the company of other young noblemen including the King's own son, the Lord Edward, later Edward I. Henry might also have spent at least part of his childhood in France since, at a later date, Queen Margaret, wife of Louis IX, offered him hospitality during a convalescence from illness claiming that Henry would prefer to stay at the French court rather than in some unknown and foreign place.[13]

Details of the childhood of Edmund's uncle, Simon de Montfort, the husband of Richard of Cornwall's sister, Eleanor, are largely unknown but, as a 10-year-old, he was with his mother when his father, Simon de Montfort senior, was killed at the siege of Toulouse in 1218.[14] Edmund's cousin, Edward I, was not sent away to live with a strange family; he lived in the royal household at Windsor and was often seen by his parents.[15]

As the 'farming out' of children was not the practice with the sons of Henry III, Edmund too may have lived with his parents. In 1254, Sanchia journeyed in great splendour to France to meet her sisters at the French court. She might have taken her son with her to meet his aunts. At the feast of the Circumcision (1 January) 1253, Queen Eleanor had given Dionisia, Edmund's nurse, a clasp.[16] This suggests that Edmund, who had recently passed his third birthday, was close to Queen Eleanor. This might mean that Edmund was raised with his English royal cousins, Edmund, Margaret, Beatrice and later Katherine. Louise Wilkinson, in her book on Eleanor de Montfort, commented on the childhood of members of the royal family, stating that they had their own separate households from an early age. This was done partly from necessity due to the disruptive, itinerant lifestyle of the royal court which was not suited to the emotional and physical wellbeing of children especially in an age when children were vulnerable to disease.[17] Edmund might have been treated similarly but his mother, Sanchia, might not have been as itinerant as her sister, Queen Eleanor.

When Richard made his first journey to Germany on being elected King, he took his wife and sons with him. The 8-year-old Edmund left Yarmouth on 29 April 1258[18] and landed at Dordrecht on 1 May. At Aachen, on Ascension Day, 17 May, his father and mother were crowned King and Queen of Germany by the Archbishop of Cologne. Following the coronation, Richard was styled as Richard 'of Almain' (Germany) as was his son, Henry, and in due time, this suffix was used by Edmund. The coronation might have been when Edmund saw the Holy Blood relic which he went on to acquire eleven years later. From Cologne the royal party went to Mainz where, in September, Richard held his first royal parliament or diet. Winter was spent in the Lower Rhineland, before they travelled south again in the spring of 1258, reaching as far as Worms. The family did not return to England until January 1259, arriving in London on 2 February.[19] Having been away from England for nearly a year, Edmund was now 9. His father could speak English[20] so one can assume Edmund could too. He must have been impressed by the strange sights, places, customs, rituals, ceremonies and languages which he experienced whilst abroad. Perhaps he picked up some German. We can be sure that he knew French and, as he commissioned books in Latin, that he was comfortable with this language.

When the family arrived back in England, the country was gripped by political turmoil.[21] At the April Parliament of 1258, held at Westminster, some earls, barons and knights came to the King's Hall wearing their swords. Although the swords were left at the door, the threat of violence was clear. These men had lost patience with the King's plans to accept the Sicilian throne for his son and to seek funding for the venture from the English. They were also infuriated by the actions of the alien favourites of Henry III, particularly those of his Lusignan half-brothers, the Poitevins. On 12 April 1258, the magnates swore an oath to support each other in their demands for reform. Changes would be negotiated by twenty-four men, half of whom would be nominated by the King and the other by the Barons. At the subsequent Parliament, held in June 1258 at Oxford, the King was forced to accept the Provisions of Oxford which dealt with grievances such as the method by which the sheriffs were appointed and how they behaved. But, above all, a Council appointed by the magnates had to agree to new royal charters and the appointment of royal officials. Henry had ceased to reign in the traditional sense.

Even before Richard crossed the Channel to return to England, he was being asked to side with the Baronial reformers and he was pressured to swear an oath to uphold the reforming Provisions of Oxford. Eventually he agreed and he took the oath on 28 January 1259. Richard's family was given a grand welcome to London.[22] Although some feared that Richard might return to oppose the reforms, he stayed clear of politics and retired to his estates, no doubt taking Edmund with him. The Oxford Provisions were strengthened by those of Westminster in October 1259. Henry III journeyed to France in that December to ratify the Treaty of Paris which would bring an end to the disputes between the two realms. Richard had intended to go and might have planned to take Edmund with him to meet his aunts, the Queen of France and the Countess of Anjou. However, Richard stayed in England conducting negotiations with the Pope to secure the formal recognition of his title as Holy Roman Emperor. During this period he brokered a rapprochement between the King and his eldest son, the Lord Edward, who had briefly joined the reformers, as well as an individual treaty of peace between Edward and Richard de Clare, Earl of Gloucester.

The foundation stone of the Treaty of Paris was the ceding of Henry III's claim to lands in Normandy, Anjou, Maine and Touraine. In return, he had his claim to Gascony in hereditary right recognised by Louis IX. To ensure that there would be no future trouble, Louis demanded that the renunciation of claims should also be made by Henry III's siblings. Simon de Montfort and his wife, Eleanor, Henry's sister, used this requirement as a bargaining tool in their long-running battle for the dower lands due to Eleanor from her first marriage. Henry claimed that Louis had never required any renunciation from Henry's daughters nor from his nephew, Edmund. Henry of Almain had already renounced his rights. This was the first time that Edmund is mentioned in official documents.[23] The King emphasised the unreasonableness of his sister and brother-in-law, whilst indicating the co-operation of Richard of Cornwall's family.

Having brokered another peace to avoid bloodshed between the Barons and the Royalists in London at Easter 1260,[24] a visit to Germany was made by Richard in the summer. He left London on 17 June but there is no record of Edmund going with him.[25] Perhaps he was left with his ailing mother. Richard hoped that the climax of this journey would be his coronation as Holy Roman Emperor by the Pope but disappointment was to follow. A victory by the Italian supporters of the Hohenstaufen claim to the imperial crown on 4 September resulted in the blocking of Richard's way to Rome. Papal encouragement was no longer forthcoming and, without this crucial support, Richard headed for home, reaching England on 24 October. Whilst Christmas was spent with the King, Richard again continued to live mostly away from court and on his own estates. 1261 saw a return of royal power over the barons; Henry regained his rights and strengthened his position by appointing a raft of new sheriffs. During this time Richard kept mostly out of the way although he was likely to have been supportive of his brother and, by October, he was offering to land foreign mercenaries in his Cornish power base to assist Henry.

On 9 November 1261, Sanchia died. Denholm-Young noted the apparent indifference of Richard to his wife's illness. Sanchia was left alone by Richard at Christmas 1260 and again in November 1261 prior to her death. Perhaps Edmund was with his mother. Although Richard was not present when her body was moved to Hailes for burial on 15 November[26] and it is likely that the 11-year-old Edmund witnessed his mother's interment. In the spring of 1262, Richard once again acted as arbiter with the barons over the King's demand to control the appointment of sheriffs, but he entirely vindicated the king's prerogative rights. It is not known whether Edmund went with Richard on his third visit to Germany in June 1262. At Aachen, Richard deposited a duplicate set of imperial regalia. Apparently he feared that, in the future, he might be unable to obtain access to the true regalia with which he had been crowned and which was stored in the great imperial fortress of Trifels. On 7 August, the new Pope, Urban IV, announced that both Richard and Alfonso were to be granted equal recognition as kings-elect, and both were summoned to Rome. By November, Richard had reached Zürich but he turned back, arriving in England on 10 February 1263. It is not clear why he aborted his journey but he might have heard of unrest in England.

1263 witnessed the outbreak of serious violence within England when attacks were made on aliens of whatever origin. No longer was hostility directed solely towards the Lusignans and their Poitevin associates but the Savoyards suffered as well. Richard was closely related to both alien camps, by blood to the Lusignans and by marriage to the Savoyards. Initially Richard tried to mediate and bring peace, a policy which led to the Pope writing to him to accuse him of conniving in the rebellion by lending insufficient support to his brother, the King. Vincent believed that these letters would not have been written without approval from Henry's proctors at Rome, although they should also be seen in the context of Urban's attempts to mediate on the imperial election dispute. The letters might also reflect the King's anger with Richard's son, Henry of Almain, Edmund's half-brother, who had openly sided with Montfort throughout the summer of 1263. When young Henry pursued the King's chief minister, John Mansel, as far as Boulogne, the Queen intervened and had Henry captured and imprisoned by Ingram de Fiennes, a relative of Eleanor of Castile.[27] However, the barons insisted on Henry's release and, later in the year, he gained his freedom but returned to the side of his father who was now in full support of the King.

In an attempt to bring the crisis to an end, it was agreed, following negotiations supervised by Richard,[28] that the dispute should be put to the arbitration of King Louis of France. When Henry III crossed to France to await the result of the arbitration in January 1264, Richard stayed behind in England as Regent. The resultant Mise of Amiens was a triumph; it was a complete vindication of Henry III's position. Louis's only concession to the baronial opposition was to require the King to restore harmony and good will. Infuriated, the barons, led by Montfort, refused to accept the decision. Acting to safeguard the realm, Richard strengthened the defences of the Marches against the Welsh and joined the King when he returned from France in March 1264. By now, Richard was a target of violence himself. Baronial supporters sacked his favourite manor of Isleworth and his Westminster mansion. It is not known where Edmund was but it is likely that he was with his father. These attacks were said to have triggered Richard's change from a persistent conciliator into a hard line anti-Montfortian royalist. In this hardened guise, he rejected all offers of payments and compromise on the run up to the battle of Lewes which took place on 14 May 1264.

Edmund experienced warfare first-hand in the savage battle of Lewes and he was captured during the battle which should have been a royal success and this might be why Richard took his son with him. It turned out to be a traumatic event for a 14-year-old boy. The King's army significantly outnumbered that of the barons led by Montfort and it had already gained significant victories including the capture of Northampton on 5 April 1264. At the battle of Lewes, Richard led the left wing of the Royal army along with his elder son, Henry. Edmund must have been with them.

Most commentators put down the baronial victory against the odds to the superior strategy of Montfort who had managed to move his army from his manor of Fletching to the north of Lewes on 12 May. During the night of 13/14 May he positioned his forces on the high ground above the town.[29] Surprised by the unexpected arrival of Montfort's army, the royal forces marched out of the town of Lewes, Lewes Priory and Lewes castle to confront the enemy. The Lord Edward's knights had an early success routing the contingent raised for Montfort by the Londoners. Bent on revenge for the London mob's insults to his mother, Queen Eleanor, who had been subjected to a volley of stones as she tried to pass under London Bridge on her way to Windsor, Edward and his forces swept away his opponents. But he committed the cardinal sin of the cavalry by pursuing his defeated enemy too vigorously and too far; up to four miles. By the time Edward returned, the battle was lost. Having been pushed back by Montfort's sons, Richard of Cornwall and Edmund were in real physical danger and, as the royal lines broke, they took refuge in a windmill next to St Anne's church. Taunted by their future captors led by John Giffard, a knight of Gilbert de Clare, Edmund's future brother-in-law, they surrendered. Retreating to Lewes Priory, King Henry was joined by the Lord Edward. Realising that future military resistance was useless or possibly because Montfort threatened to kill Richard and Edmund,[30] a peace agreement was reached quickly. Although it left the male members of the royal family as prisoners, the King remained the nominal ruler.

Richard and his son remained as Montfort's prisoners until September 1265, sometime after Montfort's defeat and death at the battle of Evesham on 4 August. At first they were kept in the Tower of London under the care of Edmund's aunt, Eleanor de Montfort. Then they were moved to their family castle of Wallingford now in Montfort's hands.[31] The Lord Edward was also kept there. An attempt to free them was made in November 1265 when Warin de Bassingbourne, the Keeper of Bristol castle, brought 300 mounted men and 1,000 infantry soldiers to Wallingford. From the adjoining All Saints' church they climbed across the ditch, broke through the walls and entered into the castle bailey. The constable resisted the attack vigorously and told the attackers that 'they would gladly send sir Edward out to them bound with a mangonel, to take home with them'. On hearing this, Edward himself climbed on to the walls and told his potential rescuers to go home 'or he was a dead man of a truth'. Thereupon, Warin withdrew and the rescue mission was over.[32]

Because of this scare the prisoners were sent on Montfort's order to the security of Montfort's own stronghold at Kenilworth.[33] Initially, Countess Eleanor was there but, when she left, she sent them luxuries and bought Edmund clothes.[34] However, when Montfort learnt of the Lord Edward's escape from captivity in Hereford on 28 May 1265,[35] in a fit of anger, he ordered that Richard and Edmund should be put in chains to prevent them from absconding;[36] that Edmund was put in chains emphasises his political importance. After Montfort's defeat and death at Evesham on 4 August 1265, Simon de Montfort junior still held Kenilworth castle and he resisted a siege until December 1265. However, young Simon agreed to release his royal prisoners on 6 September 1265. There is a report contained in Rishanger that the garrison would have preferred to kill Richard.[37] The Melrose chronicle stated that in the winter of 1264, Richard procured his release in return for the payment of a ransom of £17,000 of silver and £5,000 of gold. Although it is possible that Richard might have offered such a sum, he remained a prisoner until well after the battle of Evesham.[38] Richard and Edmund reached their home at Wallingford to great rejoicing on 9 September 1265.[39] The Hailes annalist compared Richard's return to that of the release of Job.[40] At Wallingford he received royal letters to assist him in the recovery of his ravaged estates.[41]

In an oath sworn by Richard at Kenilworth Priory on the day of his release, he promised to do his best to protect his sister, Eleanor, from any reprisals by the royalists. He kept his promise and, on 31 October 1265, he was at Canterbury to welcome the newly arrived papal legate, Ottobuono, and he made arrangements for the surrender of Eleanor and her children who were at Dover.[42] In the following months and years Richard was again a voice for moderation and reconciliation. He urged clemency towards the defeated barons who had lost their lands and advocated peace with the Welsh supporters of Montfort.[43]

On 26 July 1268, Edmund was at Isleworth when he witnessed his father's grant for Merton College, Oxford.[44] With England at peace, Richard of Cornwall was able to return to Germany to pursue his imperial destiny. Edmund went with him on this fourth journey to Germany in August 1268. The visit had a major impact on Edmund, now 19 years old. It was there that he acquired the Holy Blood relic. He also witnessed his father's third marriage to Beatrix von Valkenburg. Edmund and his father were known to have stopped at Cambrai, Aachen, Cologne, Worms where he held a Diet, and then Frankfurt.

There is an account in the Hailes Annals of the discovery and acquisition of the relic from the castle of Trifels.[45] Situated near the small town of Annweiler in the Palatinate and located high above the Queich valley within the Palatinate Forest, Trifels already had connections with the English royal family. Richard I had been imprisoned there by the Emperor Henry VI during 1193 on his ill-fated return from the Third Crusade and Matilda, the daughter of Henry I and wife of the Emperor Henry V, had used it as a residence. On her husband's death, Matilda returned to England and brought with her a relic containing the hand of St James. Henry V used the castle to store the imperial regalia but it also functioned as a fortress, prison and treasure house. By the reign of Richard of Cornwall, Trifels was in the custody of the Falkenstein/Bolanden family. Werner von Bolanden was Richard's steward in Germany. During Richard's stay at Worms, the castle was surrendered to him by Werner von Bolanden junior,[46] the son of Philip von Falkenstein and nephew of the elder Werner. Although Richard left the imperial regalia in the custody of Reinhard von Hoheneck when he returned to England, the young Edmund must have obtained the Holy Blood relic from Werner who had a special personal affection for Edmund. The relic was said to have been abstracted from a brooch used at imperial coronations to fasten the emperor's mantle. But it might have come from a pendant-brooch or locket which, according to tradition, had been buried with Charlemagne at Aachen. This object survives in Rheims cathedral. It once contained a hair of the Blessed Virgin Mary which was later replaced by a piece of the True Cross but it could have once housed the relic of the Holy Blood.[47]

Richard's marriage to Beatrix took place at Kaiserslautern on 16 June 1269. She was the niece of a previous opponent of Richard, Archbishop Engelbert of Cologne. On her wedding day, Beatrix had issued a charter protecting the landed rights of her new step-sons.[48] Without an army, Richard felt unable to go on to Rome to seek confirmation of his imperial title. In 1267, Henry of Almain, had acted as his proctor at the papal court but Richard must have realised that no further progress was to be made. Edmund, his father and new step-mother returned to England via Mainz arriving at Dover on 3 August. They were in London on 8 August.[49] Edmund had been away from England for a year. Thus he had spent three years overseas, largely in Germany before he was 19.

On his return to England, Richard was even more important nationally as the King was declining in health. When the Lord Edward finally left on his crusade in 1270, Richard was one of five men who were to look after his interests. If Richard died, Henry of Almain was to replace him and, if he was not available, the remaining four were to choose another. Edmund was not mentioned but he did lend the Lord Edward's clerk, Robert Burnell, £2,000.[50] On 7 March 1271, Richard was made Protector of the realm when his brother became seriously ill.

Now approaching his majority, in 1270, Edmund set off to join the Lord Edward on his crusade to the Holy Land. It may have been to mark his decision to crusade that he gave part of the Holy Blood relic to Hailes Abbey.[51] His half-brother, Henry of Almain, was also amongst the crusaders and the magnates were given large sums towards the cost of their expenses on crusade. Henry received 1,500 marks and, for each knight, the allowance was 100 marks for a year.[52] It seems likely that Edmund went with his brother's party. Denholm-Young believed that Edmund had returned to England by February 1271 at Richard's wish.[53] He cited no source for this and this seems to be inaccurate as the chronicler Thomas Wykes wrote that it was not until the death of Henry of Almain in 1271, that Edmund came home to comfort his ailing father.[54]

When the Lord Edward arrived in Tunis in August 1270, he found that King Louis IX was dead and he ordered Henry of Almain to accompany their uncle's body back to France. By Lent 1271, Henry had reached the papal city of Viterbo, fifty miles north of Rome, where a conclave to elect a successor to Pope Clement IV was in progress. On 12 March, Henry and his party came into contact with the brothers, Guy and Simon de Montfort junior. Although wounded at Evesham, Guy had managed to escape and young Simon had done likewise after the siege of Kenilworth. Travelling to Italy, they had fought for Charles of Anjou, their father's brother-in-law, in his conquest of Sicily. Charles rewarded them and Guy was now his Vicar-General in Tuscany. On 13 March 1271, knowing that Philip III of France and Charles of Anjou were at mass in the Franciscan church, the Montforts sought out Henry. He was hearing mass in the church of San Silvestro, now the Chiesa di Gesù, in Viterbo which was opposite his lodgings. They attacked Henry and, when the Montforts realised that they could not take Henry out of the church because of the crowd, Guy stabbed Henry. Guy was reported to have said 'I have taken my vengeance.' As he clung to the altar, Henry was repeatedly stabbed and his hand being almost severed, he was dragged from the church. When he begged for mercy, Guy responded 'You had no mercy on my father and brothers.' Henry was then killed. It was reported that a witness heard the cry 'Remember Evesham!' It is also possible that the killers then mutilated Henry's body after the shameful fashion in which their father's body had been treated following his death at Evesham, an act which had even disgusted the royalist-chronicler Wykes.[55]

There was another reason for enmity between Henry and the Montforts. By his marriage to Constance de Béarn, the daughter of Gaston, the Vicomte of Béarn, a consistent opponent of Simon de Montfort, Henry had gained a claim to the county of Bigorre in Gascony to which the Montforts also staked a claim. Robin Studd suggested that, at the moment of the murder, Guy and Simon might also have been able to shout 'Remember Bigorre!'[56] One of the priests celebrating mass was killed and another seriously injured. If Edmund was still with Henry, he might have witnessed the murder and, even if he was not, the event must have been shattering. He probably had to accompany Henry's body on its long, sad journey home.[57]

The Lord Edward was infuriated by the murder and both Richard of Cornwall and Henry III's last few months were made miserable by the savage act. Henry of Almain had not been at Evesham and had no hand in Montfort's death. However, the young Montforts might have had some hostility towards him as, for a while, he had been a supporter of the Montfortian reform programme before returning to the royal camp so betraying their cause. The murder of a young man, a crusader, who should have enjoyed special protection by his cousins, whilst he was at his prayers, shook Europe. The Kings of France and Naples wrote to express their horror. Although they were related by blood to the Montforts, they called them the 'children of perdition' and promised to hunt them down. King Philip wrote to Richard of Cornwall, stating that the murder had taken place 'at the instigation of the devil'. The papal conclave also denounced the murder. Dante placed Guy de Montfort in the seventh circle of his *Inferno*, where he was to be immersed in a river of boiling blood.[58] There Guy was shown by a Centaur as

> A spirit by itself apart retired,
> Exclaimed; 'He in God's bosom smote the heart,
> Which yet is honoured on the bank of Thames.'

The gruesome events of 1272 were later commemorated by a cycle of wall-paintings commissioned by the men of Viterbo.[59]

The tragedy at Viterbo transformed Edmund's life. He was now the heir to his father's lands, titles and huge wealth. Just over a year later he would become one of the greatest men of the English realm. Edmund must have been with his father when the body of Henry was interred at Hailes on 21 May 1271.[60] He might have accompanied his father on a trip to the north of England in September and been with him when he had a stroke which left him paralysed down his right side and speechless in December. Richard seems to have rallied and made some recovery but, on 2 April 1272, he died.[61] Edmund would have attended his father's interment at Hailes beside the grave of Sanchia and he possibly witnessed the burial of Richard's heart at the Greyfriars in Oxford where, in due course, the body of Countess Beatrix was to lie.

Within a month of his father's death, Edmund was recognised as his heir and granted his lands. On 1 May 1272, he was given custody of the castles of Wallingford, Oakham, Mere and Berkhamsted as the King had taken his homage.[62] On 3 July 1272, King Henry granted him the manor of Rockingham in Northamptonshire.[63] The next few months, the last of Henry III's reign, were to be highly significant for Edmund. He was knighted, married and began to play a role in royal government.

Chapter 2

Edmund: The King's Man

Following Edmund's father's death on 2 April 1272, events moved swiftly. As the nephew of the King and the cousin of the Lord Edward who was to succeed Henry III in November, Edmund of Almain, now Edmund of Cornwall and aged just 22, was expected to play a part in royal governance by offering support, counsel and military resources. His wealth also offered him the opportunity to further assist his monarch financially. The most immediate way in which he could help was by lending money and an early request was to provide £3,000 for the expenses of his cousin, Edmund of Lancaster, on the Lord Edward's crusade.[1] This was readily forthcoming and, in recompense, he was given the custody and the profits of his cousin's lands in Leicester and Hinkley (Leicestershire) and others in Northamptonshire, Warwickshire, Nottinghamshire and Rutland.[2] He received the profitable wardship of the heir of Henry de Hastings[3] and a market at his manor of Rockingham.[4]

A tallage was an arbitrary tax which could be levied at any time and needed no consent from the evolving Parliament nor from the King's advisors. When Henry III levied a tallage on the Jews to help fund the Lord Edward's crusade, it was expected to produce 6,000 marks. But, when it fell short by a third, Richard of Cornwall advanced the money instead. To repay him, Richard was granted the rights to the Jews, enabling him to profit from taxing them. On Richard's death, Henry regained these rights and levied a tallage for 5,000 marks. However, Richard's loan had not been fully paid off, so on his death, Edmund was granted the Jews until the loan was cleared.[5] As a reward for his co-operation, Edmund was given Adam of Berkhamsted, the King's Jew, with the right to his chattels when he died. Richard had been granted Adam for life but the grant to Edmund was limited to a period of two years and five months.[6]

In his early months as Earl of Cornwall, Edmund showed either a lack of confidence or a conciliatory nature or possibly a combination of both. Despite having granted Richard the Hastings wardship, Henry III had preferred two of his clerks to the livings of Wistanstow and Nailstone. Richard, who had the right to the advowsons, had earlier presented his own men including his right-hand man, Michael of Northampton. When the matter was raised with Edmund he gave 'assent for himself'. Edward I, 'to shew grace to his nephew for his assent', granted him the knights' fees and advowsons of these churches after the cession or death of the King's clerks and all the other churches during the minority.[7]

On 6 October 1272, Edmund married Margaret de Clare, daughter of Richard de Clare, Earl of Gloucester and Hertford, and sister of the present Earl Gilbert. The service took place at Ruislip chapel in Middlesex.[8] Strangely, the 22-year-old earl was not yet a knight but this was remedied a week later on the feast of the Translation of Edward the Confessor, the favourite religious occasion of the King.[9]

Henry III died on 16 November 1272 and it was crucial for the news to be sent out that the Lord Edward was now King Edward I now aged 33. Arrangements for governing the kingdom in the absence of Edward had already been made.[10] Robert Burnell had now moved into a prime rôle but, when the announcement of the change of rulers was dispatched, Edmund, his brother-in-law Gilbert de Clare and Walter de Giffard, Archbishop of York, were the three witnesses.[11] So it can be assumed that Edmund would be influential during the long absence of the new King.

Gilbert de Clare had planned to go on the crusade but his lands and new castle at Caerphilly were attacked by Llywelyn ap Gruffudd of Gwynedd and so he had stayed behind to rebuild his flagship fortress.[12] In the period since 1256, Llywelyn had made astonishing progress in establishing himself as the most powerful Welsh prince. He had attacked the lands of the Marchers and of the Lord Edward in Wales. Taking advantage of the turbulence in England in the period of Baronial Reform, he allied himself with Montfort even becoming affianced to his daughter, Eleanor, another cousin of Edmund. His high water mark was the Treaty of Montgomery in 1267 which recognised his tenure of lands acquired by force as well as his status as the premier prince in Wales and his title of Prince of Wales. But this came at the price of 25,000 marks to be paid off at 3,000 marks p.a.[13] After the battle of Evesham, Llywelyn was a major winner from the wars as the Treaty was left in place.

On 29 November and 2 December 1272, Edmund and Bishop Giffard sent letters requiring Llywelyn to come to the Ford of Montgomery, the traditional place for meetings between the English and Welsh rulers,[14] to render his homage to the new monarch and to send the 3,000 marks he owed to the King by Christmas at the latest. The King needed the money for his crusade.[15] Llywelyn neither came nor paid and the impasse continued until well after the new King's return.

Meanwhile neither Edmund, or his officials, were not always well-behaved in the land of the absentee King. In January 1273, Edmund's men were accused of occupying lands belonging to Peter de la Mare which led to the Chancellor, Walter de Merton, ordering the escheator to remedy the position.[16] Despite this, in June, Edmund was still being obstructive.[17] A long-running dispute with the Bishop of Exeter led to a threat of excommunication.[18] Even though Edmund was at the heart of government, he was pursued by the Exchequer over his father's debts.[19] However, this did not prevent Edmund from being amongst those ready to go to France to meet and welcome back Edward I. Edmund was granted protection until August 1273[20] but he was still in Paris in December where he received 2,000 marks from the King.[21] Whilst Edward I did not finally arrive back in England until 2 August 1274, it seems likely that Edmund had already returned as he asked Robert Burnell to summon a council in March.[22] Edmund was present at the King's coronation on 19 August 1274.[23]

From the start of the reign, tasks were entrusted to Edmund by the King. At the beginning of 1275 Edmund was ready to resolve a dispute with Flemish merchants but was unable to act as the Count of Flanders had not sent a representative.[24] In March, the King stayed at two of Edmund's manors, Cippenham and Risborough in Buckinghamshire,[25] and it can be assumed that Edmund was present. The first of many royal charters to be witnessed by Edmund was attested at Westminster on 22 October 1274.[26]

Unfinished business relating to Wales loomed large again and, in 1276, Llywelyn asked that Edmund be one of the persons to guarantee his safe conduct to the Ford of Montgomery to render his long overdue homage to the King.[27] Why did the Welsh prince have this confidence in Edmund? Did they know each other? That seems unlikely. The King stayed with Edmund again, at Kirton in Lincolnshire, in May 1276.[28] When the King spent some time in Chichester in June for the celebrations surrounding the Translation of St Richard, he might have stayed at a property owned by Edmund,[29] although he could have resided in the Bishop's palace. Six bucks from Rockingham forest were given to Edmund in July.[30]

The proposed meeting at the Ford of Montgomery did not take place and Llywelyn continued to prevaricate about homage and his debts even when Edward agreed to make the extra effort of going to Chester to make it easier and safer for the Welsh prince. Then, in November, Edmund was present at the Council meeting which decided on judgement against Llywelyn for failure to pay homage and, five days later, he witnessed the formal declaration of war against Llywelyn.[31] Staying at Henley and Wallingford, the King was Edmund's guest in December 1276.[32]

The war against Llywelyn was due to take place in the following year. In July 1277 Edmund was summoned to the muster of the army at Worcester.[33] He served in person with fourteen other knights[34] making his retinue one of the largest.[35] Nothing is known of what action, if any, Edmund was involved in but he was at the army's camp at Basingwerk on 20 August.[36] Working methodically to protect his supply lines, the King proceeded along the Dee estuary and began a new castle at Flint and then to Rhuddlan where another castle, some way away from the old Norman motte, was begun. In the south, the English forces under Edmund of Lancaster made more rapid progress reaching Aberystwyth where yet another castle was begun. By mid-September, the King having occupied Llywelyn's grain-producing island of Anglesey, was able to start withdrawing from Wales. Perhaps Edmund accompanied him. The Welsh war ended formally in November 1277 with Llywelyn having to cede two eastern cantreds which would now be controlled from the new castles at Flint and Rhuddlan, whilst another two were granted to Llywelyn's brother, Dafydd, who had been on Edward's side. Llywelyn was permitted to regain Anglesey but only if he paid 1,000 marks a year. He was also expected to find a mighty sum to pay reparations for the damage that he had inflicted. Homage was finally rendered to the King at Chester on Christmas Day 1277. Meanwhile, additional wealth and lands came to Edmund when his step-mother, Beatrix, died on 17 October 1277.[37]

Military service did not commend itself to Edmund and, apart from a campaign to suppress a Welsh rebellion in 1287 when he was Regent, Edmund does not seem to have served again in person. Perhaps he was unfit for war. Sometime during 1278/9, Edmund was summoned to a meeting in London but was too ill to attend.[38] But, as he was an enthusiastic hunter, he was not an invalid. Instead of soldiering, he made himself useful to the King carrying out tasks for him or deputising for him in London. At around this time, he enquired into the robbery of foreign merchants for the King.[39]

Yet more wealth came to Edmund in 1278 when he was granted the stannary of Devon but only at the King's pleasure and for a fixed rent.[40] This contrasted with his position in Cornwall where Edmund had inherited its stannary from his father. Royal stays at Cippenham, Henley and Lechlade in the Spring and Autumn of 1278 and Spring 1279 show that he remained close to the King.[41] In July 1278 Edmund with two earls and thirty five other knights, participated in a tournament at Windsor.[42] Internationally important events involved Edmund and he was present when King Alexander III of Scotland rendered homage to Edward I at Westminster in September 1278.[43]

A far more significant step in Edmund's public career and status occurred in the following year. Ponthieu, the French county, was the birthright of the Queen's mother, Jeanne. When she died in 1279, Eleanor and Edward crossed the Channel to take possession of the strategically sited area of Northern France. Arrangements were made for a regency in the King's absence and Godfrey Giffard, Bishop of Worcester, Thomas de Cantilupe, Bishop of Hereford, Edmund, Earl of Cornwall, and Henry de Lacy, Earl of Lincoln, were named to act for the King on 27 April 1279.[44] The six-week regency proved to be uneventful. On his return Edward stayed with Edmund at Rockingham and then Oakham.[45] Prior to the marriage of the King's daughter, Margaret, to John of Brabant, Edmund was advanced £2,285 14s.4d. for the expenses of the event by the Ricardi, the Italian bankers.[46]

As a boy, Edmund had travelled widely, but, after the mission to welcome Edward I home, his next trans-marine journey was not until 1280. On 2 June, protection was granted to Edmund as he was going 'beyond seas', probably to France.[47] However, he was still at court as he witnessed a royal charter, six days later.[48] By now he was a regular witness of such charters. Nothing is known about the reasons for his journey abroad but it is unlikely that he was away for long as the King stayed at his manor of Knaresborough on 24 August.[49] Another royal stay was at Lechlade in 1281 but the King might have stayed at the Hospital rather than with Edmund.[50]

It came as a complete surprise to King Edward and the English government when Wales exploded on to the political scene again in 1282. Edward had been relatively lenient following Llywelyn's surrender after the First Welsh War. He had softened the terms of the surrender, agreeing to release hostages and even attending and paying for the marriage of Eleanor de Montfort to Llywelyn at Worcester Cathedral on 13 October 1278.[51] Dafydd ap Gruffudd, Llywelyn's brother, had been on the English side in 1277 and had been given two of the Four Cantreds of Perfeddwald previously held by Llywelyn. Whatever his grievances with English administrators, the Eastertide attack by Dafydd on Hawarden castle on 21 April 1282 which began the Second Welsh War, enraged the King. He regarded it as a betrayal of his trust and friendship as well as sacrilege because of the timing of the assault. Although he probably realised what a perilous course he was about to take, the disgruntled Llywelyn, who himself had problems with English justices, had little choice but to join his brother.

An appointment of Edmund as a conservator for the peace in seventeen counties was made on 30 April 1282[52] and, on 1 May, the Constable of the Tower of London was commanded to allow Edmund to enter it and dwell there.[53] It is clear that, whilst the King journeyed to Wales to deal with the rebellion, Edmund acted as his representative in the capital.[54] Another visit abroad had been planned.[55] Edmund was to have gone via Windsor and Rochester to Dover as the constables of these castles were ordered to let Edmund enter and stay there and to be attentive to him.[56] It is very unlikely that he did go overseas as, on 24 May, the King ordered him to prevent money, raised from the tax of a tenth, from being taken out of England. This tax had been granted by the clergy in aid of the Holy Land. Edmund was ordered 'to be caused to come before him all merchants of London, and to inhibit them under pain of loss of life and limbs and of all their goods in the realm from taking out of the realm money arising from the said tenth'. Any merchants who were found to be wishing to take the money out of the realm were to be arrested.[57]

Even though he was not with the itinerant royal court, Edmund still benefited from his relationship to the King. At Ruthin on 8 September, Edmund was granted, during the King's pleasure, all the liberties and immunities of his father, saving the royal prerogative in wards. He was also promised to be protected against the Pope and all others, in respect of the payment of 8,000 marks, which he made upon the King's mandate concerning his father's will. Finally he received a pardon for illegal hunting and was given the wardship, although not the marriages, of the heirs of the baron Baldwin Wake.[58]

In Westminster Edmund must have been left with fewer Chancery clerks than normal as even the Exchequer was moved to Shrewsbury.[59] His military obligations were performed by others.[60] Instructions were sent to him from the King's war-time bases.[61] The fact that sensitive tasks were given to Edmund shows that the King trusted his judgement. The war was going the King's way and Llywelyn was killed in December. It had been intended to call a Parliament to meet in January 1283 to vote for money and supplies but, due to the war, it was decided to have two assemblies meeting at Northampton and York instead. These assemblies involved both the laity who, as the barons were assumed to be in the field, were represented by knights and burgesses, and the clergy. Edmund presided over the assembly held in Northampton. The laity were amenable and granted a thirtieth but the clergy, who had already paid a fifteenth to the King plus a crusading tenth to the Pope, delayed consenting until December.[62] As Edmund had been only partially successful, another meeting of the clergy was summoned to be held at London when Edmund and John de Kirkby were instructed to once again explain matters.[63]

Edmund was ordered to take the King's place in London on 14 January 1282, to hear and determine the case between English merchants and those of the Count of Flanders, according to a composition made between the King and the Count. The case was to have been heard at Boston but the Count had complained to the King about the shortness of the time, and asked the King to preside in person. Being unable to do so because of the Welsh war, the King appointed Edmund instead.[64] Two years later, this appointment was reflected when Edmund was granted the scutage of his knights in Cornwall because he 'has remained in England at his own charge for the preservation of the peace therein'.[65]

During June 1282, Dafydd, now Prince of Wales and who had been on the run, was captured. By July 1283, Edmund had left London and the Mayor was acting on his behalf[66] and, in October, he was at Acton Burnell in Shropshire for the state trial and execution of Dafydd, and the Parliament which was held next to Robert Burnell's new castle.[67]

A further journey overseas was planned by Edmund in May 1284.[68] Again, no details survive indicating the purpose of his trip. Charters were granted in his name later that May and in June[69] but the first concrete evidence that he had returned to England was in December when he witnessed royal charters at Bristol.[70] Although the Welsh War was over in 1283, the King spent a long time traveling not only in Wales but widely throughout the kingdom and it was not until April 1285 that he was again back at Westminster.[71] During most of this period, Edmund was the focus of royal authority in London with the exception of his time at Bristol. Throughout the whole of 1285 and until May 1286 witness lists show that he was often at court.[72] Then, on 13 May 1286, the King left for Gascony[73] and did not return for more than three years. Edmund, now 36, was to act as Regent for the whole of this time. The King divided his council, leaving half of the members to advise Edmund but he took with him all his major officials including the Chancellor, stewards and the wardrobe staff.

Chapter 3

Edmund: The Regent

Protervos domitans ne Wallia praedominetur,
Regis et absentis regnum ratione tuetur.

(Taming the arrogant lest Wales should take supremacy,
he also watches over the kingdom by reason of its absent king.)

O pinions differ as to the success of Edmund's period as Regent between 1286 and 1289. Mary Midgley faulted the Regency for failing to keep the peace and ensuring the proper administration of justice.[1] Edward I's strong reaction to the state of affairs in England on his return adds weight to her verdict. Marc Morris believed that the absence of the King was a factor; 'robbers as well as rebels would seize the opportunity if they thought that the government seemed weak'.[2] Tout thought that the Chancery worked well during a period of administrative disorder. He believed that 'the Regent Cornwall was doubtless a weaker man than his cousin, but he was terribly handicapped by the entire absence of the wardrobe, and the division of the council and the chancery. Lack of official as well as of personal control, led to the judicial and ministerial scandals that Edward was called upon to remedy on his 'return'.[3]

It is not certain how personally involved Edmund was in day-to-day administration.[4] Writs recorded in the rolls were testified by him usually at Westminster but he might have been able to get away to his homes at Berkhamsted, Ashridge, Cippenham, Beckley or Wallingford.[5] That he was sometimes away from Westminster is shown by a letter that he wrote to William de Hamilton asking him to deal with the petition of the merchants of the Circuli. Dated 27 May 1288, it was sent from Ashridge and yet, on the same day, the Fine Roll has an entry that Edmund was said to have testified at Westminster.[6] On 13 February when Edmund was at Berkhamsted, he was recorded as authorising a writ at Westminster.[7]

This evidence is reinforced by other letters written to Hamilton implying that they were not together and that, when in doubt, Edmund took advice as was intended by the King.[8]

The Revolt of Rhys ap Maredudd

The real test of Edmund's metal began when Rhys, who had previously been a staunch Welsh ally and married to Ada, the sister of John de Hastings, Lord of Abergavenny, rebelled.[9] The settlement after the First Welsh War in 1277 had seen Rhys ceding his castle of Dinefwr, but retaining Dryslwyn, both in South Wales. Now Rhys saw the prospect of regaining Dinefwr. There were early indications that trouble was brewing. In February or March 1287, Robert Tibetot wrote to Edmund asking for assistance as Rhys was refusing to mainpern in court proceedings.[10] On 20 May, Edmund ordered the justices led by Ralph de Hengham, to investigate trespasses and wrongs committed against the King by Rhys. Illustrating his desire for fairness, Edmund enjoined the justices 'to do justice in this matter to both the King and Rhys, as the King wills that justice shall be done to both'. Reinforcing his concern, Edmund required that 'justice shall be exhibited to all and singular of his realm concerning trespasses and wrongs committed upon them.'[11] But it was too late and violence broke out on 8 June 1287. Rhys seized back Dinefwr and took Caercynan and Llandovery. Then he ravaged the outskirts of Carmarthen and burnt Swansea.

Quick action was taken by Edmund's government. On 14 June, Edmund summoned forces to muster at Gloucester on 21 July for war.[12] Rhys became a wolf's head, an outlaw, on 5 July; a price of £100 was put on his head.[13] This amount was several year's income for a knight. Individuals in the Marches were instructed not to communicate with or help Rhys or his supporters.[14] The merchants of Lucca were to provide money for the army.[15] By 31 August they, and merchants from Florence, Sienna and Pistoia, had provided a total of nearly £2,000. Money was needed to pay for large numbers of infantry. On 24 June, the Sheriff of Shropshire and Staffordshire was ordered to send 500 men without delay whilst the sheriffs of Gloucester, Hereford, and of Nottingham and Derby were to provide 300, 300 and 1,000 footmen respectively.[16]

Edmund was at Gloucester by 16 July when he ordered the Savoyard, John de Bonvillars, the brother-in-law of the King's friend, Otto de Grandson, and who had been constable of the new castle of Harlech, to come to him with twenty knights and 2,000 men. The Sheriff of Shropshire had to send 2,000 diggers and woodcutters and 200 carpenters.[17] All markets in Warwickshire, Shropshire, Worcestershire and Gloucestershire were closed as everything was to be taken to Hereford to victual the expedition into Wales. From Somerset goods were to go to Bristol and Bridgwater[18] and on to Monmouth by 28 July.[19] Edmund stayed at Hereford from 21 until 23 July.[20] From here he issued further demands to the Marchers to send troops. The total number of troops requested were as follows in table 3.1:

Table 3.1: Troops demanded to serve against Rhys ap Maredudd

Person	Amount and Recruitment Area		Place of Muster
Sheriff of Salop and Staffs	500 foot	Salop and Staffs	with Edmund Mortimer
Sheriff of Gloucester	300 foot	Gloucestershire	with Edmund Mortimer
Sheriff of Hereford	300 foot	Herefordshire	with Edmund Mortimer
Sheriff Of Notts and Derby	1,000 foot	Notts and Derbyshire	with Edmund Mortimer
John de Bonvillars	2,000 foot	20 horses Gwynedd	Aberystwyth
Henry de Lacy, Earl of Lincoln	400 foot	Rhos and Rhufoniog	Aberystwyth
Reginald de Grey	200 foot	Dyffryn Clwyd + Tegeingl	Aberystwyth
Reginald de Grey	1,000 men (200 diggers, 200 tree fellers) Cheshire		Aberystwyth
Maud de Mortimer	300 foot	his (sic) land	Aberystwyth
Roger de Mortimer	400 foot	his land	Aberystwyth
Peter Corbet	400 foot	his land	Aberystwyth
Richard FitzAlan	400 foot	Clun	Aberystwyth
Richard FitzAlan	200 foot	Oswestry	Aberystwyth
Bailiffs of Bishop's Castle (Bishop of Hereford?)	200 foot	Clun	Aberystwyth
Hawise de la Pole	100 foot	Strettondale	Aberystwyth

Person	Amount and Recruitment Area		Place of Muster
Queen Eleanor (bailiffs)	100 foot	Maelor Saesneg	Aberystwyth
Queen Eleanor (bailiffs)	500 men (inc. 100 carpenters) Macclesfield		Aberystwyth
Edmund of Lancaster	all footmen	Monmouth	Monmouth
Theobald de Verdon	all footmen	Ewyas Lacy	Monmouth
Geoffrey de Geneville	all footmen	Ewyas Lacy	Monmouth
Bailiff of St Briavels	all footmen + 400 wood cutters St Briavels		Monmouth
Sheriff of Salop and Staffs	2,000 diggers +wood cutters Salop and Staffs		Monmouth
William de Valence	all footmen	Goodrich + Archenfield	Monmouth
Earl Warenne	500 foot	Bromfield and Yale	Monmouth
William de Valence	all footmen	Pembroke	Carmarthen
Bishop of St David's	all the power	?	Carmarthen

Source; *Welsh Rolls*, 312–4

In all Edmund had summoned over 8,300 footmen, 20 horses, 2,200 diggers and wood cutters, another 200 tree fellers and carpenters as well as 'all the men' of seven other Marcher barons.

With his troops gathered or on their way, Edmund advanced into Wales via Gloucester[21] arriving at Carmarthen on 9 August 1287[22] and Dryslwyn on 26 August.[23] However, Tibetot and the Marcher barons had already been in action. Edmund de Mortimer and John Gifford protected the Middle March around Brecon and the Upper Wye.[24] Reginald de Grey was commanded to sustain the royal interests in the North and Tibetot had moved to secure Cardiganshire. Edmund knew Tibetot well as they had witnessed royal charters together since 1280.[25] Tibetot concentrated his forces at Carmarthen. Rhys switched his attacks to Brecon and Edmund's army moved southwards via Monmouth and Glamorgan before joining Tibetot at Carmarthen. They proceeded to besiege Rhys's castle at Dryslwyn. Men from the North under Grey joined the forces at Dryslwyn as did John de Havering bringing men from Snowdonia and Roger l'Estrange with a contingent from Shropshire and the adjoining March. Rhys was not himself in the castle and the Earl of Hereford was ordered to move to contain him.

Dryslwyn was besieged with vigour. The besiegers used a siege engine. However, there was a disaster when a mine being dug under the chapel wall collapsed. Amongst those killed by the rock fall was Warin de Munchesney, the son of an heiress of William Marshal, and John de Bonvillars.[26] However, reinforced by the men of Gloucester, the siege was over by 5 September 1287. Alan de Plukenet became constable and was given Rhys's commotes on 24 September.[27] Edmund thought that it was all over and returned to Westminster. Wykes believed that Edmund had been persuaded by Gloucester to agree to a truce.

Whatever happened, it soon became clear that Rhys had not given up and war flared up again. In November, Rhys seized Newcastle Emlyn, slew the garrison and captured Roger Mortimer. The rebels went on to invest Dinefwr. According to Marc Morris, Edmund seems to have underestimated the threat. On 14 November, he simply ordered the lords marcher to remain on their marches and to secure their own castles. But the wording of this writ seems stronger as he urged them to pursue Rhys 'by night and by day' and enjoined them to capture and keep the rebels and to wholly repulse the rebellion.[28] Crossbows and quarrels came from the Tower of London.[29] Tibetot relieved Dinefwr and by 28 December was besieging Emlyn which fell around 20 January 1288. Rhys disappeared, and caused no more serious trouble. He was at liberty for a long time but he was captured and sent to the King for judgement and execution at York in 1291,[30] or in 1292 according to Rees Davies.

The rebellion occurred and had been dealt with on Edmund's watch. Davies was of the opinion that the response to it was 'swift and crushing' and that 'the Marcher lords co-operated closely and effectively with the local royal commanders'.[31] The size of the forces gathered by Edmund's orders shows no complacency but two biographers of Edward I thought that the government's response was an over-reaction. Michael Prestwich wrote that 'perhaps the government over-reacted in the early stages', whilst Marc Morris was more forceful: the government 'responded with a massive overraction' and 'a sledgehammer' was used 'to crack a walnut'.[32] These judgements made with hindsight are difficult to sustain. Perhaps L.F. Salzmann was fairer when he wrote that Edmund 'acted with vigour and promptitude'.[33]

The age of Welsh rebellions was not over. Another serious one broke out only six years later during which the King was besieged at Conwy and the great castle of Caernarvon was destroyed. One response to this uprising was the construction of Beaumaris castle and it was in 1296 that the King's 'architect', Master James of St George, when writing to the Exchequer pleading for funds, added 'As to how things are in the land of Wales, we still cannot be any too sure. But, as you well know, Welshmen are Welshmen, and you need to understand them properly.'[34] From a different viewpoint, Edmund's actions deserve credit. Left to handle a major rebellion, he did not have the normal facilities available to the King and, in particular, Edmund was not able to rely on the Wardrobe for cash as Edward had taken it to Gascony with him. The rapid use of the Ricardi and their associates to provide money for a paid rather than a feudal army, helped him to meet a real challenge.[35]

When he heard of the fall of Newcastle Emlyn to the rebels in November 1287, the King was furious and later blamed Edmund but the Queen intervened telling Edward that the fault was that of the keepers of the castles who had not garrisoned them adequately. The evidence is contained in a letter written in December by the curial Bishop of Ely and Treasurer, John de Kirkby, from Bordeaux. He wrote the King inquired about the Earl of Cornwall, and asked for news of England and when they were both alone, how the business at Dryslwyn went. Kirkby told the King told how things went at the assault. The King was greatly pleased with the deeds of the Earl but when, five days afterwards, came the news of how Newcastle Emlyn was taken, Kirkby had much to do to defend the honour of the Earl. He said that Edmund had wished to make arrangements about the castles different from those made by the keepers; and that they had undertaken at their peril to guard the castles with too few men. The loss came entirely by the default of those who undertook the guard with so few men. The Queen openly upheld this argument and said that the Earl had honourably done all his duty.[36] Although he received little credit at the time, Edmund's epitaph mentions that he 'ensured that the arrogant Welsh did not predominate'. It must be assumed that Edmund had not lost the King's confidence as he continued as Regent.

Although violence had ceased by early 1288, the government was still on its guard. The Prior of the English Hospitallers was sent to survey 'the state of those parts' in Wales including the royal castles.[37] In May the government wrote to Edmund Mortimer complaining that he had been ordered to 'cause the trees and underwood in every pass in his lands in Wales and the Marches of Wales to be felled and to cause the passes to be enlarged ... but nothing has been done ... to the great danger of those passing through the passes'. The King 'greatly wonders and is not unnaturally moved'. Mortimer was ordered to carry out the works without further delay.[38] Roger Mortimer, Owen de la Pole, Henry de Lacy, John de Warenne, Reginald de Grey, Robert de Tibetot, Alan Plukenet and William de Grandson were sent the same writ.[39] Edmund Mortimer and the Marchers together with the royal constables were reminded of the need to be vigilant in November as Rhys was still roving about. They were to put out spies to warn of his presence so that he could be pursued.[40] At the beginning of 1289, hostages were still being held at Dryslwyn and it was rumoured that Rhys was in the Gower intending to go to Ireland.[41] Even in May 1289, fear of a Welsh attack must have been behind Edmund's order to replace thatched roofs at Carmarthen castle with stone.[42]

Reviewing the progress and suppression of the revolt, it is difficult not to be struck by the vigour of Edmund's government but also the mixture of tact and blandishment with threats used to achieve his aims. In the original instruction to investigate Rhys's complaints, he made it clear that the justices were to be even-handed. When in June 1287, he needed the help of the barons and knights of Shropshire and Staffordshire and the adjoining March, he added 'The King thanks them for their strenuous assistance in Roger's company during the last disturbance in Wales and desires that their continued bravery and fidelity may merit his commendation.'[43] Even before the royal army mustered, Edmund gave permission to Tibetot to accept the surrender of Rhys's allies to 'receive the King's peace'.[44] After the muster, Gilbert de Clare, and Humphrey de Bohun, Earl of Hereford, were given the same permissions for South Wales and Brecon.[45] Sensitivity to niceties and to public opinion was shown even when Edmund ordered a price to be put on Rhys's head. He stated that Rhys 'has been often warred on the King's behalf' and he would not submit 'himself to the King's peace, which the King graciously offered him'.[46] When the knights of Cheshire were asked to go to West Wales, Edmund recognised that 'they have not hitherto been wont to transfer themselves out of their own boundaries', but if they came, the King would 'consider this action as arising from their grace and not their duty, and he wills that it shall not be drawn into a precedent or prejudice in future'.[47] The day after this writ, Edmund summoned a large number of Marcher barons including Edmund Mortimer and Humphrey de Bohun to send horses and arms and offer counsel and aid to Gilbert de Clare in parts of Brecon 'so as to merit the King's commendation for his fidelity, bravery and diligence'.[48] When the sheriffs were ordered to close the markets, they were 'enjoined to execute this order in such a way as to merit the King's commendation'.[49] When the embers of the rebellion were rekindled in November and Edmund asked the Marchers to suppress it, he added that they should conduct themselves diligently and manfully so as to convince the King.[50] Appointing Peter Corbet as Keeper of parts of Cardiganshire on 6 December, Edmund made it clear that was because the King 'trusts his fidelity, circumspection and diligence'. Peter was to conduct himself as 'to earn the King's perpetual commendation and so that the King may be bound by his good merits and great thanks'.[51]

However, there was a fist of steel in the velvet glove. When the destination of the goods was switched from Hereford to Ludlow and thence to Brecon, each sheriff was warned 'to behave himself so in the execution of this order that the King may not punish him'.[52] A peremptory note began the writ to the Sheriff of Shropshire on 5 August 1287 when he was ordered 'immediately upon the sight of these letters, laying aside all delay, to provide ...'[53] Edmund, or his official, had obviously lost patience as he continued that 'the King now understands that no victuals are being sent or carried to those parts' and that the expedition was suffering from their lack, 'at which he is greatly moved'. The delay was imputed 'to the Sheriff's default and negligence'. He was warned to conduct himself so that 'the King may plainly perceive that this order will take effect'. There was a bitter sting in the tail. Edmund concluded that 'otherwise the King will punish him by imprisonment and by all his goods and chattels that the Sheriff and his heirs shall feel themselves for ever aggrieved'.[54] Even when praising Peter Corbet on his appointment in 1286, Edmund added that Peter 'shall not allege now the state of wintry weather or lack of money for him or his footmen'. Peter was enjoined not to neglect his duties as 'he loves the King's and his own honour'.[55] In reminding the Marchers of the need to comply with the orders about clearing wood from passes, the government threatened them to carry out the works without further delay so that the King 'may not have to punish him and his goods'.[56] Over a year after the fall of Emlyn, William de Braose and the Bailiff of Swansea were cautioned not to omit in their actions against Rhys so as to avoid 'the King's everlasting anger'.[57] Of course, whilst these threats might be characterised as the smack of firm government, there is xthe possibility that they resulted from panic.

Other Regency Duties

Apart from much routine business, Edmund was given specific tasks which required diplomacy. During 1287, he summoned meetings of the Council to investigate the dispute between the Ricardi bankers and John of Berwick, King's clerk and Keeper of the Queen's gold, over 500 marks which he claimed that he had given to them on the Queen's account.[58] Dealing with important contestants must have needed tact. At the beginning of 1289 the King wrote from Gascony to say that, whilst he had given permission to the merchants of Bordeaux to import their wine into the city of London, the citizens of London had complained to the King. The King asked Edmund to summon a council and 'to see justice done to both parties'.[59] In April Edmund presided over a council at Westminster which some historians have seen as a Parliament.[60] Acting to prevent conflict in March, in June he intervened in the dispute between his brother-in-law, Gilbert, and the Earl of Hereford forbidding Gilbert to build a castle at Morlais.[61]

On 12 August 1289 the King arrived back in England and Edmund's regency was over. Edmund, however, appears to have been immune from the King's great inquiry into the problems that had arisen in his absence. Edmund was pardoned for all forest offences committed during the king's absence and was permitted to answer by proxy for any complaints against his administration in Cornwall.[62]

Chapter 4

Post-Regency Years

From 1287 until the crises of 1297, Edmund played a less prominent role although, after Queen Eleanor's death on 28 November 1290, it was at Ashridge that Edward I spent his first Christmas as a widower and he stayed there for over a month.[1] Whilst there, Parliament was convened. Paul Brand suggested that the holding of the Parliament resulted from the news of the death of the lawful holder of the Scottish throne, the Maid of Norway, in late September 1290. She had been betrothed to the King's son, Edward, following the Treaty of Brigham. This marriage would have brought to an end the threat of war along the Border and there were safeguards to the Scots ensuring that the two kingdoms were to be kept separate. The failure of this strategy led to the subsequent manoeuvrings of the various claimants to the Scottish throne. There was an urgent need to consider what Edward could best do to forward English interests in Scotland in the light of the changed circumstances. It is not clear how long the Parliament lasted. Some business was done by the King and his Council as early as Christmas Day. Parliamentary business might have been continued after Edward left Ashridge on 26 January 1291.[2]

Regular summons to parliaments were sent to Edmund.[3] He was summoned for war against the Scots in 1291, although the expedition was cancelled.[4] When the King went north for the long discussions on the succession to the Scottish throne in May, it seems odd that Edmund did not appear to have been with him as this important business was due to be discussed at Norham castle on the Tweed, and later at Berwick in 1292. Perhaps the King had asked him to stay in London as his representative. Following lengthy debates, the King had given his judgement that the rightful King of Scotland was John Balliol but Edward used his position as the arbitrator to require John to render him homage as his overlord.

A royal visit to Knaresborough took place on the King's return from the Borders in September 1292 and to Wallingford thirteen months later.[5] Fear of invasion led to a protection being issued to Edmund and the Bishop of Exeter for their lands in Devon and Cornwall in 1294.[6] Another Welsh rebellion, that of Madog ap Llywelyn, appeared to have been planned knowing that the King was taking his army to Gascony leading to Edmund's summons for military service in 1295.[7] It seems likely that he did not go nor did he serve when the King took action against John Balliol, in the next year when Balliol refused to answer in the English law courts.[8] Following the English victory of Dunbar, Scottish prisoners were sent to Edmund to be placed in custody in Wallingford castle.[9]

At the beginning of the turbulent year of 1297, Edmund was ordered to be with the King at Salisbury as the King wished to have 'parliament and treaty concerning certain arduous affairs touching him and the Earl and the realm'.[10] After two decades of much success, the 1290s saw the King losing his golden touch. The deaths of his Queen and of his friend and effective Chancellor, Robert Burnell, may have been contributing factors. The crisis of 1297 had its origins as far back as 1294.[11] War started with Philip IV of France declaring the duchy of Gascony as forfeit and, in response, Edward I began to establish a series of alliances along the eastern frontiers of France with the idea of fighting in Flanders. But he was not able to give the French problems his full attention for several years. First he had to deal with the serious rebellion of Madoc ap Llywelyn in the autumn of 1294 and this dragged on throughout the winter. Soon after peace returned, he was concerned with Scotland as John Balliol had formed an alliance with King Philip. The English won a major victory at Dunbar. However, in January 1297, when Edward was ready to start his Flemish campaign, news came of a serious defeat in Gascony where the seneschal was captured. Edward decided to send reinforcements but, at the February Parliament, the Marshal, Roger Bigod, Earl of Norfolk, took violent exception claiming that he was only liable to go on campaign with the King. The clergy also refused to grant a financial aid relying on a new papal bull, *Clericos Laicos*, which forbade churchmen from paying taxes without papal consent. Revenge was taken on Bigod by enforcing ancient debts to the Exchequer and taking control of all the clergy's lay estates.

Sending help to Gascony, Edward continued his preparations for the Flemish expedition and summoned a muster for 7 July. Backed this time by the Constable of England, Humphrey de Bohun, Earl of Hereford,

Bigod again refused to serve. He asserted that the muster was irregular and objected to being asked to fight in Flanders which was not part of the King's realm. The magnates and their allies produced the *Remonstrances* setting out their grievances. But Edward went abroad leaving his son and advisers to deal with the political unrest. William Wallace's climatic victory over the English at Stirling Bridge on 24 September had benefits for the King as the clergy dropped its opposition and granted a new tax. The Confirmation of the Charters of 10 October restored harmony.

Gascony in 1297 was the last place overseas that Edmund is known to have planned to visit.[12] Whether he went or not, he was back by the autumn when he stood by the King during the disputes with those led by the Earls of Norfolk and Hereford. When Edward went to Flanders, Edmund stayed behind as an adviser to Prince Edward.[13] Edmund showed his support for the King in his dispute with the church ensuring that the fine for the redemption of clerical goods was paid as far as Eye Priory was concerned.[14]

On 26 April 1298 at Westminster Edmund's name appears for the last time as a witness on the Charter rolls[15] although, in November 1299, he witnessed a release by Amadeus, Count of Savoy to the King.[16]

At the end of 1298, the King decided to attempt again to quell the Scots. Edmund received his summons to muster at Carlisle for war service[17] and, at the end of December, a writ requiring him to dispatch 'suitable and sufficient aid of men-at-arms in as much force as he can, in order to set out for Scotland as shall be then ordained by the King'. Nevertheless, showing that the court was aware that Edmund was ageing and unwell, the writ continued that 'the King is aware of the feebleness of the Earl's body, by reason whereof he cannot come in person'.[18] Sweet revenge was the King's when his massive army defeated Wallace at Falkirk on 22 July.

Although the King was now aware of Edmund's decline in health, in February 1299 he received a summons to come to London in March 'to treat of certain of the King's affairs beyond sea and to give counsel concerning them, as the King wishes to have a parliament ... upon the said affairs'.[19] Another Parliament, to discuss peace terms with France, was held that May and Edmund was summoned to attend.[20] The finalisation of a peace agreement with the French removed their threat as the ally of the Scots. John Balliol, who had been a prisoner since 1296, was released. However, war north of the border proved necessary as Baliol's subjects were still not subdued. Once more, Carlisle was chosen to be the location for another muster of the English army. Forgetting the pardon of the previous year, Edmund was required to serve but he was later excused.[21] There is no explanation of the decision in August to send Brother Henry de Radelegh, a monk of Hailes, to cross from Dover with two grooms, two horses, and their harness, to go to parts beyond sea for the affairs of Edmund, Earl of Cornwall.[22]

In Edmund's last year, he was summoned to the Parliament of March 1300 which saw the drafting of the *Articuli Cartas*, another concession to the opposition to the King's policies. The Scottish campaign, begun in the previous year, was fought in the winter and had been largely unsuccessful so another muster at Carlisle for action against the Scots at Midsummer was issued.[23] The payment of 100 marks brought a pardon for Edmund from being personally ready for military action.[24] Perhaps the last time he saw the King was when the monarch stopped at Knaresborough on the way to Scotland in April. But it is possible that Edmund was not there, having stayed in the Home Counties.[25]

As Matthew Paris might have phrased it, Edmund 'went the way of all flesh' at Ashridge. Confusion surrounds the actual date of his death when he was 50. The King had reached the Scottish borders and on 25 September whilst at Rose Castle, the seat of the Bishop of Carlisle, he heard of Edmund's death. He immediately sent a letter to the Archbishops, Bishops and thirty abbots requesting the celebration of exequies for the soul of Edmund, Earl of Cornwall, the King's kinsman, lately deceased, and to aid with their prayers.[26] However, Mary Midgley noted the record in the Pipe Roll that the date that '*quo die dictus comes obiit*' was 30 September.[27] This citation is from the Pipe Roll in 1300–01 but, in the previous year, the Steward of Oakham, was recorded as stating that the Earl '*obiit in crastino Scti Michaelis*'.[28] White Kennett believed that Edmund died on 1 October 1300[29] and the Bury St Edmund's monks celebrated Edmund's death on the feast of the Translation of St Remigius, which is also 1 October.[30] The Worcester Annalist agreed that the death occurred on 1 October, writing '*Rumor vulgaris fuit quod Kal. Octobris Edmundud Comes Cornubiae raptus fuit subite de hac vita.*'[31]

Whatever the date of his death, Edmund's body was subjected to excarnation rather than embalmment via the method known as *mos teutonicus*. This well-known practice had been used on the body of Louis

IX when he died on crusade at Tunis. Removing the flesh enabled speedy action prior to possible transport over long distances. After evisceration, the body would have been dismembered and boiled in water or wine until the flesh was cooked and fell off the bones. The entrails and any remaining flesh were buried immediately. We know that Edmund's entrails were removed on the very night that he died and were buried before the following dawn by the Abbot of St Albans.[32] This suggests that the Abbot had some notice that Edmund was at death's door. His bones were then able to be transported. Representing the King, Prince Edward was present with magnates including Edmund's old colleagues, Antony Bek, Bishop of Durham, and William de Beauchamp, Earl of Warwick, when Edmund's heart was buried at Ashridge on 12 January the following year.[33] The event was noteworthy as Prince Edward brought his trumpeters to perform at the ceremony.[34] The bones were taken to Hailes and the King himself was present when the bones were laid to rest alongside those of Edmund's father and mother at Hailes on 23 March 1301.[35]

Chapter 5

Edmund at Court: Presence and Rewards

An overview of Edmund's attendance at court and the number of rewards he received as a premier earl and the King's kinsman provides some idea of Edmund's importance to the rule of the kingdom. Evidence on how often he was at court can be gleaned from the list of witnesses of royal charters.

It was at Westminster on 26 April 1298 that Edmund's name appeared for the last time as a witness of a royal charter in the Charter rolls[1] although, in November 1299, he witnessed a release by Amadeus, Count of Savoy to the King.[2] During his career, Edmund is known to have witnessed at least 230 royal charters.[3] Richard Huscroft has argued persuasively for the accuracy of the lists of witnesses of Edward I's royal charters as being good evidence of those people named being at a given place and date.[4] From these lists it can be shown that Edmund was at court on at least 112 occasions but this is bound to be an underestimate. For instance, from the witness lists he was noted at Westminster on 23, 25 and 28 May 1281. It is very probable that he was also there on 24, 26 and 27 May.[5] In 1291, the court was at Edmund's manor and religious foundation of Ashridge from 8 to 16 January. Not all the charters were included on the Charter Rolls; on 2 December 1280, a charter which Edmund witnessed, was recorded on the Patent Rolls instead.[6]

Edmund witnessed the first of 230 charters on 22 October 1275[7] but it was not until November 1279 when he performed the same task again for another two charters.[8] The pace picked up and in 1280 and 1281 he attested seventeen and twenty-two charters respectively. The following three years saw him witness less frequently. Two charters in one day in 1282, were followed by five over ten days in 1283 and four more in two days in 1284. However, in 1285 he was very prominent being present when seventy-two charters were issued and he was there when a further forty-one were granted in the following year. Throughout the King's absence in Gascony there was a three-year gap in the Charter Rolls and charters were recorded in the Patent Rolls. But as Edmund was not with the King, this is academic as he could not have been a witness. When Edward returned to England, attestation began again and, in 1290, Edmund witnessed thirty-one charters. As Huscroft noted, in the last decade of Edmund's life, he was less often present as a younger generation took over.[9] He did not witness at all in 1291 and 1292 nor between 1295 and 1297. In the years between, 1293 and 1294, he attested ten and seventeen charters respectively. Having witnessed on 28 April 1298,[10] there were no more attestations of royal charters in the last two years of his life.

Witnesses lists show the relative status of the attestors. Senior clerics were recorded first and a hierarchy applied to the laymen. In the lists, Edmund was always highly placed, usually being entered as one of the first of the earls to be named after the bishops. He was only outranked by the King's brother, Edmund, Earl of Lancaster, and on most occasions, William de Valence, the King's half-uncle. On some witness lists, Edmund was referred to as the 'King's kinsman'.[11]

Although Edmund's activity in witnessing charters might seem impressive, work done by Andrew Spencer[12] shows that, in comparison with other earls, Edmund was not as prominent. He witnessed about 20 per cent of royal charters compared with 46 per cent by Henry de Lacy, Earl of Lincoln. Other earls who out-performed him were John de Warenne, Earl of Surrey (35 per cent), William de Valence, Earl of Pembroke (38 per cent), Edmund, Earl of Lancaster (37 per cent), and Edmund's brother-in-law, Gilbert de Clare, Earl of Gloucester (34 per cent). Of the senior earls, only Roger Bigod, Earl of Norfolk, and Humphrey de Bohun, Earl of Hereford, both of whom fell out with the King and withdrew from court for a while, witnessed fewer charters (18 per cent and 16 per cent). The lower level earls, those of Arundel, Oxford and Warwick were less prominent. Turning to the average number of charters witnessed in a year, Edmund was witness for nine. Of the senior earls, only Bigod and Bohun witnessed at a lower rate. By contrast, Lacy witnessed an average of twenty-three charters a year.

Edmund was a constant mainstay of his cousin, the king. He had carried out a range of sensitive tasks and his support never wavered. His other great service, as a lender of money throughout the reign, will be considered later. It might seem strange that he received so few rewards for his fidelity. The Earls of Lincoln and Surrey and other lords were granted large areas of Wales after the conquest but Edmund was given no new permanent holdings. But then he hardly needed more lands or money; he already held the then highest rank in the nobility.

It could be argued that King Edward could have given him a range of lesser rewards. *Curiales* and magnates expected gifts as symbols of appreciation and sometimes they were given new sources of income. Edward I was criticised even by his contemporaries for his lack of generosity compared with the munificence of his father.[13] The King's benevolence to Edmund as gifts were made on six occasions in 1278– 82 and in 1294, totalling twenty-nine to thirty bucks, two harts and eight live bucks and eight live does to stock his park.[14] Three palfreys were sent to him in 1288.[15] But one must wonder why a man who held over twenty parks and two forests needed any gifts of venison at all. He certainly needed no trees. More beneficial than gifts of deer were the six retrospective pardons for taking them from the royal forests without consent. At least six stags, sixty-one bucks, four does and a hart together with one sore stag and three sore bucks were covered.[16] Edmund did do well in the grant of wardships[17] but these were often given as a way of paying off royal debts to him.

It should not be assumed that royal goodwill would protect Edmund from penalties for failures of administration; even when he was acting as Regent, he was amerced shillings for letting a prisoner escape from his lands in Suffolk.[18] But, during 1288, a mandate was issued to the Justices of *Quo Warranto* in Oxfordshire to desist until further orders on twelve writs 'against Edmund, the King's kinsman, to whom the King granted that he should levy no such writs against him'.[19]

Tangible benefits flowed from Edmund's membership of the curial network. When judges were appointed to investigate his complaints about attacks on his parks, they could include men that he knew well. Robert de Seaton, who was to look into attacks on his park at Oakham in 1277,[20] was the brother of Edmund's steward, Richard.[21] Walter de Helion, who had witnessed charters with Edmund in 1279 and 1280,[22] was chosen to judge on attacks on the park at Corsham in 1282.[23] Helion's co-justice was a close member of Edmund's affinity, Henry de Shottesbrooke. Edmund's own clerk, Michael of Northampton, was selected to investigate trespasses in Edmund's Dartmoor forest in 1282.[24] Nicholas de Stapleton, another fellow charter witness,[25] was asked to inquire into events at Knaresborough in 1286.[26] Knaresborough in 1299 was where William de Bereford, who had been a witness for the personal charters of Edmund on five occasions,[27] was commanded to adjudicate.[28]

So it is clear that Edmund of Cornwall was often a prominent member of the King's court. He was a member of its highest echelons although not present as often as some other earls. However, he cannot be accused of being an habitual absentee or ever less than a loyal supporter of his cousin. Only in his last few years, when he was possibly unwell and the King journeyed far from Westminster, was his attendance at court rare. Compared to others, however, his rewards were very meagre for the services that he performed for the King.

Chapter 6

Edmund and His Family

Nature and nurture, or the interplay between them, are the determinants for the evolution of the character and actions of a person. So this chapter looks at Edmund's immediate blood family.

Edmund's Father: Richard of Cornwall

Nicholas Vincent, dealing with the reputation of Richard of Cornwall, drew attention to contemporary satire which made much of Richard's eye for the ladies. Richard had illegitimate children and one known mistress, Joan de Vautort. The Worcester Annalist branded him as 'a great lecher towards all women of whatever profession or condition, a most greedy storer-up of treasure, and a most violent oppressor of the poor.'[1] As Richard's foundation, Hailes Abbey, was in the diocese of Worcester this was a particularly harsh judgement emanating from Worcester Priory, whose members must have known of Richard's generosity to monastic houses. Vincent thought that Richard was neither innovative or grasping, spending only £2,000 on land acquisition.[2] The anonymous author, who celebrated the baronial victory at Lewes, called Richard a trickster and cheat.[3] On several occasions such as in 1227, 1233 and 1238, he proved to be an untrustworthy ally of the barons. He tended to support baronial confederacies but withdrew once his own grievances with the Crown had been settled. Although a crusader in 1240, and one of the most outspoken advocates of a military solution to the political crisis of 1264, in general, he preferred negotiation and arbitration to armed conflict.

According to Matthew Paris, Richard's unwarlike nature was to be explained not by any specific physical infirmity but by a general lack of either martial spirit or good health. Seen as being wiser than his brother, Henry III, he was more ready to seek consensus. 'As an arbiter and author of settlements to other men's disputes Richard was unrivalled in his day, making peace again and again between king and barons, and frequently serving as mediator in both baronial and ecclesiastical disputes.[4] When not at court, Richard spent most of his time in the Thames valley and infrequently visited his Cornish estates but he rebuilt Tintagel Castle, almost certainly because of its supposed association with King Arthur.[5]

There is no doubt that Edmund thought highly of his father. He spent long periods with him as a young man in Germany and, after the Battle of Lewes, they were together for more than a year in three different prisons. Whilst Danielle Westerhoff believed that Hailes was the only one of Richard's foundations that had Edmund's special consideration,[6] not only did he echo his father's piety and enhance his father's major religious foundation at Hailes, but he went further expanding on Richard's original scheme for a religious house at Rewley. Edmund also patronised houses that had been founded by Richard.[7] Although Richard might have treated Sanchia, Edmund's mother, badly and had a number of illegitimate children, this did not diminish Edmund's filial affection. One indication for this is the diplomatic used in the charters by which Edmund made grants to religious houses. This centres on the *pro anima* clauses, those provisions which stipulated a requirement for prayers for named individuals and their souls. In some Edmund specifically asked for prayers for the soul of his father.[8] In others he refers to the '*clare memorie*' of his father when describing himself as the son of Richard.[9] The statutes for Ashridge College required that the anniversary of the death of Richard be remembered[10] and the charters for the chapel at Wallingford and Rewley Abbey both required prayers for Richard.[11] When a grant was made to Eye Priory it was 'for the benefit of his soul and those of his mother and father'.[12] Late in life, Edmund's grant to the Knights Templar stated simply that it was for the good of his soul and the souls of his ancestors and successors[13] and this diplomatic form is used in several other charters.[14] Edmund adopted the suffix 'of Almain' as a further indication of his regard for his father, the King of Almayne.

Edmund's Mother: Sanchia of Provence

Born in 1228,[15] Sanchia of Provence was 15 when she married the 34-year-old widower, Richard of Cornwall. She was renowned for her beauty and it was that which swayed her future husband,[16] but Margaret

Howell wrote that Richard 'was too hard-headed and materialistic to have treated something as serious as marriage in a haphazard way'.[17] Richard's first wife, Isabel Marshal, had died three years earlier. The marriage with Sanchia lasted for eighteen years and Edmund was born when she was 19. He was often with his parents when they went to Germany but how much other time was spent with his mother is unclear.

Denholm-Young took the view that Sanchia was neglected but he appears to base this largely on Richard's absence when she was dying.[18] T.W.E. Roche took a different view. He believed that Richard was at Sanchia's bedside at Berkhamsted at the end of October 1261. However, when a German mission arrived in London early in November, this required Richard's urgent attention. Roche surmised that by then Sanchia's death was imminent and 'a foregone conclusion'. He even suggested that she might have been unconscious. But surely the Germans, after a long journey from Germany, would hardly have complained if they had been asked to travel another day to Richard's splendid castle at Berkhamsted. Whatever the truth, Richard was in Westminster Hall when the news of Sanchia's death was brought to him. Roche had no doubt that that the marriage had begun as a love match and that Denholm-Young's statement was 'very doubtful'.[19] Richard's first wife, Isabel Marshal, had died in child birth and this might have been the cause of Sanchia's death. However, the possible coolness shown by Richard to Sanchia suggests that pregnancy complications or childbirth were not the cause of Sanchia's death. If Sanchia did die in childbirth, this could relate to a report that an infant child of Richard's, also called Richard, was born at Grove Myle near Hailes and was then buried in the abbey.[20]

Whether Edmund sympathised with his mother over his father's infidelity is not known. She was only 33 when she died. She bequeathed an emerald ring worth 45 shillings and 2 pence to Henry of Almain but there was no such gift to Edmund. Why should Sanchia favour her stepson and not her own child? Was this because Edmund was only 11? Whatever the truth, it was hardly an extravagant gift.[21] Edmund sought prayers for his mother's soul in his charter for the Trinitarian Friars at Oxford,[22] and also in his charter for St Nicholas' chapel at Wallingford castle[23] and he required the commemoration of her death at Ashridge College.[24] She was also remembered in the *pro anima* clauses in some other charters.[25] At Mere castle, a chaplain was paid 50 shillings a year for saying prayers for her soul.[26]

When Edmund's body was buried, it was at Hailes close to Sanchia and alongside his father. John Leland believed that her heart was buried separately at Cirencester.[27] Sanchia was noted for her piety; Matthew Paris lent her his book on St Thomas and she made an offering to the shrine of St Albans in 1257 fulfilling a vow that she made earlier in the year when she was ill.[28] So Sanchia might have been as much a role-model to Edmund as his father.

Step-mother: Beatrix von Valkenburg

Edmund was 11 when his mother died and 19 when his father remarried, this time to Beatrix von Valkenburg, the orphaned niece of the Archbishop of Cologne.[29] She too was renowned for her beauty.[30] Edmund might have wished his father well or been somewhat jealous. Very little is known about Beatrix's relationship with Edmund; it is likely that he was at the marriage ceremony. Less than three years later, Richard of Cornwall was dead. Did Edmund feel any responsibility towards his widowed step-mother who, as an alien, would have felt somewhat isolated in England? She must have been of a similar age to Edmund. Lewis wrote 'We can well imagine that Edmund was not on the best terms with his father's young widow, because of the substantial dower which had to be paid to her. Moreover, he can hardly have been pleased with his father's marriage to a young girl at the age of fifty-nine.'[31] But Edmund was so rich that he may not have resented paying any dower.

As soon as Edmund succeeded his father, Beatrix found it necessary to mount eleven suits seeking dower in the counties of Northamptonshire, Derbyshire, Lincolnshire, Yorkshire, Wiltshire, Berkshire, Buckinghamshire, Devon, Cornwall, Gloucestershire and Oxfordshire.[32] Perhaps their relationship improved later. When he was abroad in 1273, Beatrix acted on his behalf when she presented the Rector of Chesterton.[33] But in the following year she sued Edmund for the manor of Newport, Essex, as part of her dower.[34] A year later, they were disputing chattels and debts belonging to Richard in the courts.[35] In 1276, they disputed the manor of Longborough, Gloucestershire. The Sheriff was ordered to deliver the manor to Beatrix, 'saving to Edmund, Earl of Cornwall, easements of the barns in the manor until the octaves of Midsummer next, as the manor was lately extended by the Sheriff at £32.4s.9d. and at 10s. from the view of frankpledge of the manor'. A dispute had arisen between Edmund and Beatrix concerning the extent, which Edmund challenged, and an agreement had been made between them in the King's court before the King himself. This stipulated that the manor should remain to Beatrix as of the value of 56 marks, 11d. of land and rent, in completion of a sum of 500 marks of land and rent, this being the amount awarded to her as a result of her dower cases.[36] In another dispute recorded in 1276, Edmund sought goods and chattels from Beatrix in Middlesex which must have been a continuation of the 1274 dispute.[37]

Beatrix survived the last record of her litigation against Edmund for only a few months, dying in October 1277.[38] No demand for prayers for the sake of her soul has been found in Edmund's charters. Assessing her court cases, it is difficult not to conclude that she, or her advisers, were devious in trying to set aside her marriage settlement.

Half-brother: Henry of Almain

Because Henry of Almain was fourteen years older than Edmund and they had different mothers, it is likely that they were not close. But this did not mean they had no regard for each other and, after Henry's murder, Edmund made a grant in which he referred to Henry as '*fratris nostri karissimi*'.[39] Henry was one of the young stars of the middle years of the century. Three years older than his cousin, the Lord Edward, the heir to the throne, he spent some of his childhood with him. In 1258, aged 22, Henry became politically important when he was nominated as one of the twelve royalist members of the council of twenty-four to oversee the Provisions of Oxford. He remained close to the Lord Edward in the confused evolution of the period of baronial reform but, in 1262, sided for a while with Montfort. Later, he returned to the royalists earning him the hostility of the Montforts. Being captured at the battle of Lewes, Henry and Edmund shared incarceration but Henry was released earlier than his father and step-brother and, having traveled abroad, he took no part in the Evesham campaign. When the war was over, Henry joined the Lord Edward's crusade and Edmund probably went with Henry.[40] After Henry's murder in 1271, Edmund was in contention with Henry's widow, Constance of Béarn, over a mere £10 in 1275.[41] Constance was to die before her father and the Béarnais lands, of which she was the heiress, passed to her younger sister and her husband, the Count of Foix.[42] Based on his actions as a young man, it is possible that, had he lived, Henry would have been a more forceful and energetic Earl of Cornwall.

Illegitimate Half-brothers and Sisters

Although White Kennett believed that another Richard of Cornwall was Edmund's 'base son',[43] he was in fact the son of Richard, Earl of Cornwall, probably by Joan de Vautort.[44] This Richard was a frequent witness of Edmund's charters (eighteen have been found) and he witnessed five charters made in Edmund's favour. When Edmund went overseas in 1280, Richard went with him.[45] As a gesture of Edmund's affection he gave Richard the manors of Asthall in Oxfordshire and Iver in Buckinghamshire.[46] Richard served Edmund as Steward of Knaresborough in 1284–85.[47] At the siege of Berwick in 1296, Richard was struck in the head by a spear and collapsed into the town where he died.[48] After Edmund's death, Richard's son contested Asthall with Hailes Abbey.[49] When, in 1305, a grant was made to another Edmund of Cornwall in his manor of Thonock in Lincolnshire, his father was referred to as Richard of Cornwall and the rights referred to were held formerly by Edmund, sometime Earl of Cornwall, and Richard de Cornubia.[50] This can be construed in two ways: following Kennett, that this Edmund was the son of the Earl Edmund but more probably of Earl Richard's illegitimate son. Perhaps this younger Edmund was so named by Richard as a gesture to Earl Edmund. Another Richard of Cornwall, a clerk, who was preferred towards the end of the century, may have had the same father.[51]

It seems certain that the Walter de Cornubia, who was given land to the value of £18 a year in his manor of Branel, Yorkshire, by Edmund, his brother, was yet another illegitimate son of Earl Richard. Living until 1313, Walter served as Coroner of Cornwall.[52] Joan de Cornwall, the daughter of Earl Richard and Joan de Vautort, was said to have married the Cornish knight Richard de Champernown.[53]

Uncle: Henry III

Edmund's only full uncle on his father's side was Henry III, King John's elder son, who married Edmund's mother's own sister, Eleanor of Provence. A compassionate and kind man, King Henry probably had affection for Edmund who had suffered during the Barons' Wars and who lost his father, mother and half-brother before Henry's own death. An indication of Edmund's warm regard for him was the stipulation in his charter in favour of Rochester Priory that the monks should pray for the soul of his uncle, the King, and the priests at Wallingford castle were required to do as well.[54]

Aunts: The Sisters of His Mother – Margaret, Queen of France; Eleanor, Queen of England; Beatrice, Queen of Naples

Turning to his aunts, the most illustrious were his mother's three sisters, Margaret, Eleanor and Beatrice, the other daughters of Raymond-Berengar V, Count of Provence. In turn they were married to King Louis IX of France, Henry III of England, and Charles, Louis's brother. From Beatrice, Charles eventually inherited Provence but he was also Count of Anjou and later King of Naples. All three sisters outlived Sanchia and they may have had some affection and sympathy for Edmund who was left motherless as a boy in 1261. Whilst Beatrice died in 1267, Margaret and Eleanor survived well into Edmund's adulthood, dying in 1296 and 1291 respectively.

Whether Edmund met Margaret and Beatrice is not clear. The 1259 meeting of all the sisters was cancelled as Richard was too preoccupied with securing the German Crown. Richard stayed in England when Henry III travelled to France to meet Louis IX for the publication of the Mise of Amiens in 1264. But it is possible that Edmund met Queen Margaret on his way to join the crusade or on his return from it. The most likely time for a meeting was when Sanchia travelled to Paris in 1254 to meet her sisters whilst Richard stayed behind as Regent.[55]

Aunts: The Sisters of Henry III

Of Edmund's father's sisters, Eleanor, the wife of Montfort is mentioned below. The others Joan, Queen of Scotland, and Isabella, the wife of the Emperor Frederick II, died before Edmund was born.

Cousin: King Edward I

Apart from the Montforts, Edward I was lucky in his dealings with all his male relatives. His brother, Edmund of Lancaster, was unfailingly loyal and helpful and Edmund of Cornwall never wavered in his service. Whether this was due to the character of the King in treating his closest relatives with tact and generosity or whether it was in their inherent natures is not easy to ascertain. As we have seen, Edmund of Cornwall gained little in material terms from the King. Without Edmund's frequent loans, the King would have had found it harder to perform his role. The only brief wobble in their relationship was when Edward was exasperated by the fall of Newcastle Emlyn to Rhys ap Maredudd during Edmund's Regency. It is very significant that it was to Edmund that the King turned for solace when he was widowed and he spend at least a month grieving at Edmund's favourite residence at Ashridge. When Edmund died the King sought the prayers of the higher clergy and he described Edmund as '*Nobilem Virum Edmundum, quondam Comitem Cornubiae, consanguinem nostrum carissimum, qui nostris et regni nostri negotiis semper promptus, devotus extitit et fidelis, et in quo virtutum et gratiarum dona multiplicia praelucebant nuper ab hoc saeculo, prout sibi placuit, evocavit: quod nobis, non sine multa mentis amaritudine nunciamus.*'[56] Edmund returned Edward's affection and regard, asking for prayers for his soul in his charters for Launceston Priory and Wallingford castle chapel.[57] As Tout wrote, 'Earl Edmund of Cornwall had always a high place in his cousin's affections and councils' and, when dealing with those who acted as his Regent or representative in Gascony, 'all served Edward with the utmost loyalty and were entirely trusted by him'.[58]

Cousin: Edmund of Lancaster

Born in 1245, Edward I's younger brother, Edmund, later Earl of Lancaster, was almost five years older than Edmund of Cornwall. However, he was named for St Edmund the martyr unlike the younger Edmund who was named for Archbishop Rich. When Prince Edmund was 9, the Pope offered him the Crown of Sicily, an offer which his father accepted leading to much of the unrest that triggered the period of baronial reform. In 1263, having surrendered Dover castle to Montfort,

Edmund accompanied his mother, the Queen, to France where she set about raising an army of mercenaries to support the King. They did not return until after the battle of Evesham meaning that he was not captured at Lewes and did not share his cousin's captivity.[59] One of Edmund of Cornwall's first actions on becoming Earl, was to agree to the request of Queen Eleanor to lend Prince Edmund £3,000 or 3,500 marks so that he could continue with his brother's crusade.[60] The two had set off for the Holy Land together.[61]

The two Edmunds knew each other well in adult life. They were together on at least sixty-three occasions when they witnessed royal charters.[62] Private charters of other *curiales* were also witnessed by both men, for instance for Otto de Grandson in 1290.[63] Service in the First Welsh War also brought them together. Whilst Prince Edmund was in Gascony with the King, he wrote to Earl Edmund, as Regent in England, about accusations against Aaron, his Jew,[64] and seeking his assistance for William de Percy.[65] As Regent, Edmund authorised an instruction to assess the bounds at Kirkham and Rigby, Lancashire, because of a dispute between Edmund of Lancaster and Vale Royal Abbey.[66] Having played a major role in both Welsh wars, Edmund was abroad during Rhys' rebellion, but was required to send all his men from his Monmouth lordship to support the royal army.[67] Both Edmunds gave unstinting support to the King and might have been similar in character although ultimately Edmund of Lancaster was more of an affective warrior and leader.

Cousin by Marriage: Eleanor of Castile

Although as wife of Edward I, the Queen and Edmund must have known each other well, there is scant evidence of their dealings. Stephen de Chenduit's debt to the Jews had been acquired by Eleanor[68] and, in a 1275 charter confirming the grant to Eleanor of Chenduit's manor of Langley which was within the honour of Berkhamsted, Edmund called her 'Precibus karissime domine Alianore, regine Anglie.'[69] She intervened to support Edmund when her husband's confidence was shaken on the recrudescence of Rhys ap Maredudd's rebellion at the end of 1287. Edmund attested her charter granting lands at Godshill.[70]

Edmund's Sister: Isabella?

In a 1308 document listing jewels returned by Piers Gaveston, there is a reference to a gift '*autre fermaille du doun Edmon, Counte de Cornewalle a madame Isabelle, la seor, que poise quatre deniers*'.[71] It is certain that Edmund had no sister named Isabella and, in his index, Chaplais noted the jewel as having been given to Queen Isabella, the wife of Edward II, but this cannot be accurate as she arrived in England eight years after Edmund's death. Another entry in the index has the jewel being given to Elizabeth, Edward II's sister, who married John, Count of Holland in 1297. The clerk may have put in the wrong name. Was it a gift from Edmund as a wedding present? But, if so, how did it come into Gaveston's hands. Whilst Gaveston gained Edmund's earldom, he was not entitled to the Earl's chattels.

Edmund's Remaining Aunt and Her Husband: The Montforts and Their sons

After the outbreak of the hostilities, the Barons War, family relationships were generally poor with Edmund's uncle, Simon, the husband of Eleanor sister of Henry III and Richard of Cornwall and his sons, Edmund's cousins, Henry, Simon and Guy. But Simon junior did resist pressure to have Edmund and his father killed in the aftermath of the death of his own father at Evesham[72] and the kindness of his aunt, Eleanor, to Edmund whilst he was in captivity has already been noted. A gift of wine was sent to the son of the King of Germany, who might have been either Edmund or Henry of Almain. For Palm Sunday 1265, Countess Eleanor spent £12.7s.2d. on a wide range of spices for her brother. After Easter, she sent dates, whale meat and sturgeon.[73] Whilst these gifts were mainly for her brother, at Pentecost she sent six and a half ells of cloth dyed in grain to be made into a robe for Edmund himself and also three hoods for the King of Germany and his son as well as a lined miniver fur hood for Edmund. This cost her 27 shillings.[74] The defeat and exile of the remaining Montforts removed any chance of a reconciliation and the shocking murder at Viterbo closed any chance for a reconciliation or an improved relationship that they might have had with Edmund.

Other Cousins and Relatives

When Ashridge College was instituted, Edmund required obituary masses for two other relatives: Peter, Count of Alençon, and Beatrice, Countess of Richmond.[75] Beatrice was the daughter of Henry III and Edmund's cousin. Peter too was a cousin, a younger son of Louis IX and about the same age as Edmund. Peter died in 1284 but perhaps he had met Edmund on crusade. Edward I's daughters put pressure on Edmund to come to terms with the citizens of Exeter in 1286, when he remitted 50 of 250 marks which the city was due to pay him when he withdrew his anger and indignation against them 'for certain trespasses committed' in the previous June.[76]

Conclusions

It seems reasonable to state that Edmund of Cornwall was at ease with most of his blood relations. He was a dutiful son and a reliable nephew and cousin. The only family members with whom he had problems were the Montfort men.

Chapter 7

Edmund's Marriage

The Marriage of Edmund and Margaret de Clare

It is not known when the marriage of Edmund to Margaret de Clare was arranged. Until his brother's death in March 1271, Edmund was not the heir to the earldom and his marriage would have been of minor importance. But Henry's murder made Edmund the future richest man in the realm and, when his father died on 2 April 1272, he succeeded and was recognised as Earl of Cornwall within the month.[1] Edmund, a 22-year old Earl, was in need of a wife. The life of Henry III was drawing to a close and the Lord Edward was on crusade but the Queen, Eleanor of Provence, was still very active. She had a reputation as a matchmaker and had been behind the marriages of both Edmund of Lancaster and Henry of Almain. Perhaps she was the prime mover in arranging Edmund's marriage. It seems that Richard of Cornwall had shown no interest which seems strange unless he was too unwell.[2]

Who was the best candidate? Edmund's father had married into the powerful Marshal family. His second marriage to Sanchia of Provence made the Queens of France and England, and later Naples, his sisters-in-law. The German third marriage furthered his Imperial interests. His elder son, Henry of Almain, found a bride in the heiress of Béarn and Bigorre.[3] Was there any member of a foreign royal, ducal or comital family available for Edmund to marry? The only unmarried daughter of Louis IX was Agnes, born in 1260, who later married the Duke of Burgundy but she was too closely related to Edmund, being his first cousin. None of the children of the Emperor Frederick were available but there were daughters of Ferdinand X of Castile, the brother of Queen Eleanor. The wave of alien marriages stimulated by the arrival in England of the Savoyards and Lusignans was now a thing of the past. If, following the example of his father's first marriage, Edmund should take an English wife, which family should he become allied with? From the list of witnesses to royal charters at the time,[4] Gilbert de Clare, as Earl of Gloucester and Hertford, outranked all the non-royal earls. A Clare bride was thus a logical choice.

On 6 October 1272, Edmund married Margaret de Clare at the chapel at Ruislip in Middlesex. Her brother, Gilbert, gave her in marriage.[5] Edmund's bride was 22, a few months older than Edmund.[6] She was the daughter of Richard de Clare, the sixth Earl of Gloucester and the fifth Earl of Hertford. Richard was, in turn, the son of Gilbert de Clare, the fifth Earl of Gloucester, whose widow was Richard of Cornwall's first wife. Whilst Edmund and Margaret were related by marriage, they were not by blood.[7]

Richard de Clare died in 1262 and the head of the family, Gilbert, was now in his thirtieth year. Due to trouble with the Welsh who attacked his lands in the Marches, Gilbert had not joined the Lord Edward's crusade in 1270. In contrast to his former rebelliousness, Gilbert had behaved in an exemplary way in the last years of Henry III's reign and during the absence of the new King.[8] Margaret's mother was Maud, the daughter of John de Lacy, Earl of Lincoln, who would live on until about 1288.[9] Margaret had two other older brothers, Thomas, born before 1247,[10] and the notorious clerical pluralist, Bogo, who was two years older than Margaret.[11] Two of Margaret's sisters survived into adulthood but the elder, Isabella, left England to marry the Marquis of Montferrat and died in 1270. Rose, who was two years younger than Margaret, married Roger de Mowbray in 1270.[12] Margaret was the last of the daughters of Richard de Clare to marry and one might wonder why she married relatively late. Her sisters, Isabella and Rose, married at 17 and 18. The normal age for marriage was 15 although Plantagenet and senior aristocratic English women could get married when they were very young and under the canonical age of 12.[13] Edmund's aunt, Eleanor, later to be the wife of Simon de Montfort, was betrothed to her first husband, William Marshal, when she was only 6 but her sister, Isabella, was about 21 when she married the widowed Emperor Frederick II.[14] Was there something unappealing about the 22-year-old Margaret?

It is not clear what her *marigatium*, or dowry, consisted of. The only one extant *inquisition post mortem* for Margaret relates solely to the Suffolk manor of Clopton which she held in dower.[15] But the manor of Sundon, Bedfordshire, was given to her by Earl Gilbert and reverted to the Clare family after her death.[16] It is possible that Bow Brickhill in Buckinghamshire, from the honour of Gloucester and part of Edmund's estates, came to him from the marriage or it might have been acquired by his father from his marriage to Isabel Marshal, the former Countess of Gloucester.[17] If this was all that Margaret brought with her, it was not a generous settlement.

As Richard of Cornwall was the step-grandfather of Margaret, it seems likely that the bride and groom had met before the marriage but it is difficult to be certain how successful the marriage was during the early days. It is too easy to look forward to the future unhappiness and assume that the marriage was doomed from the start. *The Complete Peerage* states that the marriage was not blessed by children but miscarriages would not have been noted. However, it is known that, twelve years after the marriage, Margaret was pregnant. On 26 January 1286, the Bishop of Winchester, excused himself from a meeting as he had promised to be present at the delivery of the Countess of Cornwall.[18] But no birth was recorded. It seems unlikely that this would have been Margaret's first pregnancy. There is no evidence of any live births. The eccentric antiquarian, General Plantagenet Harrison, believed that Edmund and Margaret had a daughter, Isabel, who married Maurice, Lord Berkeley.[19] This Isabel, however, was the daughter of Richard FitzRoy, an illegitimate son of King John, who married Berkeley by 1247.[20]

The Breakdown of the Marriage

The marriage deteriorated after 1286. Perhaps the failed pregnancy triggered a downward spiral. Whether it was the absence of children and, or, other issues which caused the rift cannot be ascertained. Rosemary Hill noted that Margaret accused Edmund of neglect and of such cruel treatment that she feared for her life. But Hill suggested that 'the fault was probably not entirely on his (Edmund's) side, for the quick tempers of the de Clares were notorious'[21] and Margaret's brothers, Gilbert and Bogo, were renowned for their testiness.[22]

By 1289, Edmund wanted a separation and took the initiative but John Pecham, Archbishop of Canterbury, was determined to reconcile the couple. Margaret lost her mother in March of that year.[23] Writing from Fulham on 1 December 1289, the Archbishop stated that 'I have spoken to my lady the Countess, according to the bull (from the Pope), as to the two points which it contains.' The Pope ordered Pecham 'to interfere to make peace between you and her'. If this failed, he was to secure a vow of chastity from Margaret who replied that 'she desires peace between you and herself, more than anything else in the world, and says that she does not believe that the trouble caused to her comes from your (Edmund's) heart'. On the vow of chastity she replied that 'she is not advised to vow chastity, because this would be, if she did it, as much to corroborate the blame and falsehoods which are put upon her'. She pressed Pecham to seek a peace between her and Edmund. In a bid for the Archbishop's sympathy, she persuaded him that 'the lady's state is weak and dangerous'. Pecham advised her not to leave the country until he had spoken to Edmund whom he asked to come to see him. He stressed that he was willing to travel to see Edmund himself but was prevented because of a visitation to remedy defaults in the diocese of London. Pecham ended the letter: 'I wish to abate this slander, if God gives me power, nor can I neglect it without great sin.'[24] This letter indicates the determination of all three parties: Margaret to win back Edmund, his resistance and the Archbishop's siding with the Countess.

If a wife agreed to a separation and to remain chaste, her former husband might be free to re-marry. Was Edmund trying to induce Margaret to take a vow of chastity so that he would be free to re-marry? There is no evidence of this as a motive and the fact that he did not re-marry seems conclusive.

By May 1290, Pecham's plan of using the Bishops of Hereford and Rochester to persuade Edmund to receive back his noble wife, whom he had left, had failed. On 8 May, Pecham turned to three other bishops, Winchester, Worcester and St Davids, to go to the Earl and to induce him to take back his wife within fifteen days.[25] By October, the Bishops of Winchester and Lincoln had been appointed papal legates to examine the matter.[26] If the Archbishop had expected the Bishops to share his enthusiasm, he was misguided. Perhaps he did not appreciate that Edmund knew these Bishops very well. He had often been at court with them as shown by their attendance together as charter witnesses. Pontoise of Winchester had written a very friendly letter to Edmund when he received the bishopric.[27] Bishops Oliver Sutton of Lincoln and Geoffrey Giffard of Worcester appealed to the Pope in August 1290 against Pecham's mandate to the Bishops in whose dioceses Edmund held lands, to return to his wife and treat her properly, and to excommunicate him if he did not. The Bishops argued that 'excommunication was an encroachment on episcopal jurisdiction, since the person concerned was only indirectly the Archbishop's subject'.[28] Edmund himself appealed to Rome in August 1291. Although judges were appointed to hear the appeals, Pecham treated Edmund as if he was already excommunicated and, despite the appeals, on 12 August 1291 he wrote to the Minister-General of the Grey Friars urging him to have nothing to do with Edmund.[29]

Meanwhile Bogo de Clare and Edmund came close to blows. Bogo had attempted a reconciliation and when this failed he served a writ on Edmund from Pecham threatening him with excommunication and requiring him to attend the Archbishop's court. This action occurred during the Easter Parliament of 1291 whilst Edmund was crossing the middle of the Great Hall at Westminster, making his way to a meeting of the King's council.[30] Edmund brought a complaint against Bogo and the Prior of Holy Trinity London for citing him to appear at a court Christian whilst he was at a session of Parliament. He claimed that anyone had the right to have the benefit of the peace of the King and to come lawfully and peacefully to pursue his business without receiving any citations or summons there. He alleged that the Prior had acted at the instigation of Bogo. This was a manifest contempt of royal privilege and of the liberties of the Abbot of Westminster. The damage to the King was assessed at £10,000 and to the Abbot, £1,000. The action also impinged upon the office of the Steward, Peter de Champvent, and the Marshal, William de Fanecourt. The damage to Edmund himself was said to be worth £5,000.

The Prior and Bogo appeared and Bogo admitted the offence but said that 'he was completely unaware that the aforesaid place was exempt' and that he did not mean any contempt or prejudice to the officials. He put himself at the King's mercy. The King was very angry at this breach of parliamentary privilege and Bogo and the Prior were sent to the Tower of London. The Prior and his Convent were pardoned 'for the honour they did to the body of the late Queen when lately passing through the priory'.[31] To secure his release Bogo agreed to pay 2,000 marks to the King and £1,000 to Edmund. However, at the request of the Bishops of Durham and Ely, Edmund agreed to accept £100.[32] The Archbishop was fined £10,000. Henry Summerson saw Bogo's intervention as an act of fraternal loyalty[33] but it could have been another example of the Clare temper.

'Divorce' Settlement

By February 1294, Margaret had accepted terms for a separation. Negotiations had taken place and a conference had been held probably at Rochester in the presence of its Bishop, as well as Bogo. Edmund was at Bermondsey on 13 February, the same day as Margaret agreed to terms at Rochester. Before doing so, she set out her case, making it clear that she blamed Edmund for the breakdown of their relationship. She alleged 'that as there are wranglings and disputes between my lord sir Edmund, Earl of Cornwall, my husband … and me, his wife, because I demanded to be taken back to him and that he should receive me in his house and treat me as his lawful wife, give me back my conjugal rights and find and provide for me in all things as his wife, and … my lord persisted in rebuffing me in these demands in divers ways and by many exceptions, these wranglings and disputes have at last been brought to an end and terminated in the following manner'. Edmund agreed to provide £800 worth of land and rents a year for the support of Margaret and her household.

The lands granted included Edmund's holdings in Norfolk and Suffolk worth £382.15s.8d. pa. plus the manor and soke of Kirton in Lincolnshire valued at £368.15s.9d.a year. This was topped up by £40 from the annual farm of Malmesbury and Winterslow in Wiltshire and a further £8.13s.7d. from that of Queenhithe in the City of London. In return, Margaret agreed not to alieniate any of these lands nor to waste them so that they would retain their full value. Edmund kept any advowsons attached to these lands as well as any knight's fees or escheats. The lands were to revert to Edmund in the event of Margaret dying before him. If Edmund predeceased her, she was entitled to the customary dower, of a third of the value of his lands, as long as she had less than that already. To ensure that she would keep to the agreement, Margaret went further and waived any rights to claim anything further during or after Edmund's life as she was satisfied and content with the apportionment.

The agreement continued, stating that from now on Margaret wished 'to live and serve and direct my thoughts to God alone readily and of my free will' and with the assent of Edmund. To this end, she swore on the gospel and took an oath before the Bishop to stay chaste and continent during the Earl's life and she would not claim conjugal rights from him or be in his house or 'to be taken back into his bed unless my lord pleases otherwise'. Nor would she 'from now molest or vex in him on any of these points'. Going further she accepted safeguards and potential sanctions if she broke the terms of the agreement. She agreed not to seek absolution from her oath from the Pope or any other religious superior nor would she let anyone else do so on her behalf. If she was found to have done so, the lands awarded to her were to revert back to the Earl. On the other hand, if Edmund himself disturbed her in her lands and was adjudged to have done so before the King or a competent judge, she was merely entitled to damages and her legal costs. Further strengthening Edmund's position, Margaret renounced all her remedies at law of the English or Papal courts. She also agreed that all previous sentences of suspension or excommunication were to be considered as non-existent. This was easier because Pecham had died in 1292. The document was sealed by her and the Bishop of Rochester and Bogo. The agreement had Edmund's seal on that part of the document that stayed with her.

The concord was paralleled by a chirograph of Edmund's made at Bermondsey on the same day. This set out the same terms without referring to the rights and wrongs of the marital strife. The two documents were inspected and confirmed by the King on 14 February 1294 whilst he was at St Albans.[34] At court on 15 February were *curiales* well known to Edmund such as Richard de Bosco and Robert Tibetot.[35] This quick succession of acquiescence and approval of the documents suggests careful planning. The terms had to be agreed to enable them to be sealed in two places thirty miles apart and then sent north to St Albans, a further twenty-five miles from Bermondsey, for confirmation on the following day. It seems rational to assume that Bogo was the prime negotiator for Margaret.[36] Why was she at Rochester? Bishop Ingoldsthorpe had no known connection with Edmund although he might have come across him when he was Dean of St Paul's from 1276 until 1283.[37] Possibly it was because Rochester was only twenty miles from Tonbridge, the *caput* of her brother Gilbert's honour. There are no obvious reasons as to why Edmund was at Bermondsey. He could have been at the abbey but it was a Cluniac house and Edmund showed no regard for this alien order.

However, Edmund's fellow earl, John de Warenne, had property in the neighbourhood of the priory.[38] One other possibility is that he could have been at the abbey because his brother-in-law, as Earl of Gloucester had the right to receive maintenance there.[39]

The final settlement of the marital dispute seems hard on Margaret. Although she became possibly the wealthiest woman in the country, she had only a modest portion of Edmund's wealth and had waived her rights to seek more. But she left open the option of re-marrying if Edmund predeceased her.

Life after Separation

Although, after Edmund's death in 1300, his lands went to the King as his next in blood, Margaret kept those lands awarded to her in 1294 as well as her *maritagium*. The total amount of these lands is not clear and it is disappointing that the only surviving inquest *post mortem* for Margaret refers to her lands in Clopton, Suffolk.[40] After Edmund's decease, she did exercise her right to claim additional lands as her dower. There are records of her efforts to gain property in Oxfordshire, Lincolnshire, Buckinghamshire, Gloucestershire, Cornwall, Suffolk, Yorkshire, Wiltshire, Hertfordshire, Wiltshire and Somerset.[41]

Whilst it might be assumed that the relations between Edmund and Margaret continued to be poor after their formal separation, it is worth noting that, in the year after the 'divorce', she supported him in a case against her brother, Gilbert, over the advowson of Hambleden.[42] Whether Margaret lived in a 'religious' manner is not known but her husband's religious enthusiasms were still evident after his death. In 1303, she successfully appealed to the Pope to be able to choose her own confessor, who may commute her vows, especially that of visiting Jerusalem, which she had taken at 'the desire of her husband Edmund, since deceased'.[43] Margaret had twelve years of widowhood, dying in 1312.[44]

In later years neither Edmund nor Margaret seem to have had any remnants of affection for each other. Despite the assertion by Kennett that Margaret died at Kirton,[45] there is no firm record of the date or place of her death. Although it is not known where she was buried, it was not with her husband at Hailes. An internet source quoting a secondary source has her buried at Chertsey Abbey in Surrey but no provenance is given.[46] There seems no reason why she should have been interred there; it had no Clare connections. Perhaps her body joined that of her brother, Gilbert, at the family mausoleum at Tewkesbury Abbey[47] or that of Edward I's daughter and her sister-in-law, Joan of Acre, at Clare Priory in Suffolk, a Clare foundation. The main part of the lands settled on Margaret at the time of her 'divorce' was in Suffolk, so she is more likely to have died there than in Surrey where she had no estates. The absence of joint burial should not be used as evidence for lack of affection; the bodies of Henry III and Eleanor of Provence, whose marital affection has never been doubted, where interred many miles apart.

Evidence of marital affection can be found in the terms of benefactions to religious houses. For example, Edmund's aunt, Eleanor, was mentioned in the *pro anima* clauses of William Marshal junior, her first husband's charters although she was his second wife.[48] Neither Edmund nor Margaret made acts of religious piety seeking blessings for the soul of the other. Indeed there are no surviving records of any religious patronage by Margaret; the Tewkesbury cartulary contains no grants made by her.[49] But, even if she had been inclined to endow a religious house, she had very little land of her own, most of her wealth having come from her husband's settlement on her had to be returned intact on her death. But the absence of a mention in a charter does not invariably point to a coolness between spouses. Although his marriage with Alice de Saluzzo appears to have been close, Edmund de Lacy, who was related to Margaret, did not mention Alice in making a grant to Pontefract Priory. He required prayers for his own soul and those of his father, ancestors and heirs.[50] Alice's sister's husband, John de Vescy, mentioned his own soul but not his wife's in a grant to the Carmelites at Alnwick.[51] She, in turn, did not mention John in her grant to Rievaulx Abbey.[52] John de Warenne, well known for his affection for his Lusignan wife, used the same exclusive style as Edmund de Lacy in his grants to Lewes Priory,[53] as did Ranulph, Earl of Chester when endowing Chester and Dieulacres Abbeys.[54]

Another possible indicator of a widow's attitude to her husband was whether she reverted to her maiden name. It is not surprising that in her widowhood, Margaret FitzGerold, whose husband, Falkes de Bréauté, had died in disgrace and exile, reverted to her father's surname.[55] There is evidence that Countess Margaret used the Clare name following Edmund's death.[56]

There were times when we might assume that the relationship of Edmund and Margaret was good. The commissioning of the Clare chasuable must date from this period. In 1677, the Lancaster Herald, Francis Sandford, published his *Genealogical History of the Kings of England*. In this he described the seal of Margaret as being of a dimidiated design with half of Edmund's arms on the dexter and her paternal arms on the sinister. The recently retired Garter King of Arms, Sir Thomas Woodcock, believed that this was amongst the earliest examples of this form of heraldic practice which was later replaced with impalement and quartering.[57] This shows that, at some time, Margaret gloried in her prestigious marriage as well as her own ancestry.

Brother-in-law: Gilbert de Clare, Earl of Gloucester and Hertford[58]

Gilbert de Care was the eldest son of Richard, Earl of Gloucester. Gilbert was about seven years older than Edmund but he became a major player in English political events at an earlier age. Whilst Edmund was 22 before he emerged in his own right on his father's death, Gilbert was 19 when he succeeded his father in 1262. Although technically under-age, Gilbert demanded the immediate seisin of his father's lands and titles. The rebuffs that he suffered at the hands of Henry III, who gave a very generous dower to Earl Richard's widow, drove Gilbert into the Montfortian camp. But Gilbert, the Red Earl, was never constant. By late 1263, he was back supporting the King, only to take a neutral line during the Christmas period before joining Montfort again in early 1264. He led the centre of the rebel army at Lewes despite his youth. With the King in captivity, he was one of the three most important men in the Kingdom but he fell out with Montfort again at the end of the year and he withdrew to the Marches. A short-lived agreement with Montfort was followed by his attempt to seize the captured King and the Lord Edward. On Edward's escape from Hereford, Gilbert joined the royalists and commanded a division of the army at Evesham.

By 1266, he had fallen out with the King over the terms of the Dictum of Kenilworth which set a scale for fines allowing rebels to regain their lands. Gilbert supported the immediate return of lost lands pending payment. Not making any headway, he occupied London and was joined by other rebels who were still at large. Negotiations ended with Gilbert gaining most of his points but he had to give expensive sureties for his future good conduct. More disputes ensued over his failure to redeem his promise to crusade. However, when the King died, Gilbert was present and swore to maintain the kingdom for the Lord Edward and part of the Regency in Edward's absence.

He fought alongside Edmund in the First Welsh War but, during the Second, was replaced as the commander in the south after losing a battle at Llandeilo Fawr. He served again for the next two rebellions in 1287 and 1294. However, the last decade of his life saw major quarrels with the King following complaints by Humphrey de Bohun, Earl of Hereford. Gilbert defied the royal courts and engaged in private warfare. Edward I stamped down on both earls, imprisoning and fining them. But he then allowed his widowed daughter, Joan of Acre, to marry Gilbert. Gilbert died in 1295.

It would have been difficult to maintain good relations with such a mercurial man. His red hair led to his nickname 'red dog'. According to the Furness Chronicler, Montfort, seeing Gilbert's arrival before the onset of the battle at Evesham, exclaimed: 'This red dog will eat us today.'[59] His red hair was said to indicate his quick temper.

At first, Edmund and Gilbert worked well together. They were part of the government in the King's absence on crusade.[60] Gilbert served Edmund during the rebellion of Rhys ap Maredudd. Witness lists show that they were together at court on at least sixty-one occasions.[61] The collapse of Edmund's marriage must have caused tension. During Gilbert's dispute with Earl Humphrey of Hereford, a letter was sent to him saying that Hereford went to Archbishop Pecham and others, including Edmund, alleging that Gilbert had not kept his word over certain lands.[62] It is not clear what stance Edmund took but, in the same year, the brothers-in-law were together at the translation of St Frideswide in Oxford showing that they could at least be civil to each other when the occasion demanded.[63]

Brother-in-law: Thomas de Clare

Thomas, the second son of Richard de Clare, was at the age of about 21 in 1264, a crucial player in a critical event in English history. He had been with his older brother, Gilbert, at the Battle of Lewes and he had been knighted before it by Montfort himself. But Montfort's conduct alienated Gilbert. When the Lord Edward was imprisoned at Hereford, Thomas was present at Gilbert's request. Whilst exercising horses on the Widemarsh on 28 May 1265, Edward tired out most of the horses and, at an agreed signal, he and Thomas sped off to join the Mortimers at Wigmore.[64] It is clear that Thomas was a party to a plot. The escape marked the beginning of the end for Montfort, who was slain on 4 August at Evesham.

Thomas joined Edward's crusade but he returned in 1272, the year of his sister's marriage to Edmund. It is possible that he journeyed with his future brother-in-law. During 1276, Thomas granted lands he had been given by Edmund in the parish of St. Mary Bothaw in the City of London to Stephen of Cornhill.[65] Edmund's grant can be found in the Scrope Cartulary where Edmund described Thomas as ' *karissimo fratri nostro*'.[66] This is evidence that Thomas and Edmund were on good terms. However, from 1274 onwards, Thomas concentrated increasingly on Ireland being lord of Thomond[67] and it is probable that the brothers-in-law saw little more of each other.

Brother-in-law: Bogo de Clare[68]

With Bogo, Richard de Clare's third son, Edmund had more mixed relations. They were almost the same age. Even in his lifetime Bogo was unpopular and he became notorious as a pluralist. His church career began when he was only 7 and later he became a papal chaplain. Although he was amassing a substantial portfolio of livings, by 1283 he had twenty clerical positions, he was still not an ordained priest and he may never have been.[69] The Archbishops of York and Canterbury tried to restrain him with little effect as he was well-regarded at court being a special favourite of the Queen. Whilst Edmund was Regent, he took action on Bogo's behalf ordering the Sheriffs of York and Buckingham to proceed against the Archbishop and the Bishop of Lincoln who had excommunicated Bogo.[70] However, in 1290, as we have seen, Bogo fell out with the King over his intervention in the marital problems of his sister and Edmund.[71] Did Edmund still lend money to his awkward brother-in-law? At Michaelmas 1290, four years before Bogo's death, a writ to the Archbishop of York instructed him to levy £100 on the ecclesiastical goods of Bogo de Clare, which was to be given to Edmund.

Bogo had acknowledged, at the January Parliament, that he owed this sum to Edmund.[72] Perhaps this was a loan made in happier times?

Conclusions

The failure of Edmund's marriage marred his relationship with some of his brothers-in-law, notably Earl Gilbert and his brother, Bogo. The Clares were notoriously prickly, so this might not be unexpected and he could have quarrelled with Gilbert whether they were related by marriage or not. But their landed interests were not aligning. However, Edmund's relationship with another brother-in-law, Thomas, seems to have always been cordial. So it is clear that Edmund's familial problems were with men who had great difficulties with their fellow magnates and with the King. This supports a conclusion that Edmund was unlikely to have been the cause of discord with these relatives both by blood and marriage.

Chapter 8

Edmund's Friends and Associates

After more than 700 years, it is difficult to be sure whom of those that Edmund came into contact with were his friends, enemies or mere associates. The witness lists of royal charters are excellent evidence of those with whom Edmund associated. Whether he was friends with fellow witnesses cannot be ascertained but frequent meetings might have created bonds of trust and possible affection. There are 111 men listed in Chancery documents as fellow witnesses.[1]

Bishops

As might be expected, the Chancellor, Robert Burnell, Bishop of Bath and Wells, was Edmund's most frequent associate. The witness lists show that they were together on at least eighty-nine days. From humble beginnings as a younger son of a Shropshire knight, Burnell built his career as a servant of the King and was his chief clerk even before Edward became King. Burnell was probably the King's best friend.[2] The sale by Edmund of Holdgate castle in Shropshire to Burnell enabled the Bishop to strengthen his position in his native county. Amongst the other episcopal witnesses were the Bek brothers, the sons of a Lincolnshire baron. Antony, Bishop of Durham, and Thomas, of St Davids, were typical curial bishops and were very prominent at court. They witnessed with Edmund on forty-four and twenty-eight times respectively. Antony, who had been on the Lord Edward's crusade would be an executor of Edmund's will. Edmund lent him money and received the rich manor of Howden in exchange.

The older Bek' brother, Thomas, was never so close to the King.[3] Antony's presence as a fellow witness was almost matched by William Middleton, Bishop of Norwich (forty-three occasions). Noted as a King's clerk in 1277, Middleton had made his way to the episcopate as an associate of Archbishop Kilwardby.[4] Another frequent colleague of Edmund was the former Chancellor, Geoffrey Giffard, Bishop of Worcester (twenty-five occasions). From a baronial family, Giffard was the younger brother of an Archbishop of York.[5] Two other curial bishops and fellow witnesses became prominent later on in the reign: William Louth, Bishop of Ely (seventeen occasions) and William March, who succeeded Burnell at Bath and Wells (thirteen occasions). After studying at Oxford, March had become a King's clerk and owed his promotion to the monarch.[6]

All three of Edward I's Archbishops of Canterbury met Edmund at court but none were members of the court circle before becoming Archbishop and they were infrequent attestors of royal charters. Archbishops Kilwardby and Winchelsea were each only once mentioned alongside Edmund as a witness. John Pecham accompanied Edmund on five days but had more dealings with him away from court especially over his marriage.[7] As Edward I discovered, Pecham was an awkward man and his apparent siding with Countess Margaret cannot have made him a friend of Edmund. Two other Archbishops came to court during Edmund's time; Richard Huscroft noted that Archbishops of York avoided court when their fellow primate was present.[8] This might explain why John le Romeyn met Edmund as a witness on only two days although John de Sanford, Archbishop of Dublin, was there on seven.

Oliver Sutton, Bishop of Lincoln, was a curial colleague of Edmund, albeit as a fellow attestor on only five days. He took Edmund's side against Archbishop Pecham, but they were on opposite sides over legal actions in 1294.[9] Walter Langton, Bishop of Coventry and Lichfield, who became one the greatest men of his time, witnessed with Edmund only once. However, they too must have known each other well as he was an executor of Edmund's will.[10] Coming from another episcopal family, Thomas Bitton, Bishop of Exeter, never witnessed with Edmund but he was another executor of Edmund's will.[11]

Earls

During Edmund's tenure of the earldom of Cornwall, there were fifteen other English earldoms: Arundel, Derby, Devon, Essex, Gloucester, Hereford, Hertford, Lancaster, Leicester, Lincoln, Norfolk, Oxford, Richmond, Surrey (Warenne) and Warwick. However, the actual number of earls was less. Gilbert de Clare was Earl of both Gloucester and Hertford whilst Humphrey de Bohun, Earl of Hereford, was also Earl of Essex. There had been the earldom of Aumale. It and Devon were linked in the person of Isabella de Fortibus, the sister of Baldwin, the last Redvers Earl of Devon and the widow of William, Count of Aumale. She styled herself as Countess of Aumale and Devon but she was only Countess of Aumale by marriage. When she died in 1293, her heir to the Devon earldom was Hugh de Courtenay but he was not recognised as such for forty years.[12] Previously important earldoms had ceased to be noted as such as they were now held with other earldoms. The Ferrers family lost their earldom of Derby following the Barons' Wars and it was then attached to Lancaster, held by Edmund, the King's brother, as was Montfort's old earldom of Leicester. Chester had been given to Edward I when he was the heir to the throne and, apart from a few months after the battle of Lewes when the Montforts seized it, it has remained a Crown possession ever since. The effective number of earls was reduced to a maximum of eleven although Richard de Burgh, Earl of Ulster,[13] from Ireland and John de Comyn, Earl of Buchan and son of an heiress of the last Earl of Winchester,[14] from Scotland were also sometimes at court. Whilst William de Valence had a good claim to the Welsh earldom of Pembroke through his wife, he was never formally granted it despite being sometimes referred to in official documents as earl.[15] However, William was considered to be of comital rank and was usually listed above the non-royal earls in the charter witness lists. Another old earldom, Salisbury, was by right held by Margaret Longespée, the wife of Henry de Lacy, Earl of Lincoln, but neither she nor her husband used the title.[16]

During Edmund's time, there was one Earl of Arundel, Lincoln, Norfolk, Richmond and Warenne. Richard Fitzalan was only recognised as Earl of Arundel in about 1290.[17] Two Clare Earls of Gloucester and Hertford were separated in 1297 by Ralph de Monthermer, the household knight who married Gilbert de Clare's widow, Princess Joan, and was recognised as Earl in his wife's right. The Oxford earldom was in the hands of two successive Robert de Veres. When Edmund Crouchback died in 1296, his son, Thomas, succeeded as Earl of Lancaster. Warwick was also represented by two men, William de Beauchamp and his son, Guy, from 1298.[18] Three Humphrey de Bohuns held the earldoms of Hereford and Essex.[19] Thus, the maximum number of English earls with whom Edmund could have had dealings was eighteen, although three only became earls in the last four years of Edmund's life.

As to royal charter attestors, Gilbert de Clare, Edmund's brother-in-law, was the second most frequent fellow witness (sixty-nine occasions) and another recurrent witness was Henry de Lacy, Earl of Lincoln (sixty occasions). Edmund's cousin, Edmund, Earl of Lancaster, was present on sixty-four days and his half-uncle, William de Valence, on fifty-four. The two holders of the great hereditary offices of state, the Marshal and Constable, were also familiar partners: Roger Bigod, Earl of Norfolk (thirty-seven occasions) and Humphrey II de Bohun, Earl of Hereford and Essex (twenty-nine occasions). Of the remaining earls, John de Warenne, Earl of Surrey (sixty occasions) was more often at court with Edmund than William de Beauchamp, Earl of Warwick (thirty occasions). Beauchamp's son, Guy, was one of Edmund's executors.[20] One earl, John of Brittany, Earl of Richmond, Edmund's cousin, was not noted at court with Edmund. The only other Earl was Robert I de Vere of Oxford who was never prominent and only witnessed with Edmund four times.[21] Edmund met Richard de Burgh, Earl of Ulster, on three days in 1285 but was not recorded with the Earl of Buchan.[22]

Of the earls who were not relatives of King Edward, Edmund's most consistent support came from Henry de Lacy, Earl of Lincoln.[23] He served in both Welsh wars and, on the death of Edmund of Lancaster, he commanded the English forces in Gascony in 1296. He was one of the leaders of the army that defeated the Scots at Falkirk in 1298. He helped negotiate the King's second marriage with Margaret of France. In the year of Edmund's death, Lacy was at the siege of Caerlaverock but, when Edmund died, he was on his way to Rome to complain about the Scots. For his services in Wales, Lacy was granted the cantreds of Rhos and Rhufoniog centred on Denbigh. Henry was the same age as Edmund and they shared a grandfather, John de Lacy. As men who shared the same goals, the two men must have been close. It was to Henry de Lacy that the King had committed Richard of Cornwall's lands at Knaresborough, pending Edmund's succession.[24] They were co-Regents in 1279 when the King went to secure Ponthieu.[25] As well as witnessing royal charters, they acted jointly for individuals such as John de Vescy, Robert de Tateshall and Amadeus of Savoy.[26] However, when the Welsh passes were not kept clear in 1288, Lacy was amongst those to whom Edmund complained.[27] In the last few days of Edmund's life, Lacy won a pardon for Richard Luve, of his outlawry for taking deer in the chase of Edmund at Knaresborough.[28]

Another recipient of extensive lands after the Second Welsh War was the Earl of Surrey, John de Warenne, who was given Bromfield and Yale.[29] John, when only 9 in 1240, married a half-sister of Henry III and had supported the Poitevins during the Barons' Wars. He quarrelled with the Lord Edward after Evesham but was reconciled and served in the government in England whilst Edward was on crusade. In the last years of Edmund's life Warenne was the King's lieutenant in Scotland winning a substantial victory at Dunbar before losing badly at Stirling Bridge. Their early service together during the crusade must have cemented their friendship and there is evidence of their attendance at a royal council between the years 1278 to 1282.[30] When Warenne lost his son and heir, William, in 1287, William de Beauchamp, the commander of the army in Cheshire, wrote to Edmund, as Regent, about a dispute between Warenne and Reginald de Gray, the Justice of Chester. Warenne sought Edmund's assistance because he had bailed Bromfield and Yale to his son. Edmund came to his aid.[31] As with Lacy, the failure to clear the passes led to a rebuke from Edmund.[32] Edmund and Warenne could be on opposite sides. Warenne had major holdings in Norfolk and Edmund challenged him over his rights including wreck and view of frankpledge in the coastal settlements of Bacton and Paston.[33]

Earl Roger Bigod of Norfolk gave Edward I many problems in the 1290s and paid for it when he was forced to do a deal disinheriting his family from a claim to the earldom when he died childless. He, too, had difficulties with Edmund whom he accused of taking oxen and horse from his lands in Wycombe.[34]

Curiales and Barons

One of Edmund's close companions when charters were attested (twenty-nine occasions) was the Savoyard, Otto de Grandson, who, with Robert Burnell, was the most trusted of Edward I's friends. He rose to baronial rank although Michael Prestwich was surely right when he wrote that Otto might have been of enough status to be an earl, 'fully deserving the honour in terms of the services' he had rendered to the King.[35] Otto came from Grandson on the shores of Lake Neuchâtel in the Pays de Vaud, then in Savoy but now in Switzerland. He became part of the King's circle when he crusaded with the Lord Edward and he was sent by the King to try to save the doomed Kingdom of Acre in 1292. Otto was prominent in the conquest of Wales and continued his diplomatic activities on behalf of the English throne throughout Edward's reign and during that of Edward II.[36] It is a sign of friendship that Edmund witnessed two of Otto's private charters in favour of his relatives.[37]

Other prominent *curiales* who witnessed with Edmund frequently were the stewards of the royal household one of whom, Peter de Champvent, was Otto de Grandson's cousin (seventeen occasions). He rose to prominence during the reign of Henry III and was with him during the last few months of his life rather than joining the Lord Edward's crusade. After a period of obscurity under the new King, Peter became Steward and later Chamberlain for Edward I and was recorded on one occasion, as the King's Secretary.[38] The other royal stewards who witnessed with Edmund included Hugh FitzOtto (twenty-seven occasions), Robert FitzJohn (fifty occasions) and Walter de Beauchamp (twenty occasions). FitzOtto, who died in 1283, had been one of the Lord Edward's crusaders and had lands in Hertfordshire and Essex as had Edmund.[39] Lands in Norfolk provided the wealth for FitzJohn.[40] A relative of the Earls of Warwick, Beauchamp had lands in Worcestershire, Gloucestershire and Wiltshire and fought at Falkirk.[41]

Of the other frequent fellow attestors, the former steward, Richard de Bosco (fifty occasions), merits a mention. Bosco, who had lands in Somerset and Dorset, outlived Edmund, dying in 1302.[42] Guy de Pitchford from Sussex, who was the Keeper of Windsor castle and charged with safe guarding the royal children,[43] attested with Edmund on three occasions spread over three years. Peter de Huntingfield, a Kentish knight, was a fellow witness on ten days during a three-year period.[44] About the same time Payn de Chaworth, witnessed on eight days from 1279 until 1281. Payn was a Marcher baron and Lord of Kidwelly castle who, like Edmund, had Hampshire and Northamptonshire lands.[45] Another fellow attestor on the verge of baronial rank, was John de Vaux (Vallibus). There were two men of this name but the most likely royal witness of the 1280–85 period was the older who died in 1287 and had lands in Lincolnshire, Suffolk and Norfolk.[46]

When the King went to Gascony in 1286, it was decided that William de Hamilton should act as Vice Chancellor in Robert Burnell's absence. A Yorkshire man, he was Dean of York in 1289 and became Chancellor in 1304.[47] During Edmund's Regency, Hamilton was one of Edmund's closest associates; they exchanged many letters and, just after Christmas 1286, Edmund wrote to him from Ashridge addressing him as his 'friend and clerk'[48] and, in 1288, as *'son cher sire, saluz et bon amour'*.[49]

John de Vescy, (thirty-seven occasions), Robert Tibetot (fifty occasions), Reginald de Grey (thirty occasions), and Roger Mortimer (eighteen occasions) were examples of the senior barons who were fellow witnesses of charters. Although he was a Montfortian and was wounded at Evesham, the Northerner Vescy joined the Lord Edward's crusade and served him well in Wales and Gascony. When he died at Montpellier, he was mourned greatly by the King and, as a mark of royal favour, his heart was buried in 1290 alongside the hearts of Queen Eleanor and Prince Alfonso, Edward's heir, in the Blackfriars, London.[50]

By contrast, Robert Tibetot was a staunch royalist from his youth and was one of Edward I's fellow crusaders. Apart from his activities in Wales, he served the King in Gascony.[51] He was another whom Prestwich believed might have merited an earldom.[52] In addition to the times when he witnessed royal charters, Robert and Edmund both witnessed for Otto de Grandson.[53] Edmund owed much to Robert for the successful suppression of Rhys ap Maredudd's rebellion but in 1284, they had a legal dispute over rents owed by Edmund in Suffolk.[54]

The third major beneficiary of the post-conquest distribution of substantial lands in Gwynedd was Reginald de Grey who received Ruthin.[55] He served as Justiciary and Constable of Chester from 1270. Chester was part of the Lord Edward's lands and his efforts must have secured royal recognition. Grey, too, fought at Falkirk and was present at the same Council meeting as John de Warenne and Edmund.[56] During the rebellion of Rhys, Grey was another criticised over the issue of the safety of passes in his lands in Wales.[57]

Roger III de Mortimer, Lord of Wigmore, was one of the greatest Marcher barons. Twenty years older than Edmund, he played a major role in both the Barons' Wars and in the First Welsh War. At first a supporter of reform, he became one of Henry III's strongest supporters and it was to his wife that the grisly trophy of Montfort's body parts was sent after Evesham.[58] However, in the early years of Edmund's holding of the earldom, they disputed lands at Oakham in Rutland[59] as well as lands in Essex in 1275.[60] On Roger's death, in 1282, he was succeeded by his son, Edmund de Mortimer who was present on seven occasions witnessing charters alongside Edmund of Cornwall in 1286.[61] Another Marcher, Roger de Clifford, witnessed with Edmund only on four occasions in 1280.[62]

Another Baron, who witnessed with Edmund, but only on two occasions in 1275 and 1281, was Baldwin Wake; he also contested Edmund's rights in Boroughbridge, Yorkshire in 1275.[63] Edmund later had the wardship of his heir.[64] Robert FitzWalter, summoned to Parliament as a baron in 1295, witnessed with Edmund eleven times over eighteen years. He had lands in Essex and Hertfordshire and may have come across Edmund there.[65] A similar pattern, six times over eighteen years, applied to William de Leyburn, a baron from Kent.[66] On three occasions over four years, another baron, Eustace de Hache, was at Edmund's side.[67]

Judges

Six of the most important judges were fellow witnesses of royal charters. Roger Brabazon (five occasions, 1293–94) began his career in the service of Roger de Mortimer and Edmund of Lancaster but, by 1290, was appointed as a junior justice. He was Chief Justice from 1296 until 1316.[68] From Shropshire, Walter de Hopton (twice in 1279), was a royal judge during the reign of Henry III and joined the King's Bench in 1274. He served in both Wales and Ireland but was convicted of misconduct following the Norfolk eyre of 1286.[69] Witnessing with Edmund three times in 1293–94, John de Mettingham started his career as clerk to Gilbert of Preston, the Chief Justice of Common Pleas under Henry III. John became an assize judge in 1274 and, having escaped the state trials of judges in 1289–93, became Chief Justice of the Common Pleas until his death in 1300.[70] Mettingham's promotion to the post of Chief Justice followed the disgrace of Thomas Weyland, who witnessed royal charters with Edmund between 1289 and 1296 (thirteen occasions). Weyland was a member of the affinity of Roger Bigod, Earl of Norfolk, before he became an itinerant justice and was later a justice on the Common Bench and its Chief Justice. But he fell from favour when he became involved in a murder case and he was exiled for some years.[71] Another major casualty of Edward I's crackdown on the judiciary was Ralph Hengham who witnessed only once with Edmund in 1279. Ten years later he was fined 10,000 marks despite being convicted in one case.[72] However, Edmund thought so much of him that he was an executor of his will and Edmund twice presented Ralph to church livings.[73] The final major judge, Gilbert of Thornton, was Chief Justice of the King's Bench when he died. His early years in the law were spent as a King's serjeant but, by 1290, he was Chief Justice.[74] He was a fellow attestor with Edmund on thirteen occasions between 1290 and 1294. Another man who acted judicially occasionally was Walter de Helion of West Hyde, Bedfordshire, who was a justice in 1267 and justice of the bench, Westminster, in 1278. A year later he was a witness with Edmund, the first of three such events. A less prominent member of the royal circle, Helion, also had lands in Gloucestershire, Herefordshire and Bedfordshire and twice he witnessed charters making grants to Edmund.[75] Two other judges were executors of Edmund's will. They were Henry Spigurnel and William Inge;[76] neither having been a fellow charter witness. Spigurnel made his name as a justice on eyres but only became a King's Bench judge after Edmund's death.[77] Inge had a similar early career and ended as Chief Justice of the King's Bench in 1316.

Other Senior Clergy

It is no surprise that amongst his executors, Edmund named Hugh, the Abbot of Hailes and Ralph of Aston, the Rector of Ashridge, both of whom he would have known well.[78]

Although there is no direct evidence of any relationship of Edmund with Walter of Wenlock, Abbot of Westminster, it is possible that they knew each other well too. Having spent so much time at Westminster especially when he was Regent, Edmund must have met Walter and they both used the services of John de Batesford and William Merry. In addition Walter spent Christmas 1288 at Berkhamsted as Edmund's guest. Walter spent another night at Berkhamsted in January 1291.[79]

Conclusions

It is clear that Edmund met and mixed with all the most important and high-ranking men and women of the kingdom. During the years when he was Regent, all the greater men who stayed in England, must have had dealings with him and, throughout his time as Earl, he lent money to a number of important magnates.[80] Some of the meetings that Edmund had with the great and the good were formal and of little impact but the real players in the land were well known to him and a significant number must have become his friends. Some might have disliked him but we have no evidence of this. He seems to have been an amiable companion in the circles in which he moved, not threatening others and having no real need to assert himself. The only great man with whom he had deep problems was Archbishop Pecham. However, the Archbishop also managed to upset the King and his fellow bishops.

Chapter 9

Edmund's Men: His Knightly Affinity

Et decus addit ei comitiva modesta clientum.
Dapsilis in mensa, frugalia pabula praestans,
Sacratas domini leges in pectore gestans.

(Further enhanced through its reflection in the decency
of his attendants and entourage. Lavish in his table,
providing bountiful provisions/food/fare, bearing in his
breast the hallowed laws of God.)

Much effort has been extended by historians in trying to establish the membership of a great man's inner circle of followers, his affinity or his *familia*. David Crouch described the careers of eighteen of William Marshal's knights.[1] Of these, ten went to Ireland with Marshal in 1207 but two-thirds of them held no lands from him although they came from areas where he had lands.[2] Nine of Marshal's clerks and chaplains, the men who administered his affairs, were regarded as being in his affinity.[3] Roger de Quincy (1195?–1264), Earl of Winchester, had a *familia* including fifteen knights.[4] Although hampered by the lack of surviving charters of Simon de Montfort, John Maddicott suggested that Montfort's affinity was small in number, emanating from one region, concentrating on quality rather than quantity being based on a tight inner circle of six to eight men.[5] Roger Bigod III, Earl of Norfolk, had as many as thirty-three knights accompanying him to Wales during the 1294 rebellion and an affinity put at between six and twelve knights. The affinity of Edmund's brother-in-law, Gilbert de Clare, has been put at twenty or more knights.[6] Although Edmund was said to have attended the King's coronation with knights,[7] Mark Page described Edmund's affinity as centred on a core of between seven and twelve knights.[8]

One way of examining the closeness of a lord and an affinity member is to look at the arms they bore. Peter Coss drew attention to this practice.[9]

Whilst Edmund of Cornwall's arms were a variant of those of his father, excluding Edmund's illegitimate half-brother who used similar arms, the only regular member of Edmund's circle was Walter de la Poyle. He shared the argent colour of Edmund's shield and its sable bordure bezanty. The arms of Richard's father's mistress's family, the Vautorts, included a bezanty bordure. But this might reflect the Vautort family's Cornish origin rather than that of a particular earl. So this avenue is unproductive in the case of Edmund.

Marc Morris warned against assessing the number of a man's *familiares* from charter witnessing spread over wide areas;[10] witnesses might be important members of local society present at just one moment of time. He argued that it was better to consider the membership of a magnate's council but, although most magnates and bishops had one, the evidence is often missing. Edmund's brother-in-law, Gilbert de Clare, certainly had a council as did Edmund's tenant, Ralph Pipard. Gilbert's council included seven knights and four clerks.[11]

However, an analysis of of Edmund's charters is a good starting point for a study of his affinity. One hundred and fifty people were named as witnesses of charters granted by Edmund and another two hundred and forty eight individuals attested charters issued in his favour. The details are set out in the appendix Table 9.1 A-E together with a list of the potential members of Edmund's affinity using the witnessing of charters as the first indicator of possible membership of an affinity. Those charters where Edmund was the instigator are the most important because they are more likely to include members of his circle. But the granting of a charter could be a collaborative event as forty-five of Edmund's charter witnesses also attested charters in his favour.

Seven of Edmund's charter witnesses witnessed ten or more charters. They were led by Roger de Drayton, Edmund's Treasurer, who acted on twenty-one occasions, whilst another clerk, Michael of Northampton, witnessed ten. Both men also witnessed grants made to Edmund bringing the total number of charters in which they were involved to twenty-eight and fourteen respectively. There is added significance to these high rankings as Northampton was already old, dying in 1283, and Drayton's life was cut short when he was murdered in 1292. Three knights, Reginald de Botreaux, Walter de la Poyle and Edmund's half-brother, Richard of Cornwall, were present when twenty or more charters were granted. By contrast, the most frequent witness of Roger Bigod III's charters acted only on six occasions.[12]

There has also been a continuing debate as to how robust the seigneurial honour was in the late thirteenth-century and this, too, could form the basis for a great man's affinity. Some historians have seen the honour's importance as waining in the thirteenth century heralding the onset of bastard feudalism[13] but others, including Peter Coss and David Carpenter, have thought that an honour could still provide a focus for a locality drawing in neighbouring gentry as well as feudal tenants.[14] Writing about the Buckinghamshire gentry, Ann Polden stressed the importance of proximity in established gentry links and networks but she singled out Edmund's honour of Wallingford as allowing 'us to argue a more persuasive case for the continuing significance of feudal connections'.[15] She based this view on the Malet, Neyrnuit, Dayrel and Bracy families and saw the preference of Earls Richard and Edmund of Cornwall for Berkhamsted and Ashridge, their principal residences, as a determinant in the 'continuing vitality of feudal ties'.[16] Coss commented on the importance of tenurial links during the Barons' War and cited Fernandes's study of Midland knights which showed the importance of such links whilst making the point that 'the luxury of a free choice' was open to very few knights.[17] Adrian Jobson has demonstrated that Richard of Cornwall was not very successful in attracting his Oxfordshire tenants to the royal cause during the Barons' War.[18] The tenants of another Oxfordshire baron, Hugh de Plessis, were also less supportive of their royalist lord than might have been expected.[19]

Turning to Edmund's 'men', some were inherited from his father. The new Earl, having not expected to inherit the title, would have had little time to build up his own following. A few of the men, identified by Denholm-Young as being in Earl Richard's circle, were found later in Edmund's service. Thirty-two men obtained protections when they set off with Richard to go to Germany in 1257.[20] These included John de Warenne, the Earl of Surrey, and five barons. Edmund witnessed royal charters with Warenne on sixty occasions but Warenne never witnessed a charter for, or benefiting, Edmund.[21] Six knights who went with Richard were also witnesses of Richard's charters but none had any known connection with Edmund although the son of Roger Damory, Robert, was clearly one of 'his' knights. 1257 was a long time before Edmund became Earl and some of these men would have died before 1272 including those killed in the Barons' War. However, their descendants lived on. Philip de Hoyville, who witnessed for Edmund in 1300, was the son of Hugh who went with Richard to Germany.[22] Geoffrey de Turberville witnessed the same charter as Philip de Hoyville and two members of the Turberville family were in Richard's German party.[23] Another member of the German party, Stephen de Chenduit, did not witness for Edmund and instead fought a bitter legal case against him.[24] Hugh Durival of Oxfordshire witnessed charters for both Edmund and his father.[25]

Much of what follows builds on the work of Mark Page. After analysing Edmund's affinity, Page concluded that Edmund followed his father's example in choosing his 'men' from the honours of Wallingford and Berkhamsted and from Cornwall, but without the bias towards the south-west that Richard had shown. The Cornish knights only acted for Edmund as witnesses and in other ways within Cornwall.[26]

At its most dramatic an affinity consisted of those who followed their Lord into war. Edmund lead one of the largest retinues to Wales at the start of the Welsh War in 1277. Fourteen knights are known to have been in his contingent.[27] In addition, protections were granted to another four knights: Adam le Despenser, Gilbert de Houby, John de la Sale and Ralph Pipard.[28] Pipard later served in the Second Welsh War in 1282 as part of Edmund's *comitiva*, although Edmund himself did not fight.[29] When, in 1287, he was leaving to take command of the army raised to suppress the rebellion of Rhys ap Maredudd, Walter de Huntercombe, John le Husser, Arnald Murdac, Walter de Pedwardine, Nicholas Peysun, Hugh de St Philibert, Lawrence Basset and Laurence of Sandwich were given similar protections.[30] Some of the knights from the 1277 campaign such as Peter de Chalun, Henry de Appleby, William de Eynford and Richard Belet, were never recorded again in connection with Edmund nor were his tenants. Robert de Dinham must have been a member of the family powerful in the West Country including tenants of Edmund.[31] William de Punchardon might have been the son of Robert of Richard of Cornwall's affinity.[32]

Of the military knights, only Ralph Pipard and Hugh de St Philibert were part of Edmund's regular peacetime affinity. Pipard was a knight with manors in Buckinghamshire, Oxfordshire, Essex and Derbyshire.[33] He witnessed a charter in favour Edmund. St Philibert was probably of Norman origin.[34] Sharing landed interests in Gloucestershire and Middlesex with Edmund, St Philibert witnessed six Edmund-related charters but also had interests in Derbyshire where Edmund had no land.[35] St Philibert was present when grants were made to Hailes Abbey and in favour of the city of Exeter. As well as having lands in Oxfordshire, Walter de Huntercombe held lands in Northumberland[36] and he witnessed a charter to Edmund.

John la Sale had a house in Marazion, Cornwall.[37] Holding lands in Oxfordshire and Cornwall, Lawrence Basset was Edmund's tenant at Ipsden.[38] County, but not tenurial, interests bound the former Montfortian, Adam le Despenser, who held of others in Oxfordshire and Gloucestershire.[39] There is no obvious reason for the presence of Walter de Pedwardine who was a substantial man with lands on the Herefordshire/Shropshire border. A veteran of the Welsh wars, he served Edmund during Rhys' rebellion but went blind six years later.[40] Whilst Arnald Murdac served Edmund only as a soldier, Geoffrey and William Murdac witnessed charters in favour of Edmund, one being granted at Berkhamsted.[41] Arnald was an Oxfordshire landholder and William had lands in Northamptonshire and Warwickshire, none as Edmund's tenants.[42]

Seven non-Cornwall-based knights, noted by Page, served Edmund as soldiers and had additional connections to him. Richard of Cornwall (Cornubia), Edmund's half-brother, was described by Page as the most important of his knights.[43] Page believed that Richard witnessed fourteen charters of Edmund and four in his favour. Further research has increased this to eighteen and four respectively. Two charters were witnessed in London (including Clerkenwell), two at Haughley and one each at Beckley, Berkhamsted and Gittingham.

Henry de Shottesbrooke owned lands in Berkshire[44] and was Steward of Berkhamsted for a while.[45] He was away on Edmund's business in 1280 and also acted as Edmund's attorney on several occasions in the early 1280s.[46] Henry witnessed seventeen of Edmund's charters and seven (?) in his favour. Was it a coincidence that Henry was appointed to act as a justice in investigating trespasses and the theft of deer from Edmund's park at Corsham in 1282 and 1283?[47] Edmund lent him money; he was noted as owing Edmund £14 in 1287.[48]

Thomas de Bréauté joined Edmund's affinity as a sub-tenant of the latter's Wallingford lands. Before dying in 1294, Thomas witnessed seven of Edmund's charters and one in favour of him. Overshadowed by his highly effective but infamous father, Falkes, Thomas had made his career as an Oxfordshire knight. Falkes rose from humble origins in Normandy to be a mainstay of the government during the early years of the minority of Henry III. Liked by King John, to whom he was always loyal, Falkes had secured the mother of the infant Earl of Devon as his wife but, after a revolt in 1224, he lost all his extensive lands and offices and died in exile. For a while, Falkes had been the Steward of the infant Richard of Cornwall for the Honour of Eye.[49] Falkes' son, Thomas, held no land directly from the Earls of Cornwall but he did hold Upper Heyford (Heyford Waryn) part of a relatively modest endowment from his mother, the coheiress of the FitzGerold and Curcy families.[50] Upper Heyford was by this time held by Isabella de Fortibus, Countess of Aumale and granddaughter of Thomas's mother. She, in turn, held it of Edmund.[51]

Although he took his name from Poyle in Middlesex, Walter de la Poyle (Puille), also had lands in Oxfordshire, Sussex and Surrey.[52] Attestations to eighteen charters of Edmund and eight in his favour have been found. Walter had been one of the knights that Edmund led into Wales in 1277[53] and Walter went with him to France in 1280. Two years earlier, he shared a debt of 450 marks to Edmund with seventeen others.[54]

One knight who had an extensive record in administration before he joined Edmund's circle was Geoffrey Russell. He had served as an official for Peterborough Abbey, Countess Isabella of Aumale and the Bishop of Durham. In 1277 he was a King's justice.[55] Russell was not just a witness to the comital charters (thirteen of Edmund's and two benefiting Edmund), he was Steward of Wallingford and Knaresborough in the late 1270s and early 1280s.[56] He became Steward of Oakham where he was featured in the accounts of 1296–97,[57] and acted as Sheriff of Rutland on Edmund's behalf from 1294 until 1298.[58] His personal landholdings were in Northamptonshire and he held no lands from Edmund. Just before Edmund's death, he moved on to be one of the guardians of the Archbishopric of York.[59]

Robert Damory, who died in 1285, was the son of Earl Richard's knight, Roger Damory. Robert travelled overseas with Edmund in 1280 and served Edmund in Wales in 1277. He was a witness of ten charters issued by Edmund as well as five where he was the grantee; as a citizen of London, he was in possession of the manor of Kennington on the south bank of the Thames.[60] The Damorys were tenants of Edmund in Oxfordshire.[61]

The last non-Cornwall military knight noted by Page was Robert Malet who had lands spread over four counties: Surrey, Middlesex, Berkshire and Oxfordshire as well as Quainton, Buckinghamshire, held of Edmund.[62] On seven occasions, he stood as a witness for Edmund and on three others, he was the testator for grants to Edmund. He too served Edmund in the 1277 Welsh campaign.[63] Although he might have left Edmund's affinity around 1280, they were still in touch. He was one of those appointed to investigate the murder of Roger de Drayton and to consider complaints made in 1292 by Edmund's bailiff against men of the honour of Berkhamsted. They had rescued Edmund Walerand, one of Roger's murderers, who had been found guilty in the King's court. They had put Walerand in sanctuary in Berkhamsted church before letting him go free.[64]

The principal Cornish knight identified by Page as belonging to Edmund's affinity was Reginald de Botreaux one of the few knights with links to Richard of Cornwall. Reginald's father, who died in 1274, was a retainer.[65] A younger son, Reginald acquired lands in Cornwall and was noted twenty times as a witness for Edmund and five times for grantors to him. Although Reginald was the most prominent Cornish affinity member, his brother, William, was also associated with Edmund. The tenant of Edmund at Worthyvale and Penhele,[66] William witnessed Edmund's charters in favour of Launceston Priory and St Michael's Mount Abbey as well as for three other men, one of which charters was issued in Cornwall. Another related to Cornish lands however, one was issued in Westminster, indicating that William had travelled with Edmund. William also had lands in Somerset, Devon, Dorset and Warwickshire.[67]

Page acknowledged that Thomas le Erkedene (Lercedekne or the Archdeacon) was another Cornish knight at the heart of Edmund's affinity. A former crusader, he was Edmund's tenant in Veryan.[68] Whilst he witnessed only three of Edmund's charters[69] and five in his favour, he was Steward of Berkhamsted before the death of Michael of Northampton in 1283[70] and he acted for Edmund as Sheriff of Cornwall in 1280.[71] He was also one of Edmund's knights in Wales in 1277.[72] Thomas had one moment of national importance when he captured Simon de Montfort's daughter, Eleanor, from a ship in the Bristol Channel whilst she was on her way to marry Llywelyn ap Gruffudd.[73] At least one charter was likely to have been granted in London.[74] In addition, Edmund issued three charters (Page has two) in Thomas's favour.[75] Thomas also held Trerice from Edmund.[76] Page believed that Thomas was inherited from Richard of Cornwall's affinity and was certainly present alongside Richard at Watlington in 1269.[77] Thomas's brother, Geoffrey, also moved in Edmund's circle, witnessing two charters when Edmund benefited, as did another Erkedene, Otto, who witnessed Edmund's grant to William Chenduit at Watlington.[78]

Page listed a group of Cornish knights who witnessed a single acta each.[79] It included Serlo de Nansladeron and John de Treiagu. Nansladeron was one of Edmund's tenants but he grew in national importance and was summoned to Parliament as a baron in 1300.[80] Being known to Edmund did not prevent him from having to pay 4 shillings for not having to attend Edmund's court as did William de Botreaux.[81] It was Treiagu who witnessed William of London's grant to Edmund at Lostwithiel in 1290. Treiagu was a burgess for Truro in 1305.[82] Page also included William de Champernown, Reginald de Beville and John Alet, who are now known to have attested two Cornwall-related charters. Champernown had extensive lands in Cornwall and Devon[83] and Richard de Champernown was said to have married Richard of Cornwall's illegitimate daughter by Joan de Vautort.[84]

John de Beaupré, another of Richard of Cornwall's affinity, witnessed two Cornwall charters and his son, Stephen, one. Another knight with connections to Richard was Ralph de Bloyou, the son of Alan, one of Richard's knights[85] who stood as a witness twice[86] including one issued outside Cornwall, at Ashridge. Whilst his family originated in the south east, Thomas of Kent seems to have moved to Cornwall by the 1260s.[87] Later he attested six charters for Edmund[88] and three in his favour. His son, Bartholomew, witnessed for Edmund and held Holton, Oxfordshire.[89] Four charters, all relating to Cornish lands, were vouched for by Richard de Hiwys (Huish?) who held lands in Devon and Cornwall.[90] During the 1290s, he was active in the local administration of Cornwall and was granted lands there by Robert FitzWalter in 1295. Hiwys was not a tenant of Edmund[91] as Edmund had quitclaimed Robert's homage to the King ten years previously.[92]

Amongst the witnesses in favour of Edmund was Roger Pridias who was present on three occasions. Pridias had been a member of Richard of Cornwall's affinity and his father had been Richard's steward in Cornwall.[93] In 1274, Roger was a defendant alongside Edmund in an action brought by John FitzJohn concerning detention in Devon.[94] He was also a co-defendant in a Devon case initiated by the Abbot of Forde in 1277.[95] When he was replaced as Sheriff of Devon in 1273, complaints brought about him by the men of the county were investigated.[96]

Moving away from the West Country, other significant knights who witnessed more than one charter for Edmund included Peter Becard who attested four charters about grants in Cornwall but also Oxfordshire and Yorkshire from 1280 until 1284. Becard, the son of John Becard who was killed at Evesham, was based in Yorkshire where he held of Edmund.[97] Another knight who witnessed six widely-spread charters was William de Bereford. William, who became one of Edmund's executors,[98] was the son of a justice, a landholder in Northamptonshire and Oxfordshire and a tenant of Edmund in Berkshire. Alongside Robert Malet, Bereford was appointed to investigate the escape of Edmund Walerand.[99] Edmund had granted Bereford a fishery on the Thames.[100]

Oxfordshire was the base of William l'Enveysey who witnessed charters, all local; six in favour of Ashridge and others in favour of Edmund.[101] Although the two charters William de Beyville witnessed related to Cornwall, his lands were in Essex, Suffolk and Somerset.[102] John Neyrnuit witnessed two Ashridge charters and one for Wallingford castle chapel. He held land in Wiltshire of Edmund, as well as other manors in Buckinghamshire.[103]

John de Gatesden came from another group of Edmund's lands: Northamptonshire, Hertfordshire, Bedfordshire.[104] Although not a tenant, he was an attestor for six charters including five for Ashridge as well as four benefiting Edmund.[105] Another knight from Northamptonshire as well as Wiltshire and Cambridgeshire, Hugh Peverell[106] witnessed twice for Edmund both about Cornish lands[107] although he was not his tenant. The *curialis* Walter de Helion was dealt with in the previous chapter.

One important knight who served Edmund, but not mentioned by Page, was Ralph le Marshal. He witnessed seven charters granted by Edmund, including six for Ashridge, as well as six in his favour from others including places in Buckinghamshire and Oxfordshire. Ralph served Edmund for over a decade. His lands were in Somerset,

Huntingdonshire, Dorset and he had interests in Essex but he does not appear to have been a tenant of Edmund.[108]

Another attestor was Roger de Moeles, a man with lands not only in Oxfordshire, Hertfordshire, Buckinghamshire and Berkshire but also Somerset, although he was not a tenant of Edmund.[109] The seven charters that he witnessed were conceded at Ashridge but also at Restormel in Cornwall. From Northamptonshire, Seman de Stokes[110] witnessed in relation to charters for a wide range of religious houses: Eye Priory, Stoneleigh Abbey, Knaresborough Friary, St Leonard's Hospital, York and Burnham Abbey. He went abroad with Edmund in 1280.[111] Finally, of the knights who witnessed several charters for Edmund, Roger de Ingpenne from Inkpen in Berkshire had lands in Cornwall[112] including at Caerhays which he had been given by Edmund.[113] It was in Cornwall that he served as Sheriff in 1285–86.[114] Witnessing three of Edmund's charters and two for his benefactors, by 1297 he had moved on to join the household of Aymer de Valence.[115]

There were forty-three knights who witnessed a single charter for Earl Edmund which suggests that they had no long term links with him. They are listed below.

Table 9.2: Knights who witnessed only a single charter for Edmund of Cornwall

Name	Landed Interests	
(The landed interests are taken from 1 Moor, *Knights*, 2 *Aspilogia* 3 *CIPM*, iii, 604. 4 *Feudal Aids*)		
William le Alemand	Unknown	1 and 2
Ralph de Arundel	Cornwall	1
Reginald Beauchamp	Bucks, Berks, Northants	1
William de Blotessdon (Bluntesdon)?	Cornwall, Berks	1
Ralph de Bloyou	Cornwall	1 and 3
Roger de Bodrugan	Cornwall	1
Richard de Bosco	Somerset, Dorset[116]	1
Nicholas de Boys	Northants, Bucks	1
Adam de Burton	Cheshire, gaoled in York	1
Thomas de Burton	Sussex	1
John Carbonel	Bucks, Essex, Suffolk	1 and 3
William Cole	Devon, and Coroner of Cornwall[117]	1
John Dang...	?	

Name	Landed Interests	
Thomas Danvers	Somerset, Oxon, Bucks, Hants	1[118]
Ralph Dayrel	Northants[119]	
John Digby	Warwickshire, Leicestershire	1
Hugh Durival	Oxon	1, 3 and 4
Otto l'Erkedene	Cornwall	1
Alan FitzRoald	Northants, Devon, Oxon	1
Sampson Foliot	Oxon, Dorset	1
Richard de Goldsborough	Yorkshire	1
Adam Gurdrum (Gurdon)	Devon, Hants	1
Philip de Hoyville	Berks[120]	1, 2 and 3
Roger d'Insula	Northants	1
W de Lapville	?	
Peter de la Mare	Wilts, Glos, Oxon, Herefordshire, Devon etc[121]	3
Nicholas de Montford	Somerset, Devon	1
Theobald de Neville	Rutland	2 and 3
Robert de Nunnewyt	?	
Thomas Paynel	Sussex, Hants	1
William de la Penne	Bucks?[122]	1
Alan de Plukenet	Herefordshire, Hants, Somerset, Oxon	1
Robert de Plompton	Yorkshire	1 and 3
Robert Pugeys	Oxon, Bucks	1
Fulk de Rycote	Oxon[123]	3 and 4
Geoffrey de Turberville	Berks	1
John de Umfraville	Devon and Somerset	1
Robert de Vernon	Wiltshire and Cheshire	1
Robert Walerand	Devon, Glos, Worcs	1
Thomas de Warberon	?	
Simon Ward	Yorkshire	1
Edmund de Wedon	Bucks, Bedfordshire	1 and 4
Alberic de Whittlebury	Northants	1

Some of these knights were of more significance than might be at first supposed. Although they witnessed only one charter for Edmund, some attested for grantors to him. These included Thomas Burton, Thomas

Danvers, John Digby, Alan FitzRoald, Richard de Goldsborough, Robert de Plompton, Robert de Vernon and Alberic de Whittlebury. Whittlebury acted as Sheriff of Rutland[124] and Neville in Cornwall.[125] Danvers and Digby also served as Edmund's stewards in Cornwall and Wallingford.[126]

Of the remaining four, only Plompton had a tenurial connection with Edmund for a mere 4 shillings annually from Knaresborough.[127] He had extensive lands in Yorkshire for which he gained a market, fair and free warren and for some he was a Percy tenant. He fought in Scotland and witnessed for Countess Isabella of Aumale.[128] Burton had Sussex holdings; he made a grant of lands to Michelham Priory in, or before,1320.[129] A prominent Yorkshire knight, Goldsborough, had £40 worth of lands in the county and was a tenant of the Percy family. He served against the Scots as a Commissioner of Array and was summoned as a knight from both Yorkshire and Lincolnshire to the Great Council at Westminster in 1324.[130] With lands in Cheshire and Wiltshire, Vernon was summoned against the Welsh and to serve in Flanders. But he also had some interests in Oxfordshire acting as an assessor of subsidy.[131] He came from a branch of the Vernon family of Haddon, Derbyshire.[132]

Of the other single charter knights, Reginald de Beauchamp was Edmund's tenant in Buckinghamshire and Northamptonshire.[133] William le Alemand's name suggests a family relationship; perhaps he was another illegitimate son of Richard of Cornwall. Having served in the Welsh war of 1277,[134] he was killed in 1284.[135] Bluntesdon was a knight of Eleanor of Provence.[136] Robert Walerand had been in the affinity of Richard of Cornwall.[137] Otto l'Erkedene was part of a family whose close connections to Edmund have already been mentioned.

This analysis suggests that it would be wise to consider knights who had been present when grants were made to Edmund and especially those who performed more than once. Seven such knights are listed below.

Table 9.3: Knights who witnessed more than one charter in favour of Edmund of Cornwall (The landed interests are taken from 1 Moor, *Knights*, 2 *Aspilogia* 3 *CIPM*, iii, 604. 4 *Feudal Aids*)

Name	Landed Interests	
John de Braybroke	Bedfordshire	1 and 2
John de Dagworth	Suffolk and Essex	1
William l'Enveysey	Buckinghamshire	1
Walter de Helion	Herefordshire and Gloucestershire	1
Ralph le Marshal	Somerset and Dorset	1
Philip Strug	Wiltshire[138]	1
Hugh de Tywe	Northamptonshire[139]	
Walter de Upton	Buckinghamshire and Shropshire	1

Of the seven, William l'Enveysey, Walter de Helion and Ralph le Marshal have already been considered. John de Dagworth, a landholder in Suffolk and Essex,[140] was granted lands at Stowe by Edmund[141] and his relative, Simon, also received Henton.[142]

Neither John de Braybroke or Walter de Upton were tenants of Edmund. Braybroke had a manor in Bedfordshire and must have been a relative of Gerald de Braybroke who had Buckinghamshire lands.[143] Upton was a Buckinghamshire knight but also had lands in Shropshire.[144] There was a John de Tuwe (Tew) in possession of Astrop, Oxfordshire, in 1300 and Hugh de Tywe, a tenant of Edmund, might have been a relative of John.[145] A royal writ in 1297 required a coroner for Wiltshire to be elected to replace Philip Strug who had died. Again, he was not a tenant of Edmund.[146] However, even a knight who witnessed for only one charter benefitting Edmund might be more significant than this slight linkage suggests. One was a neighbour of Edmund's in Berkshire, Thomas Huscarl.[147]

One man not mentioned in Edmund's charters but who was listed as Edmund's knight was John Wyger who, in 1272, was robbed at Topsham[148] but, in 1275, he and Edmund fell out and were at odds in the court.[149] Wyger's earlier closeness to Edmund was confirmed in 1274 when he was alongside Edmund's clerk, Master Ralph (Roger of Marlow) when appointed to go to the papal court as King's proctors.[150] Wyger's connection with Edmund must have been further strengthened when Wyger was in place as Sheriff of Devon and Constable of Exeter castle in 1274.[151] Whilst he had extensive lands in Devon, they were not held from Edmund.[152]

One difficulty which arises when trying to establish which men were knights is that the title seems to have been given more liberally than deserved, as will be shown when considering clerks. But there were also men who were not given the title in charters who seem to have been recognised as knights. Thus John FitzNigel, who had extensive interests in Buckinghamshire and was hereditary Keeper of Bernwood forest, should probably be included as a knight[153] He witnessed for Edmund and was his tenant in Buckinghamshire.[154]

Conclusions

The knights of Edmund's affinity show that he relied mainly on men from the areas where he was most often present, namely the honours of Wallingford, Berkhamsted and the earldom of Cornwall. This meant that he must have known them personally or by reputation before they joined him. He seems to have chosen well and the evidence shows that few of the men he chose left him and only a handful of stewards were untrustworthy or inefficient.

Chapter 10

Edmund's Men: His Clerks and Officials

This chapter deals with other men who were close to Edmund including non-knightly laymen and clerics who acted as his clerks. After considering the laymen, the role and importance of the clerical clerks is examined, the most prominent men are identified and information is given on their careers. There is mention of Edmund's chaplains. Of Edmund's officials, the most important were the Sheriffs and Stewards of Cornwall and the Sheriffs of Rutland. The stewards and bailiffs of Edmund's main honours needed to be men of ability and probity. Some did not live up to the standards Edmund expected and, when disputes were not settled amicably, they ended in the law courts. Normally, at one remove, were the attorneys who acted for Edmund in litigation. Sometimes his clerks acted as attorneys but the increasing specialism of attorneys' duties led to Edmund employing professionals whose relationship was based on being paid rather than as being part of his household.

Edmund's clerks carried out a wide range of vital tasks. Without them, the administration of his extensive land and financial interests would have been unmanageable. They dealt with his correspondence, receiving and sending letters and writs. They wrote or commissioned other lower-paid clerks to draft and send out documents on his behalf. They may have drafted his charters also, although those for religious houses might have been prepared by members of the house itself. The stewards of the honours were responsible for the local administration but there needed to be an over-arching mechanism to bring their activities together especially in accounting for the overall revenues of the Earl and their disbursement. This was provided by the senior clerks. Travelling on Edmund's behalf, they visited the centres of his honours, sometimes carrying large sums of money. The clerks would also arrange for and pay messengers. When Edmund moved to another of his homes or visited the royal court, the clerks made the arrangements for his journey ensuring that the necessary horses, carts and protection were in place as well as making sure that the traveling party was fed on the way. Advance warning was given to those in charge at their proposed destination. Liaison with Edmund's attorneys over legal actions was also in their remit. The clerk ensured that the Earl's administrative machinery was properly oiled.

Some men in Edmund's circle were never styled as knights and had no priestly livings. These served as his officials and witnessed charters. From near Edmund's base at Berkhamsted came Maurice de Pichelsthorn (Pitstone) who witnessed three charters, two giving lands to Ashridge and another granted in Oxfordshire. From the Buckinghamshire village of Hedsor, east of Marlow, came John de Hedsor who was present when four land gifts to abbeys were made and also when three laymen gave lands to Edmund. Presumably Master Philip de Hedsor presented to Beckley, Oxfordshire, by Edmund, was John's relative.[1] Not far from Berkhamsted lies Harpenden and it is probable that William de Harpedene, witness of four charters, came from there. As well as acting as his attorney in London, John Godsalm,[2] witnessed two charters. Hugh Bataile, who attested two charters, must have been related to William Bataile, Edmund's bailiff of Wallingford in 1296–67.[3] Three further multiple attestors were William Merry, John de Scardeburgh and Roger of Wallingford. Merry who was Steward of Berkhamsted in 1296–99[4] witnessed three times.[5] Scardeborough was present at charter-granting twice and Wallingford on five occasions. Nothing more is known of Roger.

Although knights were accorded more prestige, much of the day-to-day administration of Edmund's affairs relied on these non-knightly men especially the clerks. Some were priests, others clerks in minor orders and some were university graduates. Perhaps the most important of those who served Edmund were Michael of Northampton, Roger de Drayton, Payn of Liskeard, William de Monkton, Roger de Inkpen, Hamo Parlbien, Roger de Byterwyk, Roger de Marlow and Walter of Aylesbury. Two of his clerks acted as his executors alongside Guy de Beauchamp, Earl of Warwick, Thomas Bitton, Bishop of Exeter, Anthony Bek, Bishop of Durham, Walter Langton, Bishop of Coventry and Lichfield, John, Abbot of Hales, William de Bereford, Ralph, Rector of Ashridge, namely Walter of Aylesbury and Roger of Marlow and three justices, Ralph de Hengham, William Inge and Henry Spigurnel.[6]

Edmund used his patronage to grant church livings to people whom he wanted to impress or to provide incomes for his clerks. Edmund presented church livings at least fifty-six times but the documentation of other appointments must have been lost. Of the men whom he preferred, some were of national significance whose services Edmund desired or whom he wanted to reward for past services. They included Ralph de Hengham[7] and possibly John de Kirkby. Hengham received the livings of Lanteglos-by-Camelford in Cornwall and Middleton in Yorkshire. Middleton was in Edmund's hands with the wardship of the lands of Baldwin Wake.[8] Table 10.6 in the appendix lists the presentations made by Edmund.

Michael of Northampton was amongst the most important servants of Edmund's father. He was noted as a King's clerk in 1254, when Richard of Cornwall was granted exemption from tallage in Northampton. This writ shows that whilst he came from Northampton, Northampton was not an inherited surname; his father was Simon de Houton.[9] Michael was granted the farm of Abington, Northamptonshire, for six years but he lost these lands during the Barons' Wars because they belonged to the Montfortian, Humphrey de Bassingbourne, but he recovered them later.[10] He travelled to Germany in 1257 when Richard of Cornwall accepted the crown and he was used as a plenipotentiary during the tense days of 1263 when violence had broken out in the kingdom. His final service to Richard was as an executor of his will. In the latter role, he fell foul of Archbishop Pecham who ordered his excommunication in 1281.[11] Before Richard's death, a royal charter of 1271 gave Michael and his heirs free warren in his lands at Garton, Northamptonshire.[12] A writ was issued instructing him and William de Braiboeuf[13] to investigate those who had entered Edmund's free chase at Dartmoor, hunted there and took away deer.[14] In 1280, Michael was Edmund's attorney, when he was going overseas.[15] Emden believed that, in the same year, Michael was acting as Sheriff of Middlesex but this was based on a faulty reading of a writ.[16] A year later, Michael presented Master Henry le Meser to the living of Frodingham on Edmund's behalf.[17] On fifteen occasions Michael attested Edmund's charters as well as another four which benefited Edmund. Michael was dead by 17 June 1283 when he was replaced as the priest-in-charge of Hemswell in the diocese of Lincoln.[18] Two years later his executors were challenged by Edmund for the return of missing documents. There is some doubt over Michael's status.[19] Although he was Rector of Beckley,

Oxfordshire in 1260,[20] a writ of 1293 respited him from being distrained to be a knight.[21] Moreover in a witness list attached to a 1278 or earlier charter, he was styled knight.[22] He had children and his grandson held Garton in the fourteenth century.[23] Another executor of Michael's will was Edmund's frequent attorney, John de Batesford.[24] Batesford was also close to Walter of Wenlock, Abbot of Westminster, and acted as the abbey's Steward.[25]

Murder ended the career of Roger de Drayton's service to Edmund. At the time of his death, he was Edmund's Treasurer but he must have come from humble origins. At Edmund's request, the Pope granted permission for Drayton to be ordained even though he was of illegitimate birth and agreed that he could hold the rectory of Harwell.[26] Perhaps Drayton originated from Drayton Beauchamp in Buckinghamshire which was in the honour of Berkhamsted. Drayton travelled overseas with Edmund's small group of trusted men in 1280.[27] During the negotiations for Edmund's acceptance of Howden from Bishop Bek, Drayton acted as Edmund's attorney.[28] He witnessed at least twenty-five charters for Edmund, the earliest not later than 1277, as well as nine more in his favour. Although a clerk, Drayton, too was styled as a knight on the Wautham charter.

Payn of Liskeard inherited as an affinity member from Richard of Cornwall, left Edmund by 1283 to join the household of John of Pontoise when he became Bishop of Winchester. From the bishop, he obtained a living and became the Treasurer of Wolvesley.[29] Earl Richard had presented Payn to the living of Michaelstow (Cornwall) and he was preferred by Edmund to St Stephens at Saltash on the Cornwall/Devon border.[30] Not as frequent charter witness as Drayton, he attested six of Edmund's charters and one granted to him.

Another Cornish clerk was Master Hamo Parlbien first witnessing for him in 1275, the first of four charters. In 1279, he received the living of Ladock in Cornwall from Edmund.[31] Hamo was prominent enough to have his 1291 death noted by the Hailes annalist.[32] Another multiple attestor of Edmund's charters was Master Walter de la Mare. From sometime before 1277 and up until 1283, he witnessed four charters benefiting the Bishop and the Prior of Rochester as well as Hailes Abbey and Christina de Chesterton. Before 1277, Walter had served Edmund as Sheriff/Steward of Cornwall and was also his steward in Berkhamsted.[33]

Presented to North Stoke, Oxfordshire, by Edmund,[34] Roger de Byterwyk witnessed nine charters for Edmund, all benefiting religious houses. A further four charters, granting property to Edmund, were also attested by him. In 1285 and 1286 he acted as Edmund's attorney.[35] It seems probable that John de Byterwyk, who was murdered at the same time as Roger de Drayton was a relative.[36] In the middle years of Edmund's earldom, Roger de Marlow (Merlawe) was prominent in Edmund's administration. As a church man, he was Dean of St Nicholas at Wallingford Castle in 1303 and Edmund gave him livings at Hemswell in Lincolnshire and Harwell in Berkshire.[37] Seven grants by Edmund were witnessed by him and two benefiting the Earl.

Perhaps the most successful of Edmund's clerks was Walter of Aylesbury. He was a landowner, having Rowton and Ellerdine in Shropshire and Wydney and Edstone in Warwickshire in 1284–85.[38] For his services, Edmund gave Walter lands at Rousham, Oxfordshire, in 1296.[39] He acted for Edmund as Sheriff of Cornwall in 1289.[40] Of Edmund's charters, Walter witnessed nine and another four in Edmund's favour beginning in 1280. Perhaps Nicholas of Aylesbury, who was presented by Edmund to Manton in Rutland in 1292[41] was a relative. Walter outlived Edmund and was busy acting as an executor of his will.[42] In 1304 he was Constable of Wallingford castle.[43]

Whilst the two great departments of state were the Chancery and the Exchequer, Edward I, gave more emphasis to the Wardrobe, an administrative department of the court.[44] It provided a mechanism by which money could be given to, and be used by, the King in a more rapid, less bureaucratic way. This effectiveness commended itself to magnates. Tout noted that, in addition to a Treasurer, Edmund had wardrobe clerks.[45] Marlow, Byterwyk and Drayton were noted as clerks of his wardrobe.[46] Marlow and Andrew de Ashbourne, possibly a relative of Edmund's attorney, Thomas de Ashbourne, were also recorded as being in Edmund's wardrobe.[47]

A possible brother of Edmund's Steward, Geoffrey Russell, John Russell was chaplain to Edmund in 1293.[48] Chaplains at Oakham were known only as Robert in 1296/7 and John in 1300.[49]

Edmund controlled the shrievalties of Cornwall and Rutland. The men who acted for Edmund as Sheriffs or Stewards of Cornwall as well as Keeper of the Stannaries and as the Sheriff of Rutland are listed below.

Table 10.1: Sheriffs/Stewards of Cornwall 1272–1300.

Name	Date	Reference
(John de Beaupré)	(1269)	*CAD*, A9711.
Sir Richard de Seaton[50]	1273	*List of Sheriffs*, 21.
Sir Richard de Seaton	1274	*Bronescombe Register*, ii, 990.
(Master Walter de la Mare)	before 1277	TNA:PRO CP 40/26 m. 18.
William de Monkton	1278	*List of Sheriffs*, 21.
Sir Thomas le Erkedene	1280	*List of Sheriffs*, 21.
Sir Thomas Danvers	1280	TNA:PRO E 36/57, f.43v.
William de Monkton	1282	*List of Sheriffs*, 21.
	1284	TNA:PRO E 36/57 f.14v.
Henry de Geleton	1284	TNA:PRO JUST/111 m.16d.
William de Monkton and Roger de Inkpen	1285	*List of Sheriffs*, 21.
Roger de Inkpen (Acting for Edmund of Cornwall)	1286	*List of Sheriffs*, 21.
John Hommedon (Umeddon)	1288	*List of Sheriffs*, 21.
Walter de Aylesbury	1289	*List of Sheriffs*, 21.
Sir Thomas de Danvers	1290	*List of Sheriffs*, 21.
Sir Thomas de Danvers?	1291	*CPR 1377–81*, 114–5.
Humphrey de Kayle	1291	*List of Sheriffs*, 21. PRO E 372/138
Sir Theobald de Neville	1292	*List of Sheriffs*, 21.
Sir Theobald de Neville	1295	*CChR 1300–26*, 490.
Robert de Stockey	1295	*List of Sheriffs*, 21.
Thomas de la Hyde	1296	*List of Sheriffs*, 21.
(Thomas de Ocham acting for)	1296–97	*Ministers' Accounts*, 222.
Thomas de la Hyde	1300	*List of Sheriffs*, 21.

Table 10.2: Acting for the Keeper of the Stannaries.

Name	Date	Reference
John de Wilton	1279 29 Sep (Mich)	Westminster TNA:PRO E 159/ 53 m. 25 d.
Roger de Aldworth	1280 30 Sep	Westminster TNA:PRO E 159/ 53 ms. 31 & 33.
John de Hommedon	29 Sep (Mich) 1286	Westminster TNA:PRO E 159/60 m. 9.

Table 10.3: Sheriffs of Rutland 1272–1300.

Name	Date	Reference
Peter de Sakerle	1272	*List of Sheriffs*, 112.
William de Beiville	1272	*List of Sheriffs*, 112.
Aubrey de Whittlebury (Acting for Edmund of Cornwall)	1280	*List of Sheriffs*, 112.
Peter de Weston	1288	*List of Sheriffs*, 112.
Geoffrey Russell	1294	*List of Sheriffs*, 112.
John de Borle	1298	*List of Sheriffs*, 112.

Of Edmund's twelve appointments to the shrievalty and stewardship of Cornwall only four, Thomas l'Erkedene,[51] William de Monkton, Humphrey Kayle and Thomas de la Hyde, lived there and only Erkedene came from the leading knightly families.[52] Monkton served as sheriff of Cornwall for two spells.[53] Around 1278, Monkton was accused of falsifying weights whilst keeper of the Cornish stannaries.[54] Appointed collector of the fifteenth in Cornwall in 1275, William owed £248 to the exchequer in 1279. He granted the advowson of the church of Morwenstow to the Hospital of Bridgwater in 1285, and went to Ireland in 1287 on the affairs of Gilbert de Clare.[55]

As already mentioned, Richard de Seaton held lands in Northampton-shire and Oxfordshire, and Roger de Pridias in Devon. Walter de la Mare was a Gloucestershire landowner and Roger de Inkpen a Berkshire knight. Walter de Aylesbury held lands in Derbyshire, Warwickshire and Oxfordshire. Thomas Danvers had lands in Berkshire, Somerset and Dorset. Theobald de Nevill was a Rutland landowner, whilst Robert de Stockey was a Devonshire man. Page was not clear why Edmund chose so few Cornishmen to serve as Sheriff and Steward and suggested that the amalgamation of the two offices freed Edmund from the obligation to appoint local knights as Sheriff. This resulted in the county's complaint to the King in 1302. On the other hand, Edmund may have regarded the office as patronage, to be bestowed upon those closer to him than the men of Cornwall. After all, the stewardship carried the very substantial reward of a £60 salary. Seven of his twelve sheriffs and stewards, Seaton, Pridias, de la Mare, Inkpen, Aylesbury, Danvers and de la Hyde, were tenants of the earl.[56]

Unlike the sheriffs of Cornwall and Rutland, there are no complete lists of Edmund's stewards for the other honours.

Table 10.4: Bailiff/Stewards acting for Edmund of Cornwall excluding Cornwall.

Name	Date	Reference
Berkhamsted		
Walter de la Mare (and Isleworth, Risborough, Hemel Hempsted, Cippenham etc)	before 1277	TNA:PRO CP 40/26 m.42d.
John le Sumenor	1292	*CPR 1281–92*, 515.
John le Sumenor	1291	Geoffrey tenant. *CChR 1257–1300*, 383.
Sir Thomas le Erkedene	?	TNA:PRO E 36/57 f.31v.
Sir Henry de Shottesbrooke	?	TNA:PRO E 36/57 f8v.
Sir Henry de Shottesbrooke	?	*HMC Hastings*, i, 277.
William Merre (Merry)	1296–67	*Ministers' Accounts*, 1.
	1299	*CPR 1292–1301*, 608.
(Mole) Hamo de Carleton		BCM/A/2/60/7.
	?	TNA:PRO SC6/827/38.
Bradnich		
Alexander le Bedel	1275	TNA:PRO CP 40/8 m.28d.
Bradnich and Exeter, Kenton, Lydford, Dartmoor, Wike and Netherton		
Henry de Raleigh	before 1277	TNA:PRO CP 40/21 m.101 and 40/22 m.23d.
Chichester		
William de Monkton	1282	*Registrum epistolarum fratris Johannis Peckham*, 379.
Peter of Bosham	1283	*Registrum epistolarum fratris Johannis Peckham*, 578.
Steward of Eye		
John de Helpstone	?	*CChR 1300–26*, 491.
Simon de Haveringes	1296–67	*Ministers' Accounts*, 151.
Steward of Howden		
Thomas de Burnham	1295	*CPR 1292–1301*, 145.
Thomas de Burnham	1296–67	*Ministers' Accounts*, 202.
Thomas de Burnham	1301	*CPR 1292–1301*, 621.
Steward of Knaresborough		
John de Molton	1278	TNA:PRO E 36/57 f.32v.
William de Stokis	?	TNA:PRO E 36/57, f.23r.
Richard of Cornwall	1284–85	*Ministers' Accounts*, 201.n.
Thomas de Burnham	1296–87	*Ministers' Accounts*, 186.
and	1298	*Bolton Cartulary*, CB 436.

Name	Date	Reference
Mere		
Richard de Chuseldene	1296–97	*Ministers' Accounts*, 55.
Oakham		
Geoffrey Russell	1296–97	*Ministers' Accounts*, 159.
Rutland		
Alexander le Bedel	1275	TNA:PRO CP 40/8 m.28d.
St Valery		
Simon de Greenhill	1296–97	*Ministers' Accounts*, 136.
Suffolk, (based at Bury St Edmunds)		
William Muchet	before 1277	TNA:PRO CP 40/26 ms. 22d and 128d.
Wallingford		
Adam de Henton	1281 29 Sep	TNA:PRO E 159/55 m.21.
Adam de Henton	1285 13 Jan	TNA:PRO E 159/58 m.4d.
John Digby	before Greenhill	*Frideswide's Cartulary*, 310.
John Digby	1287	TNA:PRO 36/57 f.32r.
Sir Robert Malet	1274	TNA E 36/57 f.31v. JUST 1/538 m.14.
Miles de Morton	1292	TNA:PRO CP 40/95 m.30.[57]
Ralph de Mershe	1296–97 23 views	*Ministers' Accounts*, 118.
Stephen le Wyte	1296–97	*Ministers' Accounts*, 121.
Walter le Ferrour	1296–97	*Ministers' Accounts*, 123.
William le Bataile	1296–97	*Ministers' Accounts*, 125.
Simon de Greenhill	1296–97	*Ministers' Accounts*, 84.
Simon de Greenhill	1298	*St Frideswide's Cartulary*, 310.
Wilton		
Gilbert de Molesham	1292	Dorset History Centre D/WLC/1306.

The names of those who served Edmund as constables and castellans are more difficult to find. William de Waldeshef, a tenant, served at Restormel.[58]

The remainder of this section comments only on knights not dealt with previously. One exception is where a layman concerned is noted for more than simply holding an office. For instance, the stewards of Berkhamsted have been considered already. Thomas de Burnham, who had served with the King personally in the First Welsh War, also acted as a justice.[59] John Pecham complained about him when he was Edmund's man in Chichester.[60] Probably he came into Edmund's service as an associate of Bishop Bek when the Bishop loaned Howden to Edmund, or he could have been associated with the honour of Knaresborough.[61] John de Helpstone might have come from the Northamptonshire village of that name. Likewise Richard de Chuseldene could have been from the Wiltshire village of Chiseldon although it is on the other side of the county from Mere. Simon de Greenhill, the Steward of St Valery and Wallingford, had lands at Hucknall in Nottinghamshire.[62] Another Steward of Wallingford, Miles de Morton, had lands in two counties where Edmund was prominent: Stanwell (Middlesex) and Horton (Buckinghamshire) during 1286–67.[63]

Edmund's relationships with officials were not always good. The bailiff of Edmund's Devon lands, Henry de Raleigh, was sued in 1277 for failure to provide proper accounts.[64] Henry was far more than a local knight. Although he went with Edmund to Wales in 1277[65] and he did not witness Edmund's charters but he had a significant rôle as a local justice. The year before Edmund brought his action against Henry, he was commissioned by the King to investigate the murder of Edmund's forester for Dartmoor. In 1284 he was investigating a death in Devon and, in 1291, an attack at Poltimore (Devon). He was even sent to discover who had stolen a beached whale which belonged to the Bishop of Exeter. Away from Devon, Henry carried out judicial duties, delivering the gaol at Oxford in 1292.[66] He also delivered Exeter gaol in 1289 and 1297.[67]

Around the same time as the Ralegh case was begun, Walter de la Mare was alleged not to have presented proper accounts for his time as Sheriff of Cornwall or as bailiff of Edmund's holdings in Berkhamsted, Risborough, Cippenham, Hemel Hempsted, Isleworth and other manors.[68] Whilst Edmund's man in Suffolk and Cambridgeshire, based at Bury St Edmunds, William Muchet, also failed to account properly for his stewardship.[69] However, Edmund was not unusual in having to take legal action to require a former official to render proper accounts; Peter de Champvent sought them from his bailiff when Champvent was Sheriff and Constable of Gloucester and Elias de Rabayn from his bailiff for the period when he was Constable of Corfe.[70]

The thirteenth century saw increasing legal activity and the potential danger of losing an action by the issuing of the wrong type of writ and the making of an inaccurate submission. This led to the growth of a proto-professional legal class at a time when the business of the royal courts was also expanding fast. Table 10.5 in the Appendix lists the known attorneys of Edmund. An attorney represented the litigant and there was an increasing trend to use men who were experienced in the law as attorneys. The use of an attorney also reduced the need to travel to court which, in the case of the King's Bench, was itinerant and could sit as far away from Westminster as North Wales and the Scottish border. The attorney would appoint a serjeant to argue the litigant's case before the judges and had the right to avow or disavow what the serjeant said on behalf of his client. He was the channel of communication with the litigant and was responsible for the safe keeping of the documents. At one time a friend or a relative might have been appointed but the evidence is clear that these non-professionals were becoming less likely as the century progressed. The attorney was appointed at the first hearing of a case and his name was enrolled. Afterwards, the litigant did not appear in person. However, appointment at the court was not the only route. Appointments could also be made through the Chancery. In a substantial number of suits involving Edmund, the attorney is unknown and the name has not survived in the extant rolls. It is difficult to believe that Edmund himself appeared at court to appoint his man in the first instance, at which time the litigant was expected to answer the call and confirm that he would be present through his attorney.[71]

Amongst those men appointed through the Chancery and appearing in the Chancery rolls, some were in place to cover a man's legal affairs however they arose and usually for a specific period. The reason for such appointments was often given. This might be because of a proposed journey abroad, sometimes on the King's service, or as a soldier in one of his wars. Other appointments related to specific court actions and were recorded, often as addenda, on the court rolls. These lists of attorneys were not always complete but they are very useful in indicating whom a litigant trusted. Some were men well-known as members of Edmund's affinity or household such as his clerk, Roger de Byterwyk, who is found in both court and chancery rolls, although, in 1287, he also acted for Hugh Despenser.[72] Edmund's most important clerk,

Michael of Northampton, was noted as attorney but only on a chancery roll.[73] Michael acted as a justice himself when investigating an attack on Edmund's chase at Dartmoor.[74] A knight who was a member of his affinity, Henry de Shottesbrooke, acted for Edmund in both exchequer and court records.[75] More professional attorneys were the men who spent their whole time in the courts representing those who paid them. Some attorneys became stars of the court and, in the case of Edmund, it is interesting to note some of his attorneys were also used by other great men. Robert de Ashbourne was used both by Edmund and by his cousin, Edmund of Lancaster.[76] Ashbourne has been identified by Paul Brand as the second busiest attorney at the Kings Bench in 1280, being appointed in at least thirty-seven cases.[77] Another man used by Edmund on at least sixteen occasions was John de Batesford and his closeness to Edmund's circle is demonstrated by the fact that he was an executor of the will of Michael of Northampton.[78] There is also evidence of an attorney, Walter de Amodesham (Amersham?), being appointed to deal with matters at the 1283 Parliament.[79]

Chapter 11

Edmund, the Man of Piety

Dulcis in elloquio, justus, pius atque benignus,
Prudens consilio, regni moderamine dignus,
Fraxinei dorsi per eum novus ordo virescit,
Summa coelicolae nova messis in aggere crescit.
Sumptibus Edmundi comitis locus aedificatur,
Regius Oxoniae, quo plebs studiosa moratur.

(Sweet in utterance, just, pious and kind, prudent in counsel, worthy
to manage the kingdom, through him flourishes the new order of
Ashridge, a new harvest grows for the Heaven-dweller [i.e. God] on
the high ridge.
A place is built at the expense of Earl Edmund at Oxford, in which
stay people who desire to learn.)

Edmund of Cornwall's devotion to religious causes might have
been stimulated by the example of his father and uncles. Nicholas
Vincent believed that the piety of Richard of Cornwall was
conventional rather than fanatical.[1] Richard had founded several religious
houses including the Cistercian abbey of Hailes in Gloucestershire, a
daughter house of Beaulieu, founded by his father, King John. Richard
also founded the Augustinian nunnery at Burnham in Buckinghamshire
and Trinitarian friary at Knaresborough, home to the shrine of the hermit
known as St Robert.[2] In addition, Richard allowed the Franciscans of
Chichester to transfer their community to the site of the former castle.
Religious piety was one of the most dominant qualities of Henry III,
the rebuilder of Westminster Abbey. Edmund's half-brother, Henry of
Almain, made only one act of religious patronage, a gift of a property
in Westminster to finance lights before the shrine of St Edward in the
abbey. Vincent suggested that this showed 'a keen devotion to the cult of
the Confessor and a desire to obtain divine protection on the eve of his
sailing for the crusade'[3] with the Lord Edward.[4]

Evidence establishes that Edmund was a man of conventional and generous piety. However, he did not have to use his wealth for generous acts of religious patronage. No one has doubted the depth of the religious commitment of Edmund's uncle, Montfort, but he made only seven benefactions to religious institutions.[5] A lack of long term assets might have been an overriding reason why Montfort was not more generous. Nor should the way in which Edmund chose to have his body and heart disposed of lead to the conjecture that Edmund had any doubt in the belief in corporeal resurrection. As Westerhoff stated, 'Valorisation of the heart in its own right as a body part which could be interred separately in a container of precious metal' did not compromise 'one's corporeal integrity'.[6]

By 1250 the great age of foundation of new monastic houses of prestigious orders, such as the Benedictines, Cistercians and Cluniacs, was past. The advent of the friars in the early years of the century 'filled the vacuum'.[7] Houses of Augustinian canons, whose members were unenclosed priests, were relatively popular and cheaper to endow than abbeys. Vincent has argued persuasively that Edmund and his father probably came across the Holy Blood relic in April 1269 when Richard, as King of the Romans, was given the imperial regalia then housed in the castle of Trifels. But it was the young Edmund who physically acquired the relic. A year later, on the feast of Exaltation of the Cross, 14 September, he led a procession from Winchcombe to Hailes where he presented part of the relic at the high altar of the abbey. At the time, he was planning to set off on crusade and made the gift to mark this commitment.[8]

Edmund and the Cistercians

Within the context of a loss of enthusiasm for endowing new Cistercian houses, it is surprising that two of Edmund's major series of patronage were to that order: Hailes and Rewley abbeys. Edmund's first actions as earl were to support or augment decisions made by his father. Hailes Abbey had been founded in 1245 by Richard to redeem a vow made when he had been threatened by shipwreck two years earlier. The monks moved there in 1246 and the church was dedicated in 1251. The works cost 8,000 marks although Richard boasted to Matthew Paris that he had spent 10,000 marks.[9] On acquiring Edmund's Holy Blood relic, the abbey's attractions to the laity were strengthened. Vincent wrote, 'The Abbey lacked any saint of its own, the Holy Blood was offered a prominence that it might otherwise have lacked, being placed, in a special shrine behind the high altar.' The Order was reluctant to sponsor ostentatious display and it 'might have been expected to eschew the more vulgar trappings of the cult of relics' but the Order stressed the humanity of Christ making it more amenable to the acceptance of Edmund's gift. By 1275 the monks had permission from the General Chapter of the Order for an annual ceremony centred on the relic. A year later, the Pope licensed two priests to serve the shrine and the pilgrims who visited it.[10]

Fire partly destroyed Hailes Abbey a year before Edmund came into his inheritance and he immediately began its rebuilding. By this time, the abbey had contained the bodies of Richard, Sanchia and Henry of Almain. Originally Hailes had a nave of eight bays with a row of eastern chapels similar to the Cistercian Abbey Dore. After the fire, Edmund paid for a new choir on a much grander scale. It had a chevet-formed space containing five semi-octagonal chapels and this might have been designed by Robert of Beverley, the chief mason of Westminster Abbey. When completed, the abbey was 320 feet long, comparable to the great abbey of Gloucester.[11] Consecration of the shrine for the Holy Blood was conducted in 1277 by the diocesan, Geoffrey Giffard, Bishop of Worcester, and Edmund funded further works: a new infirmary which was begun in 1291.[12]

Building on his father's endowments, Edmund was a generous benefactor to Hailes. Ten charters benefiting the abbey are known. Some are only recorded in the later royal inspeximii and confirmations which do not always record the original date. But the range of the dates can be narrowed down by using the death dates of the most frequent witnesses such as Michael of Northampton, who died in 1283, and Roger de Drayton murdered in 1292.

Perhaps the first two charters were those giving the advowsons of Hemel Hempsted and Northleigh to Hailes in about 1278.[13] Two years later, the abbey received Cornish lands: a meadow lying before the gate of the houses of the monks at Hauleye, called 'Fispond' (Fishpond), and a piece of land in the manor of Helston called 'La Haye'.[14] More Cornish property was added in 1286 when the advowson of St Paulin was conveyed.[15] Then, in 1290, land much nearer the abbey, the manor of Longborough in Gloucestershire, was granted.[16] Another Cornwall-related grant came in 1295; Edmund gave 'the land in the manor of Helston called "Bromelyne" with another piece lying by the church of St Breage, Cornwall, which belongs to the monks, on which a seld used to be put up'.[17] In the same year Edmund gave a gold cross with an enamel foot to contain the Holy Blood relic.[18] Finally, in the year of his death, the Earl gave the abbey the manor of Lechlade, Gloucestershire, and the advowson of the hospital and the vicarage of the church there.[19] A year earlier, an inquest was told that the Prior of the Hospital of Lechlade had removed brethren, priests, sisters and laymen and had taken items from the library and ornaments. To make matters worse, he had removed the priests who prayed for the soul of the Earl of Cornwall and his ancestors. It is not clear whether this referred to Richard or Edmund but, as prayers for Queen Beatrix were also mentioned, it seems more likely that Richard was the benefactor. However, it could have been belated recognition for Edmund's dead step-mother.[20] An undated grant of a park and pasture at Lower Swell was added to the abbey's portfolio by Edmund.[21]

Lands which were part of Edmund's manor of Haughley (Suffolk) were granted to Hailes before the death of Roger de Drayton in 1292. They were only an acre.[22] The tenth and last charter might have been granted at the same time and was really an exchange of lands for the land lying under the grange of the abbot in that town.[23]

Edmund decided to honour his father's wish to establish a religious institution at Rewley in Oxford, but to make it bigger and more important than Richard had envisaged. He had planned to fund a college or chantry with three priests to pray for his soul. It was to be sited on land on the island of Oseney, which Richard held as part of the honour of Wallingford. Instead Edmund founded a Cistercian house and doubled the number of religious members putting in place six Cistercian monks. By 1280 Edmund offered to endow a college for the members of the Order to study at Oxford. The Chapter of the Order accepted his offer and decreed that the college should have the same privileges as that of St Bernard at Paris. It was under the supervision of the Abbot of Thame, who in turn answered to the Abbot of Clairvaux. Although, at first, it was not intended to be an abbey, the Chapter decreed in 1281 that it should be ranked as an abbey 'out of due respect to the Earl of Cornwall'.[24] In the same year, the Abbot of Thame was permitted to appoint an abbot

Edmund, Earl of Cornwall. (*Wikimedia Commons, originally from the* Genealogical Chronicle of the English Kings, British Library *MS Royal 14B V. membrane 6*)

Seal of Edmund of Cornwall. (*The National Archives; E329/191. By courtesy of the Heraldry Society*)

The arms of Edmund of Almain, Earl of Cornwall. (*Berkhamsted castle.org.uk*)

Statue of Edmund, Earl of Cornwall, Ashridge. (*Michael Ray*)

Trifels castle. (*Berkhamsted castle.org.uk*)

Kenilworth castle, Edmund of Almain a prisoner 1264–65. (*Wikimedia Commons*)

San Silvestro, Viterbo. The site of the murder of Henry of Almain, the brother of Edmund of Almain. (*Wikimedia Commons*)

Berkhamsted Castle, Hertfordshire. Birthplace of Edmund of Cornwall.

Eye Castle, Suffolk. (*Wikimedia Commons*)

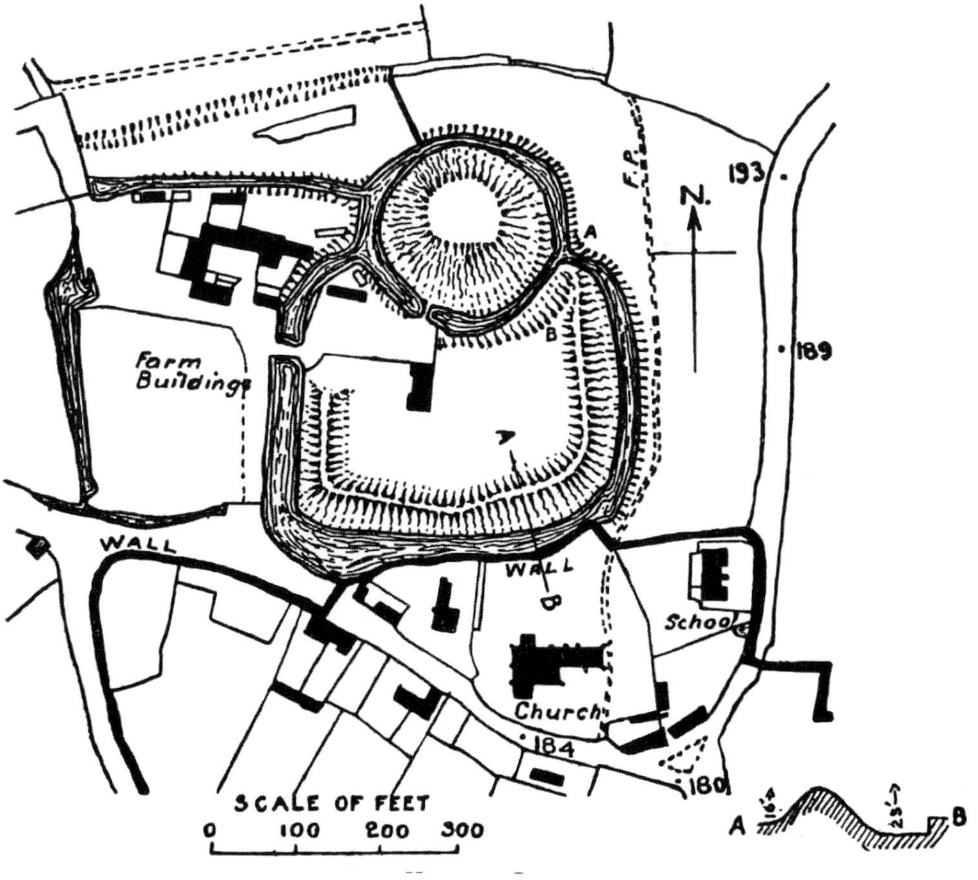

Haughley castle, Suffolk. (*Wikimedia Commons*)

Knaresborough castle, Yorkshire. (*Wikimedia Commons*)

Launceston castle. (*Wikimedia Commons*)

Lydford castle. (*Wikimedia Commons*)

Mere castle. (*Andrew Tivenan*)

Oakham castle, Great Hall. (*Wikimedia Commons*)

Restormel castle, Cornwall. (*Wikimedia Commons*)

Tintagel castle, Cornwall. (*Wikimedia Commons*)

Trematon castle, Cornwall. (*Wikimedia Commons*)

Wallingford Castle, Berkshire. (*Wikimedia Commons*)

Hailes Abbey. (*Michael Ray*)

Rewley Abbey. Sole remains adjoining the Oxford canal. (*Wikimedia Commons*)

Clare Chasuble. (© *Victoria and Albert Museum, London*)
In 1786, David Wells, writing in the *Gentleman's Magazine* stated that the accompanying stole and maniple had been decorated with the arms of Clare, Lacy and Edmund. They are now lost; *English Medieval Embroidery, Opus Anglicanum*, ed. C. Browne, G.Davies and M.A.Michael (New Haven, 2016), 138.

Peter Comestor, *Historica Scholastica* British Library. ((*BL Add Royal 3 D VI*) *f.3* © *The British Library*)

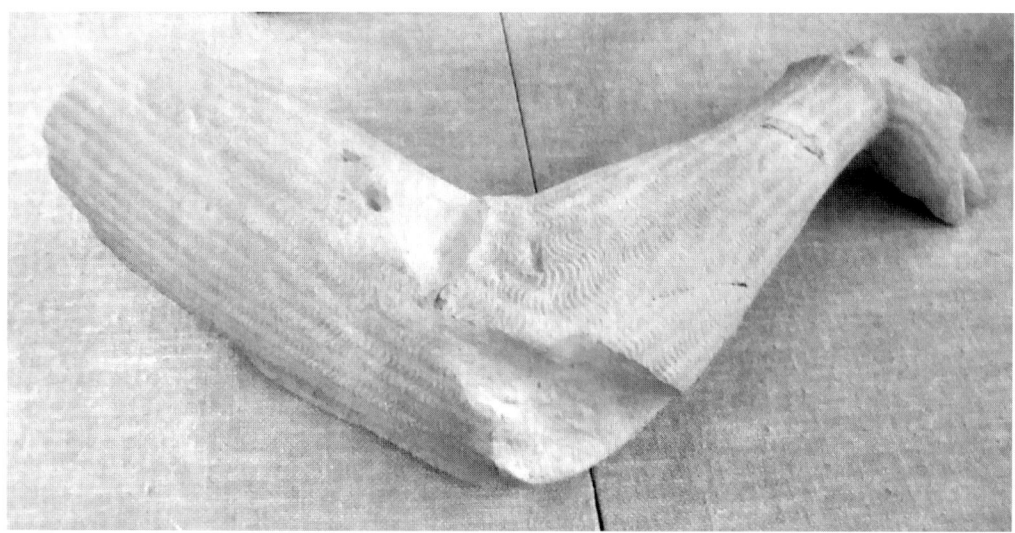

Part of an effigy, Hailes Abbey, Gloucestershire, said to be from tomb of Edmund of Cornwall. (*Michael Ray*)

Tiles from Hailes parish church, Gloucestershire. (*Michael Ray*)

Tiles from Cleeve Abbey, Somerset.
(*Michael Ray*)

Arms in stained glass, Dorchester Abbey, Oxfordshire. Edmund of Cornwall second from bottom on the right. (*Heraldry Society*)

First page of Cartulary of Edmund of Cornwall. ((*TNA:PRO E 36/57*) © *The National Archives, Kew*)

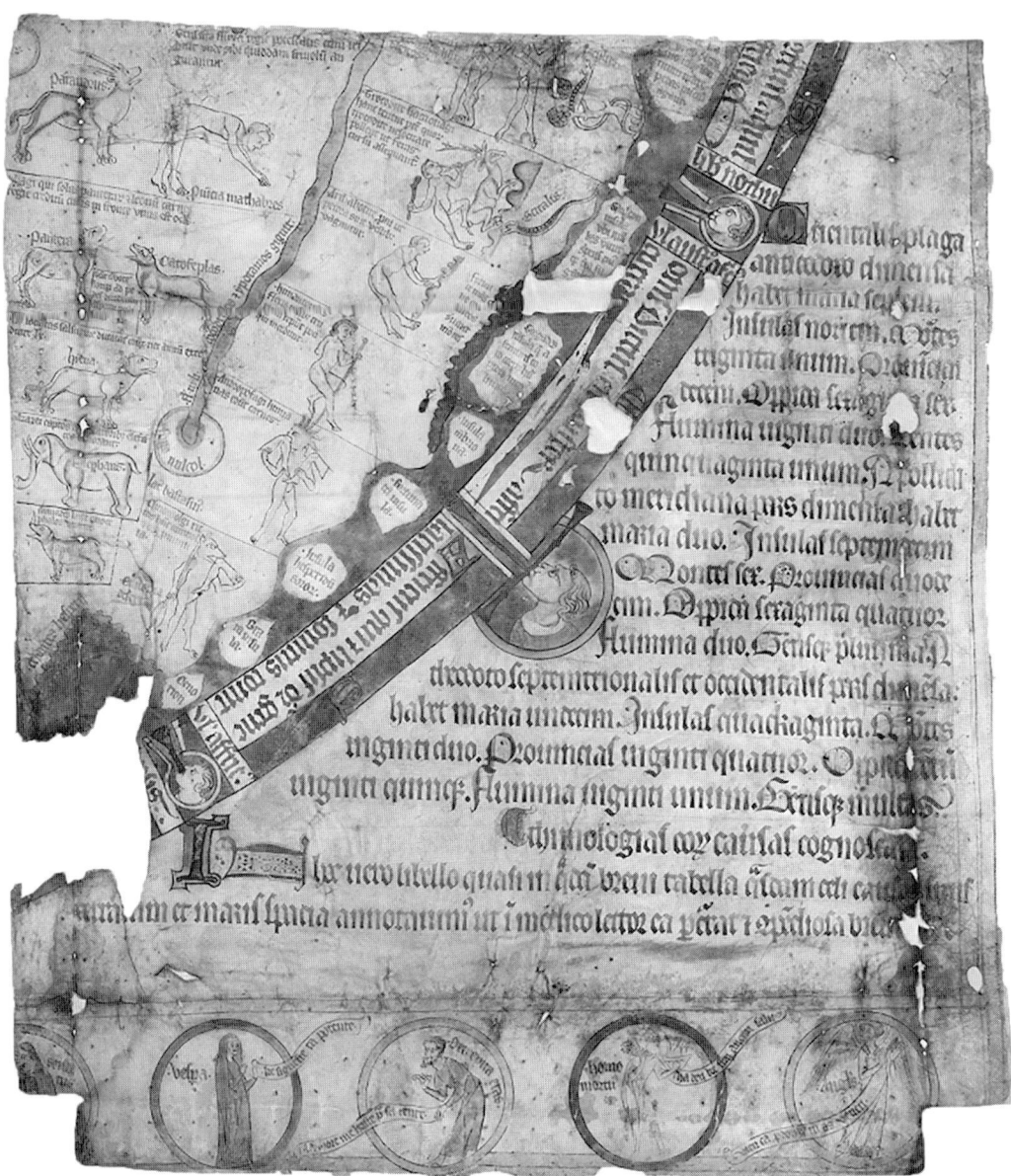

Mappa Mundi fragment. (*Duchy of Cornwall © The Duke of Cornwall 2021*)

for the house of study at Oxford and to celebrate a daily memory of the late earl of Cornwall at mass at the college (*studium*) of Oxford. The new abbey was dedicated to St Mary and, in December 1281, the building was consecrated by the Chancellor, the King's great friend, Robert Burnell, Bishop of Bath and Wells. The first monks were from Thame Abbey. In 1282 the Chapter gave the new foundation the title '*Sancta Maria de regali loco*' and decreed that houses which sent students to Rewley for study should make them an allowance.[25] Thus Edmund should be viewed as one of the earliest patrons of Oxford colleges.

Endowing Rewley was achieved by giving it the manor of Yarnton, mills in Cassington, the hamlet of Wyllanston in the parish of Mixbury, two parks in Nettlebed, tenements in London, and the advowson of St. Wendron in Cornwall (now Wendron). Before 1291 the abbey obtained possessions in Edmund's manor of Chesterton, Oxfordshire.[26]

The Cistercian advance had been stemmed by 1250 and, after Rewley, only two further abbeys were founded in England and Wales, both by Edward I. Vale Royal, Cheshire, was begun in 1274 and, like Hailes, it resulted from the fulfilment of a vow made by Edward I during a perilous voyage. In 1277 Edmund was amongst those who laid foundation stones at Vale Royal.[27] Edward needed to find a new site for Aberconway Abbey as he had used the site of the original abbey, the resting place of the Princes of Gwynedd, to build his new town of Conwy. A new home was found at Maenan.[28] Another Cistercian abbey benefited from an early act of patronage by Edmund; in 1275, Biddlesden Abbey, Buckinghamshire, was given freedom from suit of his court at Charwelton, Northamptonshire.[29] A 1279 grant to Stoneleigh, another Cistercian abbey in Warwickshire, was a temporary one. With the consent of Countess Margaret, lands in Cubbington, Warwickshire, were given to the abbey until the full age of Geoffrey de Sumilly.[30] Stoneleigh counted Stephen, the Empress Matilda and Henry II amongst its royal founders.[31] The Cistercian abbey of Fountains was given rights in Knaresborough forest by Edmund in 1284.[32] To assist the Cistercian abbey of Newenham (Devon), Edmund exchanged lands in Axminster in 1293.[33] When Peter des Roches, Bishop of Winchester and the former tutor of Henry III, died, his plans to found a Cistercian abbey at Netley, Hampshire, were brought to fruition by his former pupil. Edmund gave the abbey, rents and hidages together with the view of frankpledge in Northleigh, Oxfordshire, but the date is unknown.[34]

Edmund and the Augustinians

The Augustinian canons of Launceston Priory in Cornwall obtained confirmations of Richard of Cornwall's gifts in 1284 and in 1291.[35] In addition, trading privileges for the priory's tenants were granted in 1284.[36] Following a dispute in 1290, Edmund agreed with the priory of Thremhall, Essex, to give it lands in Birchanger providing it paid reliefs and heriot on the death of a prior and would perform suits and services.[37] During 1285, Edmund sought 30 marks from three masters of whom one was Master Richard de St Frideswide which suggests a dispute with that abbey.[38] Oxfordshire was the scene of another grant in 1292 when the Augustinian Oseney Abbey gained two fees in Mixbury and Newington Purcell and half a fee at Hampton Gay together with suit of court at Northoseneye, 'for our soul and the souls of our ancestors'.[39] A gift to Bolton Abbey, Yorkshire of common pasture at Washburn and the right to cut down the wood at Weeton was made in 1298.[40] An undated concession by Edmund waived the relief of shillings due from Poughley Priory, Berkshire, for its holding of Betterton, Wiltshire, when a new prior was elected.[41]

Another gift from Edmund was to the Augustinian nunnery of Burnham, founded by his father in 1266. In addition to the confirmation of Richard's charters, sometime before 1283, Edmund gave the nunnery the right to elect their abbess and the freedom from interference during the period of vacancy before a new abbess was elected. At the beginning of 1298, the Augustinian nuns of Goring received a licence from Edmund to elect a prioress.[42] Goring was founded by the Durivals, tenants of Edmund in the honour of Wallingford.[43]

Edmund and the foundation for the Bonhommes at Ashridge

Only one series of actions raises any doubts about Edmund's conventional approach to religious matters. These actions relate to the Bonhommes and show that he did not eschew new forms of religious worship. Representatives of the Bonhommes are said to have appeared in England around 1257. They were sometimes referred to as the 'Blue Friars'. It was in 1283 that Edmund funded their first house in England on his land at Ashridge on the borders of Hertfordshire and Buckinghamshire.

Known as 'the House of the Holy Blood of Jesus Christ', it was given papal approval.[44] The donation of a portion of the Holy Blood relic to the new house was of great importance and, from the very beginning, the statutes included provision for an annual feast to celebrate this, probably on the day of the Exaltation of the Holy Cross.[45]

The antiquarian historian of Ashridge, the Earl of Bridgewater's chaplain, Henry Todd, stated that the monks 'were brought out of the south of France.'[46] He gave no evidence for this but he seemed to have relied on Peter Newcome, Hertfordshire antiquarian vicar of Shenley, less than twenty miles from Ashridge. Newcome reasoned that 'The court of England had been frequented by crowds of nobles and gentry from Provence, and of Anjou and Poitou. And it is probable, that Edmund, now duke (sic) of Cornwall, brought this religious order, and placed them at Ashridge in compliance with some pious request of his mother, or by the interest and influence of some of the Provençals.' He continued 'My reason for this, is because they were brought out of the South of France, in which country a sect then prevailed, who called themselves Boni Homines. They were a sect of mystics, approaching, as some thought, to Manichaeism, and by some confounded with the Albigenses but in truth a remnant of the Paulicans'. Whatever the true reason for Edmund's decision, Newcome believed that Edmund brought them 'probably out of regard for their piety.'[47] The modern historian of Ashridge, Coult, followed Newcome in making an intriguing suggestion as to why Edmund favoured the Bonhommes. He noted the sympathy of Sanchia of Provence's family for the Cathars and suggested that Edmund might have favoured a religious order associated with the Cathars. Newcome believed that the wall paintings he saw in the old building in 1794/5, were of subjects chosen to deride the Dominicans and Grey Friars, the persecutors of the Albigensians.[48] If this was true, it really would have been a fine example of revenge savoured cold. Simon de Montfort's father made his name as the ruthless and savage opponent of the Cathar sect and was slain during the siege of Toulouse. Montfort's grandsons murdered Edmund's half-brother, Henry. A foundation at odds with Montfortian sympathies would have been a satisfying gesture. But it is difficult to believe that Edmund would have been that petty and was other than a very orthodox believer.

Colonel Chettle did much to resolve the confusion in his 1944 paper. He was certain that the Ashridge Bonhommes were not linked to the Bon

Hommes of Provence nor to the Friars of the Sack with whom they have also been associated. Some historians called them Augustinian canons and, in 1358, the founder of the second Bonhomme house at Edington referred to his 'brothers of the Order of St Augustine'. But, whilst the College at Ashridge kept to the rule of St Augustine, the brethren were not Augustinians. Chettle concluded that the foundation at Ashridge was a new order[49] and the doyen of monastic studies, David Knowles, thought that it was an 'institute of undiscoverable provenance'.[50]

Where did Edmund get the idea for a new order and where did he recruit the initial members from? The first rector, Richard of Watford, was an Englishman as was his successor. The establishment was never regarded as an 'alien house'. When Edington was founded in 1351, its first Rector was an Englishman from Ashridge. Members of the Ashridge community were required to be literate and of good morals.[51] Perhaps, Edmund looked to Oxford University and Rewley Abbey but Richard of Watford was not noted in Emden's list of Oxford alumni.[52]

None of the above explains why Edmund decided to found a new order. Having rejected the French origins of the Bonhommes of Ashridge, the idea that it was a response to his mother's request, she had died over twenty years earlier, can be rejected. It is difficult to conceive that a layman came up with the idea himself. Perhaps he was encouraged by one of his clerical friends. Could Thomas de Cantilupe, whose heart was buried at Ashridge, have been an inspiration? Edmund took a personal interest in setting up the house and he himself gave the members their *consetudines*.[53]

Edmund's initial endowment was not lavish. It provided for only seven brethren, all of whom were priests and they received 6 marks yearly for their support. The Dunstable chronicler believed that there was little hope that the house would continue because the foundation was insufficient, and some of the brethren had not a very good character despite the meaning of their name.[54] Edmund had more confidence and perhaps he relied on the reputation of the Holy Blood relic to bring pilgrims and money. The conventual church was dedicated in 1286 by his friend, Bishop Sutton of Lincoln, as the house was in his diocese.

Edmund and the Benedictines

The royal family was always the prominent patron of the most prestigious of the monastic orders, the Benedictines, the Black monks. Henry III's beloved Benedictine Westminster Abbey was given permission to erect a windmill at Oakham by Edmund.[55] The year 1279 saw Edmund make a benefaction to another Benedictine house. The priory of Eye in Suffolk was based at the *caput* of Edmund's honour of Eye. Founded by Robert Malet, the priory had come into the hands of the holders of the honour.[56] Edmund's benefaction began with a dispute with the Prior over the advowson of Thorndon, Suffolk, in 1276–77. The Prior withdrew his claim and, in 1279, Edmund granted it to the priory 'for the benefit of his soul and those of his mother and father'.[57] On 29 November 1295, Richard Oysel had been told to take into the King's hands the alien houses in Suffolk. Oysel ejected the Earl and his men from the priory, its barns and outer manors.[58] In 1296, the King ordered the Exchequer to restore the custody of the priory to Edmund. The King had learnt from an inquisition that Edmund took the custody of the priory into his hands before Palm Sunday, 1294. He was, as true patron and advocate, entitled to the custody in times of voidance as his father had always been.

By 1277 another gift from Edmund came to the Benedictine Rochester Priory; the advowson of Brundish in Suffolk, Norwich diocese,[59] whilst the Bishop obtained the advowson of St Berian in Cornwall.[60] Later this was returned as it had proved to be unsatisfactory due to its remoteness. The advowson of Henley as well as lands in Suffolk were given instead.[61] A daughter house of the Benedictine Mont St Michel, the Cornish St Michael's Mount Abbey, had its charter of Richard confirmed by Edmund in 1290 and he also agreed that, when the next prioral vacancy occurred, the profits would be reserved for his successor.[62]

Edmund's involvement with the Benedictine nuns of Studley, Oxfordshire, stemmed from his honour of St Valery, the nunnery having been founded by Bernard de St Valery. The year before his death, Edmund gave the nuns an acre and a half at Horton to where it had moved from Studley in Bernwood forest.[63] Another royal nunnery was Amesbury Abbey, Wiltshire, which belonged to the Fontrevault order. Henry III's widow, Eleanor of Provence, had retired there. It was given rents and the view of Chaddleworth, Berkshire, by Edmund in 1288.[64]

Edmund and the Carthusians

Other less prominent orders were also the recipients of Edmund's largesse. In 1284–85, the Charterhouse of Witham, Somerset, founded by Henry II,[65] was given lands at Marston Bigot, Somerset,[66] and in 1285, shillings rent at Monksham.[67]

Edmund and the Mendicant Orders

Mary Midgley commented on Edmund's apparent unwillingness to join in the enthusiasm for the four great orders of friars whilst patronising 'the relatively unimportant Trinitarians'. She cites only a 10 mark gift made to the Dominicans in his lifetime.[68] Whilst her general conclusion might be sound, it is possible that Edmund was a little more generous. He acted to assist the Ilchester Dominicans in 1285[69] and both the Grey and Black friars of Exeter were indebted to him. The Franciscans received lands in 1287[70] and had the charter of William Tauntefer confirmed by Edmund ten years later.[71] Meanwhile, the Dominicans had an agreement between themselves and the City of Exeter confirmed by Edmund in 1297.[72] At Chichester the same order was granted exemption from rents and services in 1284.[73] Both Leland and Dugdale believed that Edmund was responsible for augmenting the Greyfriars of Bodmin.[74] Hilda Johnstone discovered that, when Edmund died, he left a gold cross weighing over 24 ounces with 160 gems to be broken up and sold. The proceeds were to go to the four great orders on a carefully calibrated scale. Three quarters went to the Black and Grey Friars and, of the remaining quarter, the White Friars were to have two-thirds and the Augustinians the rest. The money was to pay for one mass for the repose of his soul within one year of his death. The cross was valued at £237.9s.0d[75] and Midgley noted that Edmund's private chaplain was the Franciscan, John Russell.[76] It seems strange that Edmund did nothing for the Oxford Grey Friars where his father's heart and the body of his step-mother, Beatrix, were buried. These Grey Friars had established a great reputation for scholarship but Edmund's commitment to the Cistercian educational centre of Rewley Abbey and the Trinitarian Friars in the city might have taken precedence. It was in 1280 that Edmund made his first grant to his father's foundation of Knaresborough Friary; it consisted of lands at Hampsthwaite, Pannal and the advowson of Fewston.[77] At the same time, he authorised the friars to build a mill on the river Nidd to grind their own corn. In 1284, he went further giving the friars rights in Knaresborough Forest.[78]

Edmund's gifts to other religious foundations

Well before Rewley Abbey was completed, Edmund enhanced the religious infrastructure of his castle at Wallingford by making a generous grant to found a collegiate chapel dedicated to St Nicholas.[79] There were royal chapels at Wallingford at the time of King John and, in 1227, Henry III had presented a prebend to St Nicholas's chapel. Edmund's grant enabled the chapel to be re-established and he was afterwards regarded as its founder. Under the provisions of Edmund's charter there was a large number of religious: a dean, six chaplains, six clerks and four taper bearers and a substantial endowment of over £61 was required.[80] When John Leland wrote his itinerary during the reign of Henry VIII he stated 'by the patents and donations of Edmune, earle of Cornewaul, Lord of the Honor of Wallingefeud (it apperith) that there were 14 paroch chirches in Walingford'.[81] Whilst the extent of this benefaction and the number of churches cannot be true, it indicates the longevity of Edmund's reputation for piety. Another castle had a religious presence. In the accounts of 1296/7 for Mere castle, there was a payment of an annual fee of 50 shillings for saying prayers for the soul of Edmund's mother, Sanchia.[82] In return for prayers for his soul and that of St Edmund, a garden and a little croft with a windmill at Mere were given to Salisbury cathedral in the same year.[83]

1284 was a year of benefactions. Apart from those for Knaresborough, Witham and the Chichester Black Friars already mentioned, the diocese of Exeter obtained Edmund's charter granting Hexworthy, Devon.[84] The Archdeacon of Taunton received his agreement to a decision of the Mayor and community to build a tower in Exeter. Two years later Edmund agreed to the erection of a wall to enclose the churchyard.[85] The outer geographical limits of Edmund's holdings were reflected in other grants in that period. Sometime before 1283, St Leonard's Hospital in York had been granted the right to navigate the rivers Ure and Ouse from Boroughbridge to York[86] and a gift to Bolton Abbey.[87] The grant to the Hospital may have been triggered by the case brought by its Master against Edmund in 1278.[88] St John's Hospital, Oxford, was engaged in the sale of lands between the East Gate and Rose Lane for 160 marks and the rent of a pound of incense at Christmas 1275[89] and these lands were given by Edmund in 1293 to the Trinitarian Friars, an order which his father had supported. Edmund's benefaction was the first recorded to it.[90] The earl provided a croft lying on the north side of his court for the rector of Harwell, Edmund's loyal clerk, Roger of Marlow. This was to be held by the rector and his successors, with free ingress and egress with horses and carts, for a yearly rent of 2 shillings.[91]

Leland wrote that Edmund founded three chantries at Gainsborough, Lincolnshire, but, whilst Toulmin Smith's index identifies the donor as Earl Edmund, it is possible that the benefactor was another Edmund of Cornwall, the son of the Earl's half-brother, Richard of Cornwall.[92]

Edmund did not neglect small organisations. He funded a hermit, Brother Robert of Penlyn who lived in a house built on an island surrounded by the water of Fowey, Cornwall, with rents from his tenants of Penkneth.[93] Perhaps this was the hermitage of Baldwin's Bridge about which the Prior of Tywardreath, a Benedictine house, submitted a petition in 1307. He claimed that Edmund had enclosed the woods and, in compensation for the loss, had made a grant of 4 marks a year to pay for a chaplain.[94] The hermitage of Blackmoor in Dorset received from Edmund an income from rents in Fordington.[95]

Disputes with religious houses

Despite his great generosity to religious orders, Edmund's relations with religious houses were not always harmonious. When the officials of Dunstable Priory at Dunstable market stopped a cart belonging to Edmund in order to levy a tax on his intended dinner, he was so angry that he persecuted the monks[96] and it was during 1275 that the Abbot of Forde alleged that Edmund and his men had detained his cattle.[97] The grant to St Leonard's Hospital, York, followed a legal dispute and, in the same city, the abbey of St Mary's sued Edmund over their rights to use ships in 1275. The Archbishop and Dean and Chapter were at loggerheads with Edmund over the rights to churches in the honour of Knaresborough in 1276.[98] The English Master of the Knights Temple sued Edmund in Lincolnshire in 1276 over distraint in relation to the manor of Waston and Edmund's court of Thonock and fifty sheep from the pasture of Thonock and at Swinhope.[99] In 1276/7 the Abbot of Cirencester sued Edmund.[100] Quarrels over presentation were recorded in 1277 with the Prior of Drax (Yorkshire) as well as the Abbot of Oseney.[101] Two cases involving the Abbot of Rewley related to problems over warranty and services.[102]

Edmund's devotion to Saints

Edmund of Cornwall was devoted to saints. Various holy persons attracted the attention and munificence of Edmund. He was the nephew of Louis IX of France who died at Tunis in 1270 as a crusader and became a saint in 1297. If Edmund had travelled to Paris with his mother in 1254, he might have met Louis. He made sure that he was present at the translation of St Frideswide at Oxford on 10 September 1289 with his brother-in-law, Gilbert de Clare.[103] Claiming that miracles had occurred at Bishop Robert Grosseteste's tomb in Lincoln Cathedral in 1286, Edmund wrote to Pope Honorius IV urging Grosseteste's canonisation.[104] These actions required little effort but the honouring of two other new or potential saints led to more significant expenditure. Edmund knew he was named for the recently canonised St Edmund Rich. Edmund, Earl of Cornwall decided to buy land in Abingdon from its Benedictine Abbey so that he could build a chapel on St Edmund's birthplace which he endowed with sufficient money to provide two priests to say daily masses.[105] The chapel became a place of pilgrimage and many miracles were reported there.[106]

Miracles were also engendered at Edmund's second foundation, the chapel at Hambleden, Buckinghamshire.[107] This was the birthplace of Thomas de Cantilupe whom Edmund knew well, not least when they were joint Regents in 1279.[108] They became close friends; Thomas came to Wallingford and spent Pentecost with Edmund either in 1277 or 1278. Whilst Thomas was at Wallingford, he presided over a service in the castle chapel. There was a great noble company who had been assembled by Edmund. When Thomas began to intone the *Veni Creator Spiritus*, a flock of at least thirty birds of mixed species including rooks, doves and starlings, appeared at the windows of the chapel. When the choir took up the refrain, the birds flew away and only returned when Thomas began the next verse.[109] This was regarded as the twenty-fifth and last miracle attributed to Thomas during his lifetime. Edmund, himself, told the story to Richard Swinfield, a later Bishop of Hereford.[110] Meryl Jancey observed wisely that the interesting point of the story was 'not whether this was, or was not, a miraculous obeisance of creatures to a saint, but that the observers thought that it was'.[111]

Following his death in Orvieto in 1282, the body of Thomas de Cantilupe was returned to England where Archbishop Pecham refused to allow it to be buried in Hereford cathedral. But Thomas's heart had been left to Edmund and he first placed it in Hambleden chapel and later it was interred alongside Edmund's at Ashridge. It was also said that Edmund possessed Thomas's hair shirt which had defied destruction by fire after the bishop's death.[112] The success of Hambleden chapel was shown by papal and episcopal instructions. In April 1296, the Archdeacon of Buckingham was ordered to close Edmund's private chapel at Hambleden as people had been making pilgrimage there because of the reports of miracles[113] but, by August, Edmund was licensed to have private mass at Hambleden as the excitement had died down.[114] In 1297, the Pope allowed him to have a chaplain in the chapel which might be consecrated by any bishop[115] whilst Bishop Sutton permitted him to continue to have mass at Hambleden providing there was no concourse of people expecting a miracle.[116]

Edmund and the Crusades

Crusading fever had not come to an end during Edmund's lifetime. Although often mocked, a good case can be made for Henry III's genuine commitment to the concept of the crusade. He took the cross in 1250 and 1256. Edmund's father, Richard, actually went to the Holy Land in 1240–41. When the Lord Edward decided to join his uncle Louis IX's second crusade in 1270, Edmund joined him and set out from England. His determination to be a crusader cannot be doubted although he had to return to England to comfort his father following the murder of his half-brother. After becoming earl, he had the resources to spend on crusading but there is no evidence that he planned to go again but neither did other magnates nor the King.

Edmund's involvement with the Trinitarian Friars, however, reveals his favour of an order associated with crusading. The Red Friars, as they were known, were founded in 1198 for the liberation of Christian prisoners and slaves from captivity under the Moors and Saracens. Although canons regular, in England they were often spoken of as friars. Their first house in England at Mottenden, Kent, was founded in 1224.[117] Knaresborough had been established by Edmund's father as was the house at Oxford. The site of the latter is now occupied by Wadham College.

Even after the fall of Acre and the expulsion of the Knights Templar from Palestine, Edmund continued to patronise them, making a grant in 1299, albeit a modest one. This concerned Cranford and Twickenham in Middlesex where he allowed them common of all his pasture and heath within the bounds of his hundred of Isleworth from the bridge of Babbeworthepond as far as Hounslow.[118] On his death, Edmund stipulated in his will that there should be money to pay for knights to serve for a year against the infidel, presumably in an attempt to re-conquer the lost crusader states.[119] Also, after his death, a petition to the Pope disclosed that Edmund had persuaded his wife to take an oath to make a pilgrimage to the Holy Land. The papal letter stated that she was to chose her confessor who may commute her vows, especially that of visiting Jerusalem, 'which she took at the desire of her husband Edmund, since deceased'.[120]

The scope of Edmund's benefactions

In all, Edmund's benefactions were spread right across the country from the western end of Cornwall to North Yorkshire and East Anglia. There is evidence for over seventy gifts to houses or institutions. The orders which benefited were wide-ranging but, having considered the wide spread of patronage, it is clear that one order was conspicuous by its absence: the alien foundation of Cluny. Perhaps this was because, by the thirteenth century, the order was regarded both as an alien order and in the power of the King of France. But the Cistercians were also under French control. In all the houses of eight Cistercian, eight Augustinian, seven Benedictine, four Black Friars, three Grey Friars, two Trinitarian friars, two Hospitals, one each of the orders of Fontrevault, Bonhommes, Carthusians, Carmelite Friars, Augustinian Friars were the recipients of Edmund's benevolence together with four diocesan sees as well as the Knights Templar.

Effect of Edmund's failed marriage on his piety

Nicholas Vincent has written that 'given the acrimonious nature of his marriage to Margaret de Clare, and the failure of this union to produce an heir, it may be that Edmund devoted a disproportionate amount of his wealth to the patronage of the religious, deliberately disposing of large tracts of land which would otherwise have escheated at his death'.[121] So it is worthwhile looking at whether the pattern of his benefactions changed when the marriage failed. Three dates are crucial. Firstly 1285 when his expected child did not survive and when he might have had to accept that the marriage would remain childless. Was the flurry of gifts in 1284, five or six in all, a covenant to God made by an expectant father?[122] Secondly, in 1289, when it became public knowledge that the marriage was in difficulties. Finally, in 1294, when the separation was agreed.

Table 11.1: Chronology of the piety of Edmund of Cornwall.

Date	Place	Order	Event
1269	Trifels		Acquisition of the Holy Blood relic
1270	Hailes	Cistercian	Gift of part of the Holy Blood relic
after 1271	Hailes	Cistercian	Starts rebuilding fire-damaged Abbey
1271			Joins Lord Edward's crusade
after 1272	Mere		Chaplain to pray for the soul of Sanchia of Provence
1275	Biddlesden	Cistercian	Benefaction
1272 x 83	Burnham	Augustinian Nunnery	Benefaction
1272 x 77	Rochester	Benedictine	Benefaction
1272 x 77	Rochester	Diocese	Benefaction
1275	Oxford	St John's Hospital	Benefaction
1277	Vale Royal	Cistercian	Laid one of the foundation stones
1278	Hailes	Cistercian	Benefaction
1278	Wallingford		Founding chapel
1279	Eye	Benedictine Priory	Benefaction
1279	Stoneleigh	Cistercian	Benefaction
1280	Hailes	Cistercian	Benefaction
1280	Knaresborough	Trinitarian Friars	Benefaction

Date	Place	Order	Event
1280	Rewley	Cistercian	Founded by Edmund
1282	Rewley	Cistercian	Benefaction
1282	St Thomas de Cantilupe		Edmund acquires his heart
1272 x 83	York	St Leonard's Hospital	Benefaction
1283	Westminster	Benedictine	Benefaction
1283	Ashridge	Bonhommes	Founded house
1284	Chichester	Dominican	Benefaction
1284	Exeter	Diocese	Benefaction
1284	Fountains	Cistercian	Benefactions
1284	Knaresborough	Trinitarian Friars	Another benefaction
1284	Launceston	Augustinian	Benefaction
1285	*Miscarriage or death of Countess Margaret's child*		
1284–85	Witham	Carthusian	Benefaction
1285	Ilchester	Dominican	Letter on behalf of the Friary
1285	Witham	Carthusian	Benefaction
1286	Robert Grosseteste		Edmund supports Grosseteste's canonisation
1286	Ashridge	Bonhommes	Gift of Holy Blood relic
1286	Hailes	Cistercian	Benefaction
1287	Exeter	Franciscan	Benefaction
1288	Abingdon	Benedictine	Builds and endows chapel on birthplace of St Edmund
1288	Amesbury	Fontrevault Nunnery	Benefaction
1289	*First signs of marital difficulties*		
1290	Hailes	Cistercian	Benefaction
1290	St Michael's Mount	Benedictine Priory	Confirmation and benefaction
1290	Thremhall	Augustinian	Benefaction
1291	Ashridge	Bonhommes	Benefactions
1291	Launceston	Augustinian	Confirmation
1292	Oseney	Augustinian Abbey	Benefaction
1293	Newenham	Cistercian	Benefaction
1293	Oxford	Trinitarian Friars	Benefaction
1293	Salisbury	Dean and Chapter	Benefaction
1294	*"Separation"*		

Date	Place	Order	Event
1294	Burnham	Augustinian Nunnery	Benefaction
1294?	Rewley	Cistercian	Benefaction
1295	Hailes	Cistercian	Gift of a gold cross
bef 1296	Hambleden		Private chapel built by Edmund
1296	Burnham	Augustinian Nunnery	Benefaction
1272x97	Blackmoor	Hermitage	Benefaction
1297	Exeter	Dominican	Benefaction
1297	Exeter	Franciscan	Confirmation
1298	Bolton	Augustinian	Benefaction
1298	Goring	Augustinian Nuns	Licence to elect Prioress
1299	Studley	Benedictine Nuns	Benefaction
1299	Cranford	Knights Templar	Benefaction
1300	Ashridge	Bonhommes	Edmund's heart buried alongside Cantilupe & Holy Blood
1300	Hailes	Cistercian	Benefaction
1300	York	Bishop	Left a ring in Edmund's will
1300		Dominican	Bequest of share of gold and bejewelled cross
1300		Franciscan	Bequest of share of gold and bejewelled cross
1300		Carmelite	Bequest of share of gold and bejewelled cross
1300		Augustinian	Bequest of share of gold and bejewelled cross
1300			Payment for knights for the Holy Land
1301	Hailes	Cistercian	Edmund buried
before 1303		Countess Margaret	Swore an oath to visit Jerusalem at Edmund's request
four undated	Hailes	Cistercian	Benefactions
one undated	Bodmin	Franciscan	Augmentation
one undated	Harwell	church	Benefaction

Date	Place	Order	Event
one undated	Penlyn	Hermit	Benefaction
one undated	Poughley	Augustinian	Remittance
one undated	Netley	Cistercian	Benefaction
one undated	Tywardreath	Benedictine	Benefaction
one undated	Gainsborough	?	Three chantries?

This Table demonstrates that Edmund's benefactions were made throughout his life and it would be a bold historian who would claim that the pace of gifts was significantly increased after his marriage had broken down. The great range and the continuing commitment to the assistance of religious houses clearly justifies Edmund's contemporary and historic reputation as a man of God. He inherited great wealth and used it well to enhance the religious infrastructure of his time. On one topic his later reputation is unsustainable and that is Emily Holt's praise for him as the man who brought Protestantism to England. It is not clear whether he would have really understood the concept and he might have been horrified if he did.

Chapter 12

Edmund, Man of Wealth:
The Source of His Wealth

No writer on Edmund has doubted that he was one of the richest men of his time. This chapter considers his wealth and compares it with that of other men of his time, great and small. Some of his income came from the normal sources available to landlords but he also had large sums of money from the royal grant of wardships and the rights to marry off heirs and heiresses. These grants were not expressions of cousinly affection but in exchange for considerable regular loans to the sovereign. Edmund also benefited from the large number of loans that he made to other people.

The normal sources of a magnate's income can be grouped into five main categories: farms and rents, sales of goods, feudal rights and aids, royal grants, and the profits of justice. But Edmund was the beneficiary of income from two other quarters. His stewardship of England's Jews followed that of his father's although Edmund only held this diminishing asset for a few years. More significant was his control of the stannaries of Cornwall and Devon which brought him large sums from the profits of tin mining.

No doubt using the Ministers' Accounts, Dyer put Edmund's annual income at about £6,000.[1] Vincent wrote that 'the income from these various sources, in total roughly £8,000 a year, ensured Edmund's preeminence as the richest lay Baron in England.'[2] This amount was the equivalent of well over £5.8 million by 2017.[3] Unlike Edward I, who always struggled to meet the costs of his monarchy and his wars leading him to borrow huge sums, Edmund had plenty of disposable income and could afford to lend to the King and others. Lands could be bought and he could purchase wardships and make ample profits. Ready cash and profits from his extensive landholding enabled him to endow and patronise religious houses. When he realised that he would be childless, he had no need to husband his resources for his descendants.

At the end of the thirteenth century, six earls received over £3,000 pa. Others had incomes of less than £1,000. Baronial incomes were in the £200–£500 range.[4] The annual income of Roger III Bigod, Earl of Norfolk, is put at £2,500 as was Aymer de Valence's whilst Gilbert de Clare received around £3,700 and William Marshal once had £3,500.[5] The enormously rich widow, Elizabeth de Burgh, a Clare heiress, had an income of £2,500 in 1329–30.[6] Although Vincent and Dyer gave estimates of Edmund's income, calculating its real magnitude is not as easy as it first appears. The existence of a very extensive set of accounts for 1296–97 gives the impression that there is a full picture of both Edmund's income and expenditure but there are lacunae. Firstly, by then, Edmund had settled lands worth £800 pa on his wife as part of the 'divorce settlement'. Secondly, other sources of income were not included. There are no details of repayments of his extensive loans. As money lending for interest was condemned as usury, particularly when the Jews were involved, these loans should have been simply repaid. However, it seems unrealistic to expect that Edmund lent money without any recompense. In some cases the actual amount of money lent was less than that recorded enabling the lender to receive back more than he had lent. Some payments were made by diverting income to Edmund. One form of payment was from the temporary custody of the lands that Edmund was given when he had lent 3,500 marks to his cousin, Edmund of Lancaster, in 1272.[7] Similarly, when Antony Bek, Bishop of Durham, was lent 4,500 marks he gave Edmund the custody of his rich Yorkshire manors of Howden and Alverton.[8] The King repaid some of his loans from Edmund by granting him wardships and their profits.

The income of a magnate was made up partly by an accumulation of many small payments. A gap in the Ministers' Acounts is of the payments made from the profits of wardships. Another gap is the expenditure for Edmund's principal household. Payments made to his household knights in both money and other benefits such as robes and subsistence cannot be tracked. Loan payments are not included. This suggests that very crucial records are missing, including those of the keeper of his wardrobe. Roger de Drayton as Treasurer had responsibility for an overview of the Earl's income and expenditure. These absences of records suggests that some might have underestimated both the income and expenditure of Edmund. Vincent's higher figure for Edmund's income seems to be much more realistic than estimates made by others.

One way of assessing the value of landed estates is to look at the feudal dues that were owed to the Crown. Following the Conquest, lands were granted on the understanding that so many knights would be provided by the tenant-in-chief for military service for forty days when the King went on campaign. Over time the cost of arming and providing a mounted knight had risen greatly and the number of knights a tenant in-chief was expected to send had been significantly reduced. The tenant might choose to pay the cost of equipping and sending a knight instead of performing the service himself or sending deputies. This system was mutually beneficial to both parties. In addition, sub-infeudation and the splitting of estates amongst the families of co-heiresses led to the requirement being reduced to fractions as low as a twentieth. This made it impractical to send less than one man. A requirement to provide payment appealed to the King who could recruit mercenary soldiers or pay his own household knights and use them for longer than the forty-day limit. Known as scutage, this payment was assessed on the number of knights whose service was owed. The tenant-in-chief made this payment to the Crown but he could then require his sub-tenants to pay their scutage in return. Much of the lands of the great magnates had, by the thirteenth century, been sub-infeudated which brought no regular income. However, scutage payments were still liable and, if they were assessed on the old requirement whilst the tenant-in chief paid on the revised reduced basis, he might make a handsome profit.

Sources of income: Knight's Fees

Discovering the exact total number of knights fees owed to the Crown by Edmund is difficult. His Inquisitions post mortem supplemented by the Feudal Aids are the best sources but the additional potential windfall income of scutage payments due from tenants of wards whose custody Edmund held should be added. Distortion of the requirement expected by the King from Edmund in 1300 was due to the lands settled on Countess Margaret in 1294. However, one restriction on this grant of the £800 worth of land was that Edmund kept the knight's fees.

From the Inquisitions post mortem[9] held in the autumn and winter of 1300 but lasting until January 1301 in Yorkshire and with other investigations still on-going in 1303, the following assessments can be made. The figures from the Feudal Aids for the period 1284–86 are also set out and, in almost all cases, are lower. In the case of Shropshire, Edmund sold his holding at Castle Holdgate, assessed at three fees, to the Chancellor, Robert Burnell.[10]

Table 12.1: Knights Fees 1300 and 1284–86.

County	1300	1284–86
Bedfordshire	2.10	0.50
Berkshire	12	0
Buckinghamshire	22.86	22.36
Cornwall	183	1
Devon	20.40	16.27
Dorset	0	0
Essex	See below	
Gloucestershire	8	4
Hampshire	2	0
Hertfordshire	2	0
Huntingdonshire	5.50	0
Leicestershire	0.50	0
Lincolnshire	3.50	0
Middlesex	9.875	0
Norfolk, Suffolk and Essex (Honour of Eye)	88	3
Northamptonshire	0.50	2.50
Oxfordshire	36.9	23.75
Rutland	4.5	0
Shropshire	0	3
Somerset	0	0
Wiltshire	9	0
Yorkshire	2.875	0.75
Total	413.51	77.13

Although this shows that, in 1300, Edmund held over 400 fees, as only two fees were recorded in Hertfordshire, where the caput of Berkhamsted was located, this total figure is likely to be an underestimate.

Sources of income: Royal Grants

Table 12.2 (Appendix) shows the known wardships enjoyed by Edmund. Dates are given when the wardship was first noted or could be assumed to have begun. The latter has sometimes been calculated by looking back to the inquisition post mortem of the person, whose heir/heirs were the wards. The age of the principal heir is given. This gives an idea of the potential length of the wardship if the heir survived until adulthood, although a younger sibling could take the place of an heir who died before coming of age and the wardship might last even longer. However, the wardships that were Edmund's by feudal right, possibly a significant number, were not recorded, so this table understates his position.

Unlike his father, Edmund was not the recipient of land grants from either King with the possible exception of Rockingham. The valuable wardship of the lands and heirs of Henry de Hastings were inherited from his father. When Richard obtained them, Henry's heir, John, was only 6.[11] This meant that the wardship should have lasted for at least fifteen years. In the event, in 1283 the King took John's homage and he received his lands.[12] By then Edmund had benefited from the income for eleven years.

When Baldwin Wake died in 1282, his heir, John, was about 14. When his mother, Hawise, died in 1284, her dower reverted to Edmund.[13] The King's grant to Edmund gave him the regular sources of income such as rents but also the windfall additions from the death of tenants. He could now have all the knights, fees, advowsons, dowers, wards, reliefs, escheats, etc. The only exception was the marriages of the heirs which the King reserved for himself.[14] Confirmation of these benefits can be seen in the details of Baldwin's inquisition post mortem; the heirs of Roger de Whitton held five and half fees in Northamptonshire and Sussex and those of Grace de Insula held two and a half fees in Lincolnshire.[15] Baldwin's entitlement to these wardship would have passed to Edmund.

Some wardships were bought and others came as part-payment of the vast loans that he made to Edward I but the details of which wardships Edmund received are not always clear. The Wake wardship cost Edmund 7,000 marks in 1282.[16] However, there are often no details in the Patent Rolls as to which children were involved but the grants were extensive. Thus, in 1298, the King ordered that Edmund should have all the marriages and wardships that became available until the debt of 9,840 and a half marks was satisfied. Edmund had given him 1,000 quarters of tin worth 7,000 marks and he was owed another 2,840 marks. Edmund was to receive marriages and advowsons as well.[17]

Scott Waugh calculated that Edmund obtained thirty-nine of the forty-eight wardships and marriages granted in one year. Of the remaining nine, five recipients compensated Edmund for his financial loss. In addition he obtained reliefs, fines from widows who wished to marry whom they liked, as well as amercements from those who had married without a royal licence. Details can be gleaned from the accounts drawn up by the executors of Edmund's will now in the National Archives.[18] These detail the sums received to the last farthing. When the executors rendered these accounts in 1304, the revenues flowing from wardships totalled 11,760 marks.[19] However, it was also disclosed that Edmund had made a further loan of 3,300 marks to the Wardrobe.[20]

Indirect references disclose other wardships. When Edmund presented Richard Malure to the living of Shelton, Bedfordshire, as guardian of the heir of Richard de Croxton, this was disputed by John Wake[21] who also claimed the guardianship. The executors' accounts do not mention an under-age heir in contrast to an inquisition *post mortem*. The table on wardships has been adjusted to reflect these latter records.

Tracing the wardships that came to Edmund as a feudal lord is not easy. From Inquisitions post mortem, it can be assumed that when tenants left under-age heirs, Edmund would have their wardship and marriages. Men came of age at 21 and women at 18. Maud de Haversham was only 33 weeks old when the inquisition was held in 1274 into the possessions of her father, Nicholas, so a wardship would have lasted nearly eighteen years, if she survived.[22] An action brought in the court of Common Pleas, in 1276, by Emma, the widow of John de Bayeux, disclosed that Edmund had the wardship of her son who held Conington, Huntingdonshire.[23] Continuing wardships were also possible. When Simon de Scaccario succeeded his father in 1284, he was 15 but he himself died in 1291 leaving a pregnant wife.[24] The resultant child would become Edmund's ward. Other potentially long wardships included those of William Pipard, who was 5 in 1283, and William de Codestede, 12 in 1281.[25] Wardships of teenagers included those of John de Mandeville, Andrew de Sackville, Geoffrey de Lucy and Guy de St Amand.[26]

When a man received a wardship from the King, he was entitled to wardships which would have fallen into the hands of his ward. Second layer wardships existed in practice as well as theory. Holding the wardship of John de Hastings, Edmund became the guardian of the lands and heir of William de Leire in Leicestershire. As such, he had the right to present to the parish church despite the opposition of a relative, John de Leyre,[27] and Edmund was able to present his attorney, John de Batesford, to Leire in 1277.[28] In 1279, Edmund claimed an advowson in Oxfordshire in his right as the guardian of the heirs of Hugh de St Philibert and a wardship case involving lands in Suffolk caused contention in the next year.[29] Another Suffolk case from 1281 saw Henry Bernard seek William Germayn's lands and heirs against Edmund.[30]

With wardships came the right to arrange the marriage of the heir or heirs or to sell that right. It is rare to find any details in governmental records as to how this worked in practice and the income the guardian received remains hidden. There was a right to take the fine normally payable to the King if a widow wished to have the freedom to re-marry. This would produce unrecorded income. However, a window on these transactions and the money raised can be found in the executors' accounts including those in the Pipe Roll of 1304 (see Table 12.3 Appendix). These show that sales of marriages and a widow's right to marry produced significant sums. Nineteen payments for marriage sales netted £2,465 ranging from 1,000 marks (Ralph Basset) to £5 when Joan le Heriz bought the right for her son's marriage. Eleven widows paid £868.6s.8d. with individual prices ranging from £200 (Idonea de Leyburn) to £2 (Juliana de Eston). In addition, Alice Heyrun and her new husband paid 80 marks for marrying without licence. The income from these sources alone totalled £3,386.13s.4d. for Edmund.

Chapter 13

Edmund, Man of Wealth:
Income from His Lands and Special Sources

In 1942, the Camden Society published Margaret Midgley's transcription and edition of the unusually comprehensive accounts for the earldom of Cornwall for 1296–97.[1] This enabled even very small items of Edmund's wealth to be ascertained.

Sources of income: farms and rents

Farms were commuted annual lump sums paid by bodies such as boroughs to avoid the complexity of a large number of smaller payments. This system had advantages to both the payers and payee. It left the body with the right to decide as to how it should raise and apportion the amount it needed to pay the lord without outside interference. The lord avoided the administrative expense of multiple collection. Another benefit was that the receiver knew in advance how much regular income to expect. A borough, for instance, could grow in wealth and the amount of the fixed farm payment might become an underestimate of its true value.

Income from farms was the norm for the urban settlements in Edmund's control. Corsham, Wiltshire, made two payments, one at Easter and one at Michaelmas of £36.13s.4d. each time.[2] In contrast, Launceston paid shillings (£5) and Helston in Kerrier, £6.13s.4d.[3] In all, Edmund received nearly £60 a year from nine Cornish boroughs: Tintagel, Camelford, Grampound, Saltash, Trematon, Lostwithiel, Helston, Launceston and Liskeard.[4] From Exeter, Edmund received £13.9s.[5] The value of Edmund's lands increased over the years. The jurors of the Hundred Rolls inquiry in Trigg complained that the value of their hundred had risen from just £8 a year before its grant to the Earl to £40 a year in 1274. Whilst the 1231 rents from Stoke Climsland were £11 a year; by 1296–97 they were nearly £15. The value of Rillaton manor rose from £3.13s. to £5.4s.4d. Tewington manor was worth £20 a year when held by Henry III but its rents alone brought in over £25 and, in total, it was worth over £40 in 1296/7.[6]

Farms could be also taken from particular sources such as a mill. At Mere, Wiltshire, the fulling mill brought in 28s.6d. in four payments in a year and 12d. from the Stanegriat mill and £10 from two grain mills.[7] Animals raised at a mill might bring profits; pigs raised at Great Berkhamsted made 3s.2d.[8] Some rents were paid by individuals, others by groups. Groups probably raised the money needed in the same way as a farm. In Princes Risborough, the free men produced £13.7s.6½d.[9]

Another source of income came from fairs and markets. There is evidence for markets at Edmund's towns including Berkhamsted, Boroughbridge, Chichester, Henley, Holme, Howden and Kirton in Lindsey, Knaresborough, Mere, Newport, Rockingham and fairs at Bradnich, Chichester, Corsham, Howden, Knaresborough, Lostwithiel, Lydford, and Rockingham.[10] The Market at Newport brought Edmund £7.10s.2d. in tolls in 1296–97. He received just over one pound from Henley, and a mere 2s.1d. from the fair at Lostwithiel and only 3s.5½d. from Lydford.[11]

Many lords had the right to view the frankpledge. Adults were required to become members of a tithing answerable for the good conduct of all the group. The lord could require proof of the membership which was later extended to a hundred or manor.[12] In the Chiltern hundreds, the assessment of twenty-three vills and four other groups of tenants brought Edmund 27s.[13]

Sources of income: Sales of Goods and Taxes

When demesne manors produced a surplus of crops, it could be sold. From the Ministers' Accounts, it is clear that the main items for sale were cereals. (Tables 13.1, 13.2 and 13.3 in the Appendix give more details). Comparisons can be made with items in the contemporary accounts of the able but corrupt curialis, Adam de Stratton, whose accounts for Sevenhampton in Wiltshire have survived.[14]

The pattern of sales from Edmund's lands shows strong regional variations. From thirteen demesne manors in Cornwall, no surplus appears to have been available. On the other hand, Howden in Yorkshire, held on a temporary basis from Bishop Bek, saw Edmund maximising short term profits. By far the biggest profit was from the sale of corn: £96.5s.11¼d. The next most profitable manor for corn was £44.3s.4½d. from Cippenham, Buckinghamshire.[15] In total these sales brought in over £375 for the year 1296–97. Off-setting this was expenditure on buying seed but this was only mentioned for six manors. The total amount was £17.13s. 6½d. The largest cost occurred at Mere. £13.4s.2½d.

Flour from mills could be sold; six quarters and half a bushel of rye brought in 49s. 7d. from the water mills at Bradnich, Devon. In the same manor, malt was sold for 12s.9½d. whilst the second rate crop was valued at 7s.6d.[16] Another Devon manor, Greatweek in Chagford, produced five bushels of oats sold for 2s.8d.[17] In Norfolk, at Bacton, bracken fetched 4 pence. £23.16s.8d. came from the sale of wood at Knaresborough, Yorkshire. Willows were sold in Cippenham for 10 shillings and faggots brought in 27s.1d. at Isleworth, Middlesex. Underwood from the Suffolk manor of Dallinghoo accounted for 3s. Other crops sold included hay, nettles and herbs as well as acorns and other nuts making the sale of pannage in Edmund's woods worthwhile. Pannage was a payment made for the right to let pigs feed on nuts in a lord's woods. 2s.½d. was paid for this right in Edmund's park at Sundon, Bedfordshire.[18] The right to pasture was sold in the park of Great Berkhamsted for 5s.6d.[19] Eight shillings profit was made from taking beasts on to stubble at Cippenham.[20]

Surplus farm produce sold off included wool, milk, cheese and butter. Old onions were sold for 13d. at Henley,[21] pears for 5 shillings at Cippenham,[22] cherries from Henley cost the purchaser 12½d.,[23] nuts made only 4d. at Watlington, Oxfordshire,[24] cider from Risborough sold for 8s.6d. compared with 5s.6d. at Stratton's Sevenhampton.[25] Honey, making surprisingly few entries in the accounts, was sold from Knaresborough forest for 12d.[26] Animals including pigs, oxen, cows, goats, sheep and lambs were sold; an old cow fetched only 4s. and an old ox, 8s.5d. at the manor of Iver, Buckinghamshire.[27] For pasturing goats in Edmund's wood at Little Weldon, Northamptonshire, the accounts record a payment of 20d.[28] The sale of fowl included cocks, hens, geese and pigeons; the latter worth 5d. in Purley, Berkshire.[29] 190 eggs were sold at Berkhamsted for 9½d. whereas 240 eggs at Sevenhampton made 12 pence.[30] From the Thames at Isleworth, fish were trapped and they were worth £4.7s.[31] Not every asset was saleable; the tail and feathers of a peacock from Corsham were worth nothing.[32]

Even small amounts, which might have expected to be ignored, were covered in the accounts. The hides of dead animals including an exhausted cow and a sheep which had died of murrain were recorded at Great Berkhamsted fetching 2s.10½d.[33] Although spices were not produced on Edmund's lands, some came to him as rent; cumin from Great Berkhamsted and Cippenham in Buckinghamshire fetched 3d. and 4½d. respectively.[34] Three and a half pounds of pepper, rendered as rent at Mere, was sold for 5s.3d.[35]

Sources of Income: Feudal Rights and Aids

For many landholders the aids that they could levy on the occasion of the knighting of a son and the marriage of a daughter were a major source of income. Neither of these options were open to the childless Edmund but he did benefit from others. Unless a tenant held land-in-chief from the King, Edmund was entitled to the wardship of the tenant's under-age heir and a sum of money or relief was paid so that a full-age tenant might take possession of his father's lands. Edmund was also able to control the marriage of the tenant's daughters or be paid for allowing them to marry when they were under-age. Lands reverted to him automatically when a tenant died without heirs. For example, the modest annual rents of 4s.6d. and 2s. came to him from two properties in Bradnich.[36]

Manorial tenants owed services as well as rents but, as with scutage, it suited both parties to commute these to money payments. At Berkhamsted, Edmund received £8.15s. for commuting services due from halimote and another 3s.4d. for relaxing the obligation for mowing.[37]

In towns, income came from trading and its organisations. The Guild of Henley paid 19s.2d. assessed at 5d. per merchant. The toll of the merchants brought in another 18s.8½d. and the market day toll, 3s.10½d.[38] From Benson, Oxfordshire, Edmund received 5s. for the booths set up at Henley.[39]

When non-money rents were paid, they could be sold off. Cumin has already been mentioned. Three pairs of gloves were sold in Cippenham for 3d. and one pair of white ones at Newport for 6d.[40]

Reliefs varied with their assessment depending on the value of the holding. Whilst Adam le Fleming paid Edmund £7.10s. for one and a half knight's fees in the Honour of Eye, Henry de Kildrayneck paid only 6s.3d. for his lands at Liskeard.[41] A payment was also due to the lord to permit a person to take over land. From this source, William de Menygsterde paid 6s.8d. and Agnes de Broke, 8s. to enter half and a whole virgate respectively in Risborough.[42] At Sevenhampton, four Stratton tenants paid from 10s. to £1.[43]

When land changed hands following a death or other cause, another payment was due and this was known as heriot. This has sometimes been confused with relief. It could have involved the surrender of a beast or sheaves of corn or their value. In some cases the sum was lumped together with relief.[44] Examples of heriot from Edmund's accounts include 3s.4d. from Millicent Syred at Langham, Rutland.[45] Often the animal given would be sold; the ox given for Alma ate Brok in Risborough, Buckinghamshire, was sold for 6s.[46]

Merchet was originally the payment made by a serf so that his daughter might marry within the manor but it became stretched to cover marriages wherever they were made and to the marriage of sons.[47] When Isabel Brachet paid Edmund 2 shillings at Aldborough, there is nothing about her groom.[48] The cost of obtaining a licence to marry ranged from 6d. to 12d. in Restormel[49] whilst 12d. was the rate for marrying outside the manor in Corsham.[50]

When a childless man died, his chattels went to his lord. Those of Warin Noble of Stoke Climsland were worth 3s.[51] Similarly if a person became an outlaw, their chattels became Edmund's property. Thus Gunnilda de Norton's chattels at the same place were assessed at 6s.3½d.[52] Another tax, chevage, was due when a villein lived outside his original manor. Richard ate Serston of Cippenham, paid Edmund 2d. for this right.[53]

All the above detail comes from a series of accounts of 1296/7 (now the National Archives SC 6/119/1 and 119/2). However, they represent only a snap shot of Edmund's financial position. These accounts do not represent a constant picture of Edmund's income and expenditure which varied year by year depending on matters outside the Earl's control including the weather. Other less comprehensive accounts for Edmund's income from his lands still exist but relate to a single manor or a bailiff's area. For instance, there is a faded account of Berkhamsted for 1286–87 in which the total profits of the manor appear to be given as £84.2s.9d, significantly higher than the £35.5s.11½d. in the 1296/7 account.[54]

A much clearer document is the account of the bailiff of Berkhamsted for 1299–1301. This includes information for Risborough and Berkhamsted. Not all headings have sums attached but for Risborough rents brought in £79.14s.7d. compared with £80.14s.4½d. in 1296/7, showing little difference.[55] The 1299–1301 profits of the manor had similarities with those of 1296/7 but they were not the same. In both accounts, the receipts began with payments for pepper and capons but they were 4s.2d. in one compared with 3s. and 2s.2d. in the other. The number of capons declined over just a few years from thirteen to eleven. Overall these profits amounted to £3.16s.8d. in 1299–1301 compared with £5.8s.3d. in 1296/7.[56] In the Berkhamsted account, the first three items were the same in both accounts but there were significantly fewer entries. Adding up the entries, an income of £14.2s.1½d. compares with £5.3s.11½d. in the other account. In 1299–1301, the land of Richard ad Crucem brought in nothing but, in 1296/7, the figure was 6s.8d.[57]

Another account survives from the years 1284–86 which was prepared by the Steward of Mere.[58] Again there are significant differences from the 1296/7 accounts. Only two mills are mentioned in the former, bringing in £1.16s.8d, compared with £11.9s.8d. in the latter. The profits of the manor included three and a half pounds of pepper sold for 2s.4d. in the former and 5s.3d. in the former.[59] There were greater differences in the expenses. They totalled £69.8s.1 ¾d. in the earlier account and £15.4s.1d. in 1296/7.[60]

Sometime during the reign of Edward I, accounts were also written up for other properties in Wiltshire, Somerset and Dorset. All receipts from Corsham amounted to £118. 7d. at the unknown date compared to £94.17s.7d. in 1296/7.[61] Rents in Wilton, Wiltshire, were recorded as £5. 7 ¼d. but were £1 less in 1296/7.[62] At Ilchester, Somerset, rents were £12 more in the undated account[63] and, at Fordington, Dorset, the total receipts were much higher; £212.9s.9d. compared to £82.14s.4d. in 1296/7,[64] Burford, Wiltshire, only worth £2 in 1296/7, brought in £20.11s. in the undated account.[65] These differences can be put down partly to the ups and downs of agricultural production. At Mere in 1296/7, 113 sheepskins were sold compared to 331 in 1284–86.[66] These variations might be related to the weather experienced.

Sources of income: Profits of Justice

Courts were a reliable source of income, although the amount varied. In Buckinghamshire Edmund obtained the profits from the honour of Wallingford at the time of the 1286 Eyre.[67] The Hallmote was the court of the manor of Berkhamsted and this met every two weeks at the castle. In total, it netted Edmund 56s. 2d. in 1296/7. However, the Portmote, the fortnightly court of the borough, was more profitable, producing 104s.11d.[68]

Reaching a concord or a legal agreement needed a payment to the feudal lord. The price varied and no reason was given for this in the accounts. At Oakham, Robert, son of Henry, paid 12d. whilst Simon de Ossleton paid 6d. and Cecilia Wyggeyn, 3d.[69] Six pence seems to have been the going rate in the part of the Honour of Eye within Lincolnshire.[70] To have an inquisition cost Matilda de Sorn and her sons 26s. 8d. at Tybista, whilst at the same place, contempt of court cost three men 2s.[71] False claims rebounded on their makers; Robert, son of Cous', paid 6d. in Langham whilst William, the chaplain of Ingthorpe, paid twice that amount.[72] A failed querela or complaint and trespass cost those in default; William Bragga and three associates were attached for 4s.6d. in the West Hundred of Cornwall. Failure to pursue a legal case also led to payments of 6d; William le mouner in Rutland.[73] The lord valued the attendance of his tenants at his court but they could be charged for non-attendance producing another income stream. Absence cost even tenants of high status; Robert de Beaufeu paid 6d. for non-attendance in Rutland.[74] A tenant could, instead, pay for a relaxation. Magnates and knights would pay rather than attend.

Henry de Lacy, Earl of Lincoln, paid 6s.8d. in relation to the court of the Honour of Wallingford. Robert FitzRoger paid the same and Milo de Beauchamp 4s. The total income from this court was £8 6s.6d.[75] The vaguely defined offence of trespass cost Robert Faukes 18d. in Aldborough, Yorkshire.[76] Unjust detention was assessed at 40d. for the Parson of Charwalton and at 2s. at Glatton.[77] Illegal recovery of goods left Thomas Page 12d. poorer in Rutland.[78] Shedding blood resulted in Ralph, the reeve of Conington and Pertenhall, paying a modest 3d.[79] Breaching the regulations of the assize of ale cost nine men at Calstock 4s.6d. each,[80] whilst for a similar offence against the assize of bread, seventeen people in Stoke Climsland paid 8s.7d.[81] The ale tasters themselves could fall foul of the law; those of Conington paying 6d. for concealment.[82]

Forest law caused great aggravation during the twelfth and thirteenth centuries. It applied to private as well as royal forests. Edmund had two forests, Dartmoor and Knaresborough, and at least thirty-five parks. With the boom in population, pressure for land manifesting itself in the illegal encroachment on the forest, an offence called purpresture. Thus Elias Thurbern was charged 12s. for this in Rutland.

A less frequent item in the accounts was the payment for letherwyt. As a serf was the absolute property of a master, anything that diminished his or her value was a loss. Whilst incontinency was a matter for the church, the lord had a right to recoup the loss of the value to his property.[83] Isabella Lomb of Oakham had to find 6d. but Noel' Whyta of Helston in Kerrier had to pay 5s.1d.[84] Not only individuals had to pay for illegal behaviour; failure to keep the bridge between Aston and Uppingham in good repair cost the vill of Uppingham 2s.[85]

As lord of all, or part, of nineteen hundreds, Edmund had a higher income from the hundred courts whose proceeds would normally have gone to the King. He was entitled to tithes in Cornwall which brought in 34s.4d. from Penwith, 29s. from Trigg, and 32s. from Lesnewth Hundreds.[86]

Exceptional sources of income: Marine Activity[87]

Edmund controlled a number of ports in Cornwall and Devon. With the honour of Trematon, came Saltash and the port noted as Sutton pool, the embryonic Plymouth. Further west along the southern coast were Looe, Polruan and Fowey. Upstream on the Fowey was Lostwithiel. Around the Fal estuary were Truro (Moresk), Penryn and Falmouth. South of the Helford, were Porthallow and ports fringing Mount's Bay. From the east there were Marazion, Porthplement, Penzance, Newlyn, Mousehole and Lamorna. On the west-facing coast, there were Porthgwarra, Portheras and Porthzennor. St Ives and Porthminster faced north. After the coastal manor of Tywarnhaile there was a long gap until the mouth of the Camel and Camelford and the three ports of Trigg: Portquin, Port Issac and Portgaverne. Finally there was the castle-port of Tintagel.[88] Lump sums or port farms were due from the 17 non-seigneurial ports.[89]

They paid an annual farm to the Earl. In the year after Edmund's death, this ranged from 2s. from Lamorna to £6 from St Ives. In all farms totalled £21.9s.8d.[90] These sums were presumably raised within the port communities by locally agreed tolls and levies.

As the Earl of Cornwall, Edmund was entitled to the profits from wrecks on Cornwall's rocky, windswept and stormy coast as well as the right to beached whales.[91] Depending on the unpredictable weather, the profit from the salvage from wrecks varied from year to year. Twenty years after Edmund's death, one ship was worth £400.[92] Part of this income from wrecks came from fines on pillagers as wreckers on the scene of a stranded ship. They could claim that the cargo was jettisoned before a ship was wrecked. To lessen the temptation to hide gains, the finder was permitted to keep half the value of the salvage. Fines for breaking these laws varied from 2s. to 4s.[93] In 1287–28, it was noted that £63.11s.4½d. was the income from wrecks since the last eyre.[94] The Ministers' Accounts of 1296–97 recorded £40.7½d. from the profits of the sea including wrecks.[95] There were also cases when local lords hindered salvage to keep the value of the goods.[96] Items from wreckage varied greatly but all had value including anchors, empty tuns, animal skins and especially masts.[97] Objects abandoned by their owners could be sold off as waif.[98] Another windfall profit was the right to the corpses of washed up whales. Whales were a useful source of oil but in some years there were no beachings.[99]

From every ship bringing in wine to a Cornish port, Edmund was entitled to presage. He could impress two tuns, one from before and one from after the mast but he had to pay the ship's master a pound each. The wine could be used in the comital household or resold at a profit. In 1287, Edmund sold 23 tuns for £46. In 1349, this profit was £3 per tun.[100]

Ports brought in revenues as imports and exports could be taxed. Wool, hides, fish and tin were the principal commodities. Little wool was exported from Cornwall compared with hides. Although northern counties exported more, Cornwall was the main exporter of hides in the south during Edmund's time. Wine was the main import followed by salt.[101] Disputes over maritime matters were heard in maritime courts and that brought more income to the Earl. Trantery, a toll on those who came to purchase fish for sale elsewhere, brought in 9s.3d. in 1300–01.[102] This toll was linked to fines for forestalling; the practice of buying fish by outsiders before it could be sold at market, often on the sea shore.[103]

Another right was fees from the ferry across the Tamar at Saltash which cost between a farthing and a halfpenny for a passenger and halfpenny for a horse.[104] There were other ferries on the Tamar and one on the Camel estuary on the Northern coast.[105] Sand taken from the beaches and estuaries, to improve heavy soils and for building, was another source of seigneurial income.[106]

Exceptional Sources of income: The Stannaries

In his thesis, Mark Page carefully assessed Edmund's profits from the Stannaries. He used the Ministers accounts, three partial accounts from 1287–88, 1297–98 and 1300–01 and the 1300–01 pipe roll.[107] In 1297–98, Edmund sold thousand weights of Devon and Cornish tin for £4,666.13s.4d; £4.13s.4d. per thousand weight. This money was then loaned to the King.[108] It is probable that this tin was acquired after its first smelting by the Earl. He had the right to pre-empt the entire output of Devon and Cornish 'black tin'. Edmund had been granted the Devonshire Stannaries 'at the usual rent' in January 1278. A second smelting was paid for by Edmund himself to produce 'white tin' which was sold at a profit of about £2. 10s. 0d. per thousand weight. During 1296–97 Edmund bought £328. 3s.7½d. for 4375½ feet of black tin; 1s.6d. per foot. This produced over 153 thousandweights of smelted tin at the rate of 28½ feet of ore to the thousand weight. The total cost, taking into account the payments for transport and smelting, was about £2.3s.3½d. per thousand weight. These expenses were just under half the price at which the Earl would sell the finished product. The following year, 1297–78, Edmund bought 370 feet of black tin for £27.15s. which produced nearly 13,000 weights of smelted tin, again at a cost of just over £2 per thousand weight.[109] Page believed that the quality of Edmund's smelted tin deteriorated slightly between 1288 and 1296, because of a search for greater profits.[110]

The profits collected as a result of the sale of his smelted tin, which was sold consistently for £4.13s.4d. per thousand weight, were considerable. Edmund, or his officials, were astute enough not to attempt to exercise his right of pre-emption. He avoided the perils of speculation and was satisfied with the lesser, although substantial, sums accruing from the coinage duties. These brought together created a single duty of £2 per thousand weight levied after the second smelting when the blocks of white tin were taken to the nearest coinage town for the next stamping. Although at other times five more towns were used, under Edmund it was stamped at Lostwithiel. Page believed that Edmund's profits from tin ranged from about £1,000 to £2,000 a year, rising to as much as £2,500 or £3,000 when he exercised his right of pre-emption. Thus, from this one resource he had an income for which most earls of his time would have been content. But this was not all. There were lesser dues which the Earl was entitled to collect. Some were gathered by the local bailiffs and accounted for with the revenues of the individual manors whilst others were collected by the official in charge of the stannaries, usually the Steward of Cornwall.

They were two local dues known as toll-tin and fine of tin. According to Hatcher, every Cornish landowner had the right to exact as a toll a certain proportion of the tin dug up within the bounds of his land. The ratio of the toll levied by Edmund cannot be determined but may have been as little as one fifteenth or as much as one third. In the fourteenth and fifteenth centuries toll-tin was obtained from all but two of the duchy's seventeen assessionable manors but, in the thirteenth century, only five manors referred to the duty in the *exitus manerie* of their accounts.[111] These five manors lay close to stannary districts: Tywarnhaile straddled the tin-mining region of that name; Helston-in-Kerrier lay to the south of Kerrier Stannary; Tewington occupied the southern tip of Blackmore Stannary; Rillaton and Stoke Climsland lay close to the fourteenth century stannary of Foweymore. Toll tin was a fluctuating levy but the annual fine of tin was fixed at £1 from the manor of Tewington. Hatcher suggested that the payment may have granted exemption from toll-tin but it was still paid.[112] The fine of tin amounting to £5.8s. a year collected by the Keeper of the Stannaries and accounted for in the separate section of the ministers' accounts devoted to tin, was under the heading 'Stagnaria'. This was made up of another fixed annual due, £3.5s.4d. from the stannary of Blackmore and £2.2s.8d. from the hundred of Pyder, according to the pipe roll of 1300–01. A fixed rent, a dublet, was levied on the tinners of the hundred of Kerrier, at an annual 11s.8d.[113]

Another revenue source associated with the stannaries came from their courts. Any worker in tin was subject to the jurisdiction of the stannary courts rather than the shire court or hundred courts. Amercements were usually small. There was also tribulage, a type of poll tax imposed on all 'who worked with a shovel' within the limits of the stannaries of Penwith and Kerrier and Blackmore. This tax was not imposed on other workers such as the smelters, charcoal-burners, carters, carpenters, pumpmen and firemen. It was charged at ½d. per head which allows an approximate estimate to be made of the numbers of this worker. On Blackmore, where between 6s. and 7s. was collected, the number of tinners ranged from 144 to 168, whilst in Penwith and Kerrier, where between 6s.8d. and 13s.10d. was collected, they numbered between 160 and 322.

Overall the profits from the stannaries could be huge. In 1297–98, £5,411.19s.2½d. was received. Subtracting £35.8s.4d. of expenses, Edmund's net profit was £5,376.10s.7d. This compared with manorial profits from Cornwall in this year of just under £478.

Exceptional Sources of Income: The Jewish Community

In the early 1240s, there were between 3,000 and 5,000 Jews in England. But they were declining in numbers and wealth due to the increased burdens placed on them by kings in need of money.[114] Technically the Jews belonged to the King but Henry granted them to Richard of Cornwall. Good relations with the Jewish community were established by Richard from his early years. In 1231, he protected the Jews of Berkhamsted and, four years later, he obtained a royal grant to permit them to settle there without royal permission. A move to Wallingford was proposed in 1242 with an archa, a repository for deeds relating to loans from, and debts to, the Jews, being established in the castle. When, in 1235, mass hysteria broke out after the alleged murder of little St Hugh at Lincoln resulting in the execution of eighteen Jews, Richard intervened to save another twenty-one. To show gratitude, they gave him £2,000 at the time of his crusade. Particular protection was given to Abraham of Berkhamsted. After saving him from the forfeiture of his goods in 1249, Richard secured his release from the Tower of London after he had been accused of the murder of his wife. Whilst imprisoned, it was said that Abraham offered to betray all the Jews of England and they offered 1,000 marks to keep him in prison but Richard allowed Abraham to make his peace with the King for 700 marks. Abraham became Richard's Jew but was noted as the King's Jew in 1272 after Richard's death. Although Richard had the ownership of the Jews for many years, he never borrowed from them.

Richard's benign attitude to Jewry was not shared by his own son, Henry of Almain, or the Lord Edward. They both promoted the restrictive Statute of Jewry in 1269 and, by then, Richard had lost the power to protect the community.[115]

So what was Edmund's attitude to the Jews? Did he follow his father or share his half-brother's hostility? He only owned the Jews for a few years and he never borrowed from them. But then he did not need to, so this decision might have been pragmatic and not driven by prejudice. By the late 1280s, Edward I had received around £22,000 from the Jews, almost enough to meet one year's peacetime expenditure.[116] Edmund was given Abraham for two and a half years[117] and probably kept the Jewish community for the same period. There is little evidence of dealings with the Jews. Whilst Regent, Edmund's cousin, Edmund of Lancaster, wrote to him to support Aaron, son of his own Jew, Vives, over accusations made against him and three years earlier, the King himself sought to protect Aaron.[118] Overall, with the reducing wealth of the Jewish community and the short period of his control of it, Edmund's financial benefits from this source of income would have been slight.

Chapter 14

Edmund's Expenditure, his Loans, and Overall Accounts

Expenditure, including wages, can be traced from Midgley's edition of the 1296–97 accounts for the earldom.[1] We can see that a carpenter was paid 3d. a day,[2] a beadle 23s.4d. a year and a parker and warrener, 6s.8d. However, it is difficult to believe that these sums were their only income.[3] In Sundon, the smith was paid 8s. for a year. For a period of only twelve nights, four watchmen looking after does were given a total of 4s; a penny a night.[4] By contrast, the chaplain of Oakham was rewarded with 50s. a year[5] as were the chaplains at Berkhamsted and Tintagel but the chaplain at Restormel received 3s.4d. more as did the chaplain at Trematon.[6] A chaplain at Mere castle received 50s. a year but this was to say prayers for the soul of Countess Sanchia.[7] Whilst the constable of Berkhamsted was paid 3d. a day, no more than the carpenter, he no doubt had other substantial benefits such as board and lodgings and possibly clothes which cut down his living costs. Clothes were provided to his colleague at Tintagel who was paid the same amount but who received a robe worth 13s.4d annually. Isabella of Aumale paid her constable at Carisbrooke £10 p.a. depending on whether or not she was present. The King paid his constables from £50 at the Tower of London to £5 at Cambridge.[8] A watchman at Berkhamsted castle received a robe worth 5s. as well as 45s. 6d. wages. The keeper of the park at Berkhamsted was paid 2d. daily but, unlike the keeper at Restormel, he was not entitled to a robe.[9] At Wallingford, the constable and two watchmen were paid £13.6s.8d. in total.[10] The Steward of Berkhamsted received £15.6s.8d. and had two fur lined robes and other allowances.[11]

An apparent gap in the Ministers' Accounts is the expenditure for Edmund's principal household. Payments made to his household knights in money and other benefits such as robes and subsistence cannot be traced. Loan payments are not included. This suggests that very crucial records are missing, including those of the keeper of his wardrobe.

Roger de Drayton was styled as Treasurer and he had responsibility for an overview of the Earl's income and expenditure. The absence of these records is another reason for believing that some have underestimated the income and expenditure of Edmund. Nicholas Vincent's higher figure for Edmund's income seems to be much more realistic than estimates made by others.

Types of Expenditure: The Ministers' Accounts

The overall balance of Edmund's income and expenditure cannot be completely reconstructed. The Ministers' Accounts do not give a full picture but they show over a wide range of holdings, the balance between income and expenditure for one year.

Table 14.1: 1296–97 Ministers' Accounts.

Place	Receipts	Expenditure	Profit
Honour of Berkhamsted			
Risborough	£92. 4s. 3d.	£10. 4s. 4d.	£81. 19s. 11d.
Sundon	£26.18s. 7¹/4d.	£13. 19s. 8 ³/4d.	£12. 18s. 10½d.
Berkhamsted	£160.17s. 4d.	£74. 15s. 2d.	£86. 2s. 2d.
Iver	£12. 0s. 10d.	£8. 15s. 11½d.	£3. 4s. 10½d.
Cippenham	£91. 7s. 10d.	£27. 6s. 8d.	£64. 1s. 2d.
Isleworth	£153. 16s. 1d.	£22. 12s. 11½d.	£131. 3s. 1½d.
Newport	£53. 8s. 0½d.	£6. 12s. 2¹/4d.	£46. 15s. 10¹/4d.
Total	£590. 12s.11³/4d.	£164. 7s. 0d.	£426. 5s. 11³/4d.
Honour of Mere			
Mere	£114. 2s. 1³/4d.	£67. 9s. 0½d.	£46.13s. 1¹/4d.
Corsham	£94.17s. 7d.	£8.18s. 9d.	£85.18s.10d.
Wilton	£12.13s. 4³/4d.	£5. 7s. 8³/4d.	£7. 5s. 8d.
Fordington	£82.14s. 4d.	£0. 9s. 1½d.	£82. 5s. 2½d.
Barford	£2. 0s. 0d.	£0. 0s. 0d.	£2. 0s. 0d.
Bindon	£0.13s. 4d.	£0. 0s. 0d.	£0.13s. 4d.
Total	£307. 0s. 9½d.	£82. 4s. 7³/4d.	£224.16s. 1³/4d.
Honour of Wallingford			
Watlington	£66. 1s. 7d.	£20.19s. 5³/4d.	£45. 2s. 1¹/4d.
Hambleden	£60. 3s. 6d.	£0. 0s. 0d.	£60. 3s. 6d.
Henley on Thames	£18.10s. 10½d.	£0.16s. 4³/4d.	£17.14s. 5³/4d.

Place	Receipts	Expenditure	Profit
Benson	£49.19s. 6d.	£1. 3s. 0d.	£48.16s. 6d.
Whitchurch	£30. 0s. 0d.	£0. 0s. 0d.	£30. 0s. 0d.
Chichester	£35. 6s. 9½d.	£6.10s. 8d.	£28.16s. 1½d.
Chiltern Hundreds	£32.16s. 2½d.	£0. 4s. 2d.	£32.12s. 0½d.
Purley	£6. 1s. 2¾d.	£0. 0s. 0d.	£6. 1s. 2¾d.
Wallingford	£172.19s. 1½d.	£3. 2s. 0d.	£169.17s. 1½d.
Total	£471.18s. 9¾d.	£32.15s. 8¼d.	£439. 3s. 1¼d.
Honour of St Valery			
Beckley	£40. 9s.11¾d.	£8.10s. 8¾d.	£31.19s.10d.
Harwell	£31. 5s. 5d.	£0. 0s. 0d.	£31. 5s. 5d.
Oseney	£72. 5s. 9½d.	£8. 5s.11d.	£63.19s.10½d.
Lechlade	£134. 0s. 0d.	£0. 0s. 0d.	£134. 0s. 0d.
Total	£278. 1s. 9¼d.	£16. 16s. 7¾d.	£261. 5s. 1½d.
Honour of Eye			
Bacton I	£9. 7s. 4½d.	£0. 5s. 9½d.	£9. 1s. 7d.
Bacton II	£3.11s. 1½d.	£0. 1s. 7d.	£3. 9s. 6½d.
Honing	£2. 8s. 0¼d.	£0. 1s. 9½d.	£2. 6s. 2¾d.
Alderton I	£1.15s. 3d.	£0. 0s. 8d.	£1.14s. 7d.
Alderton II	£0.17s. 7d.	£0. 0s. 4d.	£0.17s. 3d.
Dalinghoo I	£2.16s. 7¾d.	£0. 1s. 6d.	£2.15s. 1¾d.
Dalinghoo II	£1.12s. 0¾d.	£0. 0s. 6d.	£1.11s. 6¾d.
Eye	£1. 1s. 5½d.	£0.12s. 8d.	£0. 8s. 9½d.
Total	£23. 9s. 6¼d.	£1. 4s.10d.	£22. 4s. 8¼d.
Honour of Oakham			
Oakham	£168. 3s. 4d.	£21. 4s. 6½d.	£146.18s. 9½d.
Langham	£126. 0s. 4½d.	£0.18s. 10d.	£125. 1s. 6½d.
County of Rutland	£34. 8s.10d.	£2. 7s. 2d.	£32. 1s. 8d.
Rockingham	£8. 2s. 4½d.	£0. 2s. 4d.	£8. 0s. 0½d.
Conington and Pertenhall	£3.17s. 8d.	£0. 0s. 0d.	£3. 17s. 8d.
Berkhamsted in Northants	£6. 1s. 8d.	£0.13s. 4d.	£5. 8s. 4d.
Little Weldon	£20.12s.11d.	£2.10s. 0d.	£18. 2s. 11d.
Eye in Lincolnshire	£6. 8s. 2¼d.	£0.13s. 4d.	£5.14s.10¼d.
Amercements	£0. 6s. 8d.	£0. 0s. 0d.	£0. 6s. 8d.
Glatton	£99.15s.11½d.	£4. 7s. 3¾d.	£95. 8s. 7¾ d.
Total	£473. 17s.11¾d.	£32.16s.10¼d.	£441. 1s. 1½d.

Place	Receipts	Expenditure	Profit
Honour of Knaresborough			
Knaresborough	£379. 1s. 4³/4d.	£25. 8s.10d.	£353.12s. 6¹/4d.
Aldborough	£135. 6s. 2½d.	£5.16s. 1d.	£129.10s. 1½d.
Rockcliff	£22.15s.11d.	£9. 5s. 1½d.	£13. 5s. 1½d.
Howden	£427.17s. 7¹/4d.	£12. 2s.10³/4d.	£415.14s. 8½d.
Total	£965. 1s. 1½d.	£52.12s.11¹/4d.	£912. 2s. 5³/4d.
Devon including the honour of Bradnich			
Exeter	£13. 9s. 0d.	£0. 0s. 0d.	£13. 9s. 0d.
Bradnich	£55.15s. 2½d.	£11. 3s 0¹/4d.	£44.12s. 2¹/4d.
Kenton	£76.14s. 6³/4d.	£1. 7s. 6d.	£75. 7s. 0³/4d.
Greatweek in Chagford	£17. 4s. 3½d.	£0. 8s. 2d.	£16.16s.1½d.
Lidford	£6. 6s. 5³/4d.	£0. 0s. 0d.	£6. 6s. 5³/4d.
Dartmoor	£54. 0s. 6d.	£9.18s. 6d.	£44. 2s. 0d.
Total	£223.10s. 0½d.	£22.17s. 2¹/4d.	£200.12s.10¹/4d.
Cornwall			
Tintagel	£47.10s.11½d.	£14.12s. 0d.	£32.18s.11½d.
Stoke Climsland	£30. 9s. 3½d.	£3. 7s. 3¹/4d.	£27. 2s. 0¹/4d.
Helston	£56.17s. 6d.	£0. 7s. 8d.	£56. 9s.10d.
Moresek	£51. 3s. 9½d.	£0.11s. 3d.	£50.12s. 6½d.
Rillaton	£5.10s. 4½d.	£0. 6s. 0d.	£5. 4s. 4½d.
Helston in Trigg	£65.14s. 6½d.	£4. 2s. 7½d.	£61.11s.11d.
Liskeard	£27. 8s. 5½d.	£7. 7s. 5d.	£20. 1s. 0½d.
Tybista	£52.16s. 5d.	£1.10s.10d.	£51. 5s. 7d.
Penknight	£0. 3s.11d.	£0. 0s. 0d.	£0. 3s.11d.
Talskiddy	£3. 0s. 0d.	£0. 0s. 0d.	£3. 0s. 0d.
Tywarnhaile	£28. 8s. 0½d.	£0. 4s. 0d.	£28. 4s. 0½d.
Trematon	£47.14s. 4d.	£9.17s. 1d.	£37.17s. 3d.
Restormel	£12. 9s. 0d.	£11.10s. 0³/4d.	£0.18s.11¹/4d.
Lostwithiel	£27.13s. 1d.	£3. 9s. 2d	£24. 3s. 11d.
Calstock	£28. 0s. 6½d.	£1.15s. 6½d.	£26. 5s. 0d.
Tewington	£41.11s. 0³/4d.	£1. 9s. 4½d.	£40. 1s. 8¹/4d.
Penlyne	£8. 9s. 1½d.	£5. 7s. 7d.	£3. 1s. 6½d.
Trefize	£6.16s. 8d.	£0. 1s. 1½d.	£6.15s. 6½d.
Stratton	£27.10s. 1³/4d.	£0. 0s. 0d.	£27.10s. 1³/4d.
Caerhays	£27. 0s. 2d.	£0. 0s. 0d.	£27. 0s. 2d.
Fee farm	£44. 7s. 1½d.	£0. 0s. 0d.	£44. 7s. 1½d.

Place	Receipts	Expenditure	Profit
Yearly farm	£50.11s. 5d.	£0. 0s. 0d.	£50.11s. 5d.
Foreign perquisites	£288.14s. 0½d.	£0. 0s. 0d.	£288.14s. 0½d.
Stannaries	£1,983. 0s. 2³/4d.	£1,218.17s. 8d.	£764. 2s. 6³/4d.
Total	£2,963. 0s. 2³/4d.	£1,284.16s. 8d.	£1,677. 3s. 6³/4d.

These accounts show a total income of £6,297, expenditure of £1,691 and a resultant profit of £4,606.[12]

Types of Expenditure: Land Acquisition

Although Edmund's father was enormously wealthy, he only spent around £2,000 acquiring new lands. He did not need to buy more as the generous gifts of his brother had set him up for life. The landed inheritance of Edmund, dealt with elsewhere, shows that he, too, spent relatively little on land deals. Looking at Edmund's father, Nicholas Vincent wrote: 'However, with the exception of his dealings with the Cornish boroughs and the mint, Richard seems to have been neither an innovative nor a particularly grasping man of business. In 40 years he spent only £2,000 or so on the purchase of land, at a time when his annual income from estates granted to him by the crown exceeded £5,000.'[13]

Types of Expenditure: Loans to Royalty and Private Individuals

When looking at Edmund's father's career, Nicholas Vincent wrote: 'However, with the exception of his dealings with the Cornish boroughs and the mint, Richard seems to have been neither an innovative nor a particularly grasping man of business. An analysis of his property transactions suggests that in 40 years he spent only £2,000 or so on the purchase of land, at a time when his annual income from estates granted to him by the crown exceeded £5,000'.[14] Edmund's father did not need to buy more land as the generous gifts of his brother had set him up for life. The lands of Edmund, dealt with elsewhere, shows that he, too, spent relatively little on land deals.

Edmund began his holding of the earldom with royal debts due to him as the heir of his father. In 1271 a loan had been made to the King to cover a shortfall in a Jewish tallage and the King gave Edmund the custody of the Jews until the debt was paid off.[15] Edmund was a regular lender. The table below sets out the known loans.

Table 14.2: Loans to the King.

Year	Amount	Decimal £.	Repaid?	Reference	value
1273	2,000 marks	1333.33	1273 and 1274	TNA:PRO E 36/274 f248r,271r	
1274	2,000 marks	1333.33	yes	CPR 1272–81, 63 and 73	
1275	2,000 marks	1333.33	yes in a year	CPR 1272–81, 74	
1279	3,000 marks	2000.00	yes	CPR 1272–81, 321–2	
1281	£2,000	2000.00	£1,893.14s, 2.1/4d. owed 1297	CPR 1292–1301, 301	
1282	8,000 marks	5333.33	Wake wardship, 7,000m	CPR 1281–92, 35 & 52	
			worth 7,000m	CPR 1281–92, 163	
				TNA:PRO E 159/57 m. 9	
1283	£2,000	2000.00		CPR 1281–92, 83	
1289	2,000 marks	1333.33		CPR 1281–92, 313	
1297	2,000 marks	1333.33		CPR 1292–1301, 234	
1298	10,000 q tin	4666.67	wardships and marriages	CPR 1292–1301, 348, 440	7,000m
1299	2,000 marks	1333.33	Archbishopric/ bishoprics	CPR 1292–1301, 431	
Total		24,000.00			

There is a reference to a repayment to Edmund of 4,000 marks in July 1293.[16] But, despite this loan, there exists an undated certificate from the Lieutenant of the Exchequer stating that Edmund owed over £1,000.[17]

In addition to loans to the King, Edmund lent to at least eighty private individuals. Table 14.3A (appendix) reveals[18] that the known loans of Edmund to private individuals totalled £14,522, an astonishing amount. There were ninety-two loans made to eighty-eight individuals.[19] These ranged from 4,500 marks to Antony Bek, Bishop of Durham, 3,500 marks to Edmund of Lancaster, down to a mere 14 marks to Ralph de Saham. Other loans might be assumed; why did William de Beauchamp, Earl of Warwick, grant Edmund the lease of his profitable manor of Brailes, Warwickshire, for three years in 1272?[20] Some loans were recorded in Chancery rolls but others come to light from court rolls; for instance, those to Roger L'Estrange in 1279[21] and Nicholas de Audley in 1285.[22]

Not one loan was made to a woman. A study of the borrowers's status shows Edmund lent to three earls, five bishops, eleven barons and one man who might have been a baron, two abbots, one master of a hospital, two other masters, five merchants, one parson and three clerks, one of whom would later be a bishop. Of the knightly class, thirty-one were known to be knights whilst five came from knightly families. Two of the knights were also justices and four were on the brink of becoming barons with their immediate descendants being summoned to Parliament. No information on the remaining seventeen has yet been found. Eleven borrowers were also Edmund's tenants but there is no clear pattern as to which area he favoured. A single tenant was from Yorkshire, Suffolk, Hertfordshire, Oxfordshire, Berkshire, Buckinghamshire, Rutland and Norfolk whilst three were from Wiltshire. Knights dominated the tenant borrowers: one was a clerk, one a baron, one a master.

In all Edmund lent £24,000 to the King and £14,522 to private individuals. Edmund lent them £34,522 in twenty-eight years; a rate of well over £1,000 p.a.

Conclusions

Holmes contrasted the income sources of Edmund and Henry de Lacy, Earl of Lincoln.[23] He concluded that Edmund's income came largely from rents and judicial profits. There was substantial corn production but agricultural activity 'seems to be entirely absent from some bailiwicks, such as those of the honour of St Valery in Oxfordshire and Berkshire, and Cornwall itself, where apart from the Stannaries, the main profit came from small rents and courts'. The accounts of 1296/7 were used to make these judgements and those of 1304/5 to assess the activity of Earl Henry. 'Whilst a great deal of his (Henry) annual wealth came from rents and various kinds of seigneurial dues, there is also evidence of very widespread agricultural enterprise by the lord.' Henry possessed large herds of cattle in Lancashire, sheep runs in the Yorkshire honour of Pontefract and grew corn in the honour of Bolingbroke in Lincolnshire. Contrasting this activity with that of Edmund indicates perhaps a lack of acumen by Edmund, or his officials, or it might result from established local agricultural patterns. Whatever the case, Holmes underestimated or ignored other sources of money available to Edmund which he obtained with a lot less effort and risk.

Overall Edmund used his money well. He had no need to borrow himself and plenty of disposable income to lend to others which must have brought him extra influence and prestige. He does not appear to have been greedy and a significant area of expenditure would have been his funding of the completion of Hailes Abbey as well as the building of Rewley Abbey and the College at Ashridge and his widespread religious patronage. Edmund valued his own comforts and spent money on Restormel castle,[24] the nearby palace and accommodation for himself at Ashridge. A fragmentary roll includes reference to the building of a great chamber for him.[25] He spent money on other castles such as Mere, Wallingford, Oakham, Launceston and Tintagel.[26] However, this evidence based on just one year's accounts, must be a significant underestimate. His palace at Lostwithiel would have been expensive project. A few remaining objects and records are evidence that he spent money on jewellery, books and clothes. B.M.S. Campbell, having studied seigneurial estates, concluded that, with other comital and episcopal magnates, Edmund's 'far-flung manors and broad acres' emerged as the 'most exclusively geared towards production for sale'.[27] When Edmund died, the King, as his heir, acquired the wealth of the earldom in at least as healthy a state as when Edmund gained it in 1272. Edmund's stewardship of his birthright had been very effective.

Chapter 15

Edmund, the Landlord and His Tenants

The Landed Inheritance of Edmund of Cornwall

The lands which Edmund inherited, or was granted, lay in five main groups spread over twenty-seven counties. In the North, Edmund's lands were centred on the Yorkshire honour of Knaresborough and on Kirton in Lincolnshire. Oakham was the centre of a Midland estate whilst the honour of Eye in East Anglia was the third group of manors. In the Thames Valley, the honours of Wallingford and Berkhamsted were the focii alongside that of St Valery. Finally there were the lands of the earldom of Cornwall. The earldom included manors in Devon and the honours of Trematon and Bradnich, the former which had been purchased by Richard. A pattern of outliers was found elsewhere. In one of these, Richard had acquired Castle Holdgate, Shropshire, in 1256.[1] There are records of over 800 places in England which Edmund held at one time or another.

Table 15.1: The Holdings of Edmund of Cornwall

County	Number
Bedfordshire	5
Berkshire	21
Buckinghamshire	81
Cornwall	116
Devon	94
Dorset	10
Essex	11
Gloucestershire	14
Hampshire	5
Hertfordshire	15
Huntingdonshire	3
Leicestershire	4
Lincolnshire	59

County	Number
Middlesex and London	13
Norfolk	20
Northamptonshire	33
Nottinghamshire	2
Oxfordshire	117
Rutland	29
Shropshire	1
Somerset	2
Suffolk	102
Surrey	3
Sussex	2
Wiltshire	28
Worcestershire	1
Yorkshire	32
Total	823

Details of these holdings can be found in the Appendices (Tables 15.2A, 15.2B and 15.2C set out the places by name, county and honour, where known). Almost all had been acquired by Edmund's father, although confusion arises because most of the records of Richard's *Inquisitions post mortem* no longer exist. The foundation of the inheritance was almost entirely due to the beneficence of Henry III to Richard. The first grant was the earldom of Cornwall in 1225 when Richard was 16 and, two years later, he was granted the comital title.[2] In the same year (1227) when his mother, Isabella of Angoulême, died, her dower lands were given to Richard. These included the honour of Berkhamsted which was primarily in Hertfordshire as well as the honours of St Valery, largely in Oxfordshire, and Eye centred on Suffolk. St Valery was a memory of the lands once held by Count Robert de Dreux and Eye had been in the honour of Boulogne, belonging to its count. These dower lands were initially held at the King's pleasure but, in 1231, they were granted to Richard in perpetuity. In the same year, the honour of Wallingford including the manor of Watlington, Oxfordshire, was added.[3] Also, in 1231, Richard's tenure of the earldom was made permanent and he was given the immensely profitable Cornish Stannaries with their income from tin mining. Once owned by Hubert de Burgh, Haughley in Suffolk came to Richard on Hubert's death in 1243.[4] Noel Denholm-Young suggested that the honour of Knaresborough in 1235 came as a birthday present.[5] Kirton in Lindsey, Lincolnshire, was granted to him in the same year.[6] A profitable augmentation of holdings in the south west was the grant of Lydford and the forest of Dartmoor made in 1239.[7]

Additional lands had come to Richard as a result of his first marriage to Isabel, a Marshal co-heiress. They are supposed to have included Hambleden, Buckinghamshire, and Henley, Oxfordshire,[8] although Henley was part of the old royal manor of Bensington (Benson) which came to Richard by royal grant in 1244 with four and a half of the Chiltern hundreds.[9]

The next increment of Richard's lands, dates from his marriage with Sanchia of Provence. For her marriage portion, set at 500 librates, Richard obtained significant manors over a period from 1242 until 1256. Mere and Corsham, Wiltshire, and Fordington, Dorset, and Newport, Essex came in 1242.[10] A year later the manors of Glatton, Huntingdonshire, and Risborough, later Prince's Risborough, in Buckinghamshire were added. Less than a month after the Benson grant, Richard's Devon holdings were increased with the honour of Bradnich, worth twenty fees.[11] In 1252, a base in central England was provided with the acquisition of Oakham, Rutland, once part of Queen Isabella's dower. This included rights in Leicestershire. To this gift was added Lechlade, Gloucestershire.[12] Completing Sanchia's marriage portion were the Wiltshire manor of Barford St Martin and Longborough in Gloucestershire in 1256.[13]

Alongside these grants Richard acquired outliers of his honours in other counties. Thus the valuable Isleworth in Middlesex came to Richard with Berkhamsted as did Queenhithe on the north bank of the Thames within the City of London. Queenhithe had also been part of Queen Isabella's dower. In Sussex, Old Shoreham and Chichester became part of Richard's holdings; the former was attached to the honour of Berkhamsted whilst the latter was from the dower of Isabella of Angoulême.[14] Other towns in which Richard had interests included Exeter, Ilchester and Wilton, all from the dower.[15]

Richard had also been keen to increase the extent and amount of his lands where this seemed a good strategic move. In 1270, he purchased, for £300, the lands of Roger de Vautort (Valletort) which straddled the boundaries of Devon and Cornwall and included the castle of Trematon and the manor of Calstock; the manors were assessed at sixty and one half knight's fees.[16] In the same year he acquired Restormel castle from the heiress, Isolda de Cardinan.[17]

Whilst there is evidence that Rockingham, Northamptonshire, but not its castle, was in Richard's keeping as part of Isabella's dower,[18] there is a record that Henry III gave it to Edmund in 1271.

Exact details of the manors and lands which Edmund held are not completely established. It can be assumed that he inherited the lands listed in his father's *Inquisitions post mortem*. Also there are details published in Feudal Aids for the period 1284–85,[19] the Ministers' Accounts of 1296–97 and Edmund's own *Inquisitions post mortem*. However, the last two generally exclude the lands worth £800 given to Countess Margaret as part of the 'divorce' settlement. The entry concerning the honour of Wallingford included in the calendar of Edmund's inquisition *post mortem* is incomplete but the gaps can be filled by using a Bodleian manuscript, later printed in *The Boarstall Cartulary*.[20] Information from the inquisitions of Edmund's tenants, discloses further information which narrows but does not close the gap. The final relevant document is Edmund's own cartulary housed in The National Archives.[21]

In Appendix 1 and Table 15.3 (appendices), the lands and tenants of Edmund are described in more detail relating them to the counties and honours in which they lay. More information is given on Edmund's tenants, their background and the amount they owed to him in feudal duties or rents. The extent of his wider holdings such as the control of forests and hundreds within counties are explained in this chapter. Alongside his forests is information on the parks that Edmund owned giving a flavour of his widespread power and influence over local communities. His position as a multiple owner of castles is also examined.

Whilst not forgetting their snapshot nature, the 1296–97 Ministers' Accounts show that the most valuable manors owned by Edmund by net annual value were:

Howden	£416
Knaresborough	£354
Wallingford	£170
Oakham	£147
Lechlade	£134

Isleworth	£131
Aldborough	£130
Langham	£125

These figures are rounded to the nearest pound. Howden belonged to the Bishop of Durham and was held in return for a loan made by Edmund. The expenses incurred show where the most comital activity took place. The most money was spent or used in the following places:

Berkhamsted	£75
Mere	£67
Cippenham	£27
Knaresborough	£25
Isleworth	£23
Oakham	£21
Watlington	£21
Tintagel	£15
Sundon	£14
Restormel	£12
Howden	£12
Bradnich	£11
Risborough	£10
Trematon	£10

Of these properties, seven centred on Edmund's castles and most of the others contained comital residences.

Parks and Forests

An important benefit came from forests and parks, and the opportunity for creating new ones. Thus, Edmund had the rights to the vast forest of Dartmoor in Cornwall and Devon as well as that at Knaresborough. He also had at least thirty-eight parks:

1. Ashridge, Buckinghamshire, CChR 1257–1300, 324 and 331.
2. Beckley, Oxfordshire, Ministers' Accounts, 137.
3. Berkhamsted, Hertfordshire, CIPM, iii, 604, p 463.
4. Bilton, Yorkshire, Ministers' Accounts, 188.

5. Bradnich, Devon, CIPM, iii, 604 p. 456; Ministers' Accounts', 213; CPR 1266–72, 765–6
6. Cippenham, Buckinghamshire, CIPM, iii, 604, p. 464.
7. Corsham, Wiltshire, CIPM, iii, 604, p. 459; Ministers' Accounts, 69.
8. La Haye, Yorkshire, CIPM, iii, 604, p. 472.
9. Helson in Kerrier, Cornwall, Ministers' Accounts, 226.
10. Helston in Trigg, Cornwall, CIPM, iii, 604, p. 457.
11. Henley, Oxfordshire, CIPM, iii, 604, p. 465.
12. Heywro, Harewood), Yorkshire, CPR 1281–92, 258.
13. Hurtley, Cippenham, Bucks, Ministers' Accounts, 31.
14. Isleworth, Middlesex, Ministers' Accounts, 40.
15. Knaresborough, Yorkshire, I two parks, CIPM, iii, 604, p. 472; Bilton, Ministers' Accounts, 188.
16. Knaresborough, Yorkshire, II two parks, CIPM, iii, 604, p. 472.
17. Lanteglos, Cornwall, more than one entry, CPR 1266–72, 765–6.
18. Launceston, Cornwall, CIPM, iii, 604, p. 457.
19. Lifton, Devon, CPR 1266–72, 765–6.
20. Liskeard, Cornwall, I, Old Park, CIPM, iii, 604, p. 457; Ministers' Accounts, 233.
21. Liskeard, Cornwall, II, New Park, CIPM, iii, 604, p. 457; Ministers' Accounts, 233.
22. Mere, Wiltshire, I, two parks, CIPM, iii, 604, p. 459.1; at Conewich, Ministers' Accounts, 56.
23. Mere, Wiltshire, II, two parks, CIPM, iii, 604, p. 459; Ministers' Accounts, 56.
24. Oakham, Rutland, great park Ministers' Accounts, 160; CIPM, iii, 604, p. 461.
25. Oakham, Rutland, little park Ministers' Accounts, 160. CIPM, iii, 604, p. 461.
26. Penlynt, Cornwall, CIPM, iii, 604, p. 457.
27. Restormel, Cornwall, more than one entry CIPM, iii, 604, p. 457.
28. Risborough, Bucks, CIPM, iii, 604, p. 463.
29. Rishanger, Suffolk, Ministers' Accounts, 158.
30. Sedgebrook, Lincolnshire, CIPM, iii, 604, p. 469.
31. Sundon, Bedfordshire, Ministers' Accounts, 6.
32. Stoke Climsland, Cornwall (presumably the same as Clymewold), Ministers' Accounts, 224.
33. Trematon, Cornwall, CIPM, iii, 604, p. 457; CPR 1266–72, 765–6.
34. Watlington, Oxfordshire, Minister's Accounts, 85.

As if Edmund did not have enough forests and parks to hunt in or take venison from, wardships gave him even more. Baldwin Wake had 140 deer in his park at Kirby Moorside in Cumberland and 500 at Cottingham in Yorkshire. These came to Edmund with the Wake wardship. He gained a park at Skellingthorpe (Lincolnshire)[22] and Hovingham forest from the wardship of the heirs of Roger de Mowbray.[23]

Hundreds

In addition to a large number of manors, Edmund also had the private ownership of all or part of nineteen hundreds. In private hundreds he exercised rights such as the view of frankpledge and he received the profits of justice from the hundred courts. Although Helen Cam believed that all the Cornish hundreds were held by the King in 1274,[24] there is evidence that Edmund controlled all but two-thirds of one of the county's nine hundreds.[25] The Cornish hundreds were East and West Cornwall, Kerrier, Lesnewth, Pyder, Powder, Stratton and Trigg. Penwith was shared with John of Arundel.[26] Outside Cornwall, Edmund held one hundred in Devon, (Lifton); five in Oxfordshire, (Binfield, Ewelme, Langtree, Lewknor and Pyrton); and three of four Rutland hundreds, (Alstoe, East and Martinsley), and possibly the fourth, Wrandike. Despite other large holdings in many other counties, the only other hundred that definitely belonged to him in 1274 was Mere in Wiltshire.[27] However, in February 1302, the widow's dower settlement of Countess Margaret included 'the manor of Kirton with the towns, hamlets and hundreds of Kirton, Haselhen, Corringham and Manley' together with the issues of the soke moot which were assessed at the large annual sum of £288. 7s.2½d. This suggests that Edmund had control over hundreds in Lincolnshire.[28]

Wardships

The surviving records underestimate the benefits that they brought to him. For example, Edmund had inherited the wardship of the heirs of Henry de Hastings from his father. The *inquisition post mortem* of Henry mentions nine knights fees in Suffolk and Norfolk.[29] Whilst Hastings was in prison after the battle of Evesham, the King granted his wife the right to hold Blunham, Bedfordshire, Nailstone and Burbage, Leicestershire, and Fillingley in Warwickshire to maintain herself and her children.[30] The ability of Edmund to present to Leire is another indication of the underestimate of the Hastings' lands in the Inquisition.[31] Thus the surviving inquisition record gave only a partial summary of the lands and wealth that came to Edmund for eleven years.

Some lands under control from a wardship were located near to the existing holdings of Edmund, making them easier to administer. Thus the Wake lands in Lincolnshire and Yorkshire,[32] were possibly linked to Edmund's Kirton and Knaresborough holdings. There were also about three Wake fees in Hertfordshire.[33] However, other lands under Edmund's custody were far from his power bases and would have needed new administrative infrastructure; the Wakes had extensive holdings in Cumberland including Liddel castle,[34] Edmund could not have administered them from his existing centres.

Land Transactions

Although the core of Edmund's lands remained in his control during the years that he held the earldom, he made acquisitions and disposed of land. His disposals sometimes resulted from making benefactions to religious houses and some acquisitions were temporary when he was building up a portfolio of properties to be passed on to a religious house. Other additions to his land holdings were a result of the windfall nature of his feudal rights. An heirless tenant's lands escheated to the landlord and the 1296–97 accounts show that Edmund received a house and rents in Bradnich owned by John le Someter and John de Champernown.[35]

Castles

The possession of castles added considerable theoretical weight to Edmund's lands and power. When Henry III ascended the throne, he had fifty-eight castles but on his death there were only forty-seven partly because of his grants to Richard of Cornwall.[36] Edmund had at least thirteen castles:

1. Berkhamsted, Hertfordshire
2. Eye, Suffolk

3. Haughley, Suffolk
4. Holdgate, Shropshire (sold to Robert Burnell between 1284 and 1292)[37]
5. Knaresborough, Yorkshire
6. Launceston, Cornwall
7. Lydford, Devon
8. Mere, Wiltshire
9. Oakham, Rutland
10. Restormel, Cornwall
11. Tintagel, Cornwall
12. Trematon, Cornwall
13. Wallingford, Berkshire

It has also been suggested that Edmund built a castle at Helston in Cornwall.[38]

Some fortresses, such as Haughley, were decayed by the time that Edmund held them.[39] It is easy to assume that the age of castles as strongholds and power bases was over in a largely peaceful land with the exception of those that were in the forefront when the Welsh, Scots and French threatened to, or actually did, invade. As Edmund knew well, even inland castles such as Wallingford could play a strategic role; he had been besieged there eight years before he inherited it. Earlier in the century, during the warfare at the end of King John's reign and the invasion of Louis of France, Berkhamsted had undergone a siege. However, most of Edmund's castles seemed set for a quiet life but they had the potential to be strengthened. The sites of Haughley and Eye in peaceful Suffolk were and are impressive. A possible exception was Holdgate which was dangerously close to the Welsh border. The two Welsh Wars and the later rebellions meant that it was a potential target. This might be why Edmund sold it to Burnell. It was of little use to Edmund not being near other estates and allowing Burnell to acquire it was an act of curial fellowship. Scottish invasions could sweep far into Northern England which might have put Knaresborough in harm's way.

How far were these thirteen castles from each other? Were they close enough to give Edmund a network of control? The three Cornish castles and Lydford in Devon were between twenty and thirty miles apart but it was 100 miles from Lydford to Mere and eighty-seven miles from there to Wallingford. If we assume that fifteen miles was a relatively easy day's journey, the Cornish and Devon castles could be reached in a day but it would have been a serious excursion to go into Wiltshire and on to the Thames Valley. From Wallingford on the Thames, Berkhamsted was forty miles away; a distance which might be traversed in a day in an emergency or without waiting for the baggage train. In Suffolk, Eye and Haughley were only twelve miles from each other but Berkhamsted was further from Oakham, eighty-eight miles. However, the distances between these castle groups and those further afield were much longer. To reach Holdgate, Edmund, or his men, would have had to cover 128 miles from Oakham and 140 from Mere. One hundred miles separated Berkhamsted from Haughley, the nearest Suffolk castle whilst Knaresborough was 128 miles from Oakham. Thus proximity varied from area to area preventing Edmund from having a nation-wide strategy based on his castles. But, locally, the castles must have been important visual reminders of Edmund's power and centres for his estate and honorial administration.

Conclusions

Did it matter whom Edmund's tenants were? In feudal theory, his tenants should display loyalty to him which was reinforced through the honour to which the lands belonged. The honorial court was one mechanism for administering these lands and for settling disputes between fellow tenants. But the pattern of land holdings, already confused by the decision of William I to avoid the creation of substantial coterminous estates, had been further complicated by two centuries of inheritance and further grants. In particular, the equal partition of lands to provide for co-heiresses and, to a lesser extent, the detachment of smaller portions of a patrimony to endow cadet sons, had left a very confused patchwork of potential allegiances. It was possible to owe service to a number of superior lords over many different parts of the kingdom. Such men could not be expected to be as concerned about their lord in exchange for a small outlying manor as opposed to the magnate whose main estates dominated the area and where most of their income was derived. Historians, including Hugh Thomas, Paul Dalton, David Crouch and Peter Coss, have written about the decline of the honour not least in the face of the rise of the importance and popularity of the royal courts.[40] But

David Carpenter has stressed the continuing importance of the honour in the thirteenth century. He drew attention to the way in which Magna Carta dealt with honours, the practice of collecting feudal aids through the honour and the financial and intrinsic importance of feudal rights such as wardships, relief and escheat.[41]

In addition to his hundred courts, Edmund also benefited from what must have been a large number of seigneurial courts. There is plenty of evidence that Edmund had his own courts, including those at Charwelton, Northamptonshire; Thonock, Lincolnshire; Eye, Suffolk and Lincolnshire; Henley, Oxfordshire; Chichester, Sussex; North Oseney and Wallingford, Oxfordshire; Helston, Cornwall; Newport, Essex; Risborough, Buckinghamshire; Berkhamsted, Hertfordshire; Cippenham, Buckinghamshire; Isleworth, Middlesex; Wilton, Wiltshire; Watlington, Oxfordshire; Benson and Beckley, Oxfordshire; Harwell, Berkshire; Rutland; Knaresborough and Aldborough, Yorkshire; and also Howden in Yorkshire (on loan from the Bishop of Durham).[42] There must have also been one or more honorial courts in Cornwall.

Some of the listed courts might have been more manorial than honorial courts. The honorial court was held when needed; it was irregular. It dealt with matters concerning the more important non-peasant tenants and, by Edmund's time as earl, its position and status had been weakened by the growth of the royal courts. On the other hand, the manorial court, presided over by the lord's reeve, met on a regular basis and was attended by the peasant tenants.[43]

Was the relationship between the greater landowners good, or bad? No one would suggest that as he held lands in three counties where Edmund was a major landholder, Henry de Lacy, Earl of Lincoln, felt constrained to support Edmund or refrain from opposing him. They knew each other well but as comital equals. Lacy had far wider landed-estates and had his own potential supporters. The same must have been true for Roger Bigod, Earl of Norfolk, and Isabella, Countess of Aumale. Similar conclusions should be drawn for the tenants of baronial rank including members of the Bardolf, Beauchamp, Burnell, Despenser, Dinham, Mohun, Peyvere, Pipard, Segrave, Somery, Stafford, Tateshal, Tyes, and Zouche families. The picture is less clear when dealing with the cadet branches of baronial families such as Balliol, Braose, Clifford, Ferrers, Gifford, Tony, Tracy and Vautort. Some ties must have been stronger than others. The Tyes held lands in three counties and in each, Edmund was an important presence. Of the cadet branches, men such as John de Vautort, whose family had sold its barony to Edmund's father, must have maintained strong links to the earl.

Consideration of the knightly tenants suggests that feudal links were more important particularly if they had no other superior lords or, if they were, these lords were less powerful than Edmund. Within Cornwall, for instance, it would have taken a brave knight to defy the Earl or his officials. Only Reginald de Botreaux was involved in litigation against Edmund but this was a case of debt, presumably related to repayment of a loan.[44]

There were two reasons why support for the feudal overlord was of less importance during Edmund's tenure of the earldom. One was that the process of breaking down the importance of the honour with time. The second was that Edmund did not face the political problems his father had encountered in the political field. Adrian Jobson demonstrated that, when the crunch came in the Barons' War, Richard of Cornwall could not rely on all of his Oxfordshire tenants to rally to the Royalist cause. The holding of lands of the honour of Wallingford did not hold them together.[45] Edmund faced no such problems of internal dispute leading to civil war although his tenant, Henry le Tyes, supported the Earls of Norfolk and Hereford against the King during the 1297 crisis.[46]

Chapter 16

Edmund in the Local Community

In large areas of the country Earl Edmund was well known, at least by repute. His relationship with the King, and his position as Regent for long periods, meant that he was perceived as one of England's greatest men. With landholdings in more than half of England's counties, he and his officials had a significant profile and, in some counties, Edmund was the major landholder. His dominant position was clear in Cornwall, Oxfordshire and Rutland. Within Berkshire, Buckinghamshire, Devon and Hertfordshire, he had a considerable level of influence. Larger counties in which he had large holdings such a Yorkshire, Essex, Norfolk, Suffolk and Lincolnshire, had no single dominant lord. In Suffolk, the power of Bury St Edmund's Abbey possibly countered Edmund's influence. However, in these larger counties, Edmund dominated distinct areas such as the honours of Eye and Knaresborough. Cross-border landholdings meant Edmund was strong in the outer edges of counties like Northamptonshire which had manors of the honour of Berkhamsted. When not at court, Edmund favoured the Thames valley and the Chilterns as his main homes. He visited Cornwall and Yorkshire infrequently. It is possible that he never visited some of his dispersed holdings. In these areas, Edmund was experienced by his tenants through the actions of his officials.

It is difficult to form a judgement about how Edmund related to his neighbours and lesser tenants. The evidence is bound to be problematical and it can be interpreted in several ways. Care must be taken to avoid anachronistic attitudes. Apparent hostility to Edmund might be a grievance about the way in which society was then structured. Later in the chapter, there will be an analysis of the attacks and trespasses made on his forests and parks. However, these actions might stem from a long-held and deep-seated dislike of forest law rather than personal animosity towards Edmund. When he acted against one man, or a group of men, he might have had the warm support of others at the same time. Litigation against neighbours was not always the result of a bitter quarrel. Litigation was expected of a great landlord; it was almost a sport. It also signalled the increasing need to secure landed possessions on a permanent basis relying on approved and recorded documentation. Because of the vastness of his lands and their wide distribution, Edmund was a stranger to most areas of his landed estate and he was represented by his officials who might be grasping, inefficient, and with little in common with their lord.

Administration

Whilst Edmund used administrators like other landlords, in Cornwall he was unusual as with the county came his right to appoint the sheriff who acted as his honorial steward in the county with the longest coastline in England, he also appointed a Havener to deal with his maritime rights. Before Edmund's father became Earl, Cornwall had been under royal control and, in 1224, John de Baiocis (Bayeux) was appointed to administer all matters relating to the sea shore in Devon and Cornwall.[1] Elias de Bray, described as the havener in 1275–26, was probably the first havener appointed by Edmund although he might have been inherited from his father. Elias was succeeded by William Waldeshef.[2] The havener was responsible for all the ports except for those deemed seigneurial. Thus profits from Tintagel, Fowey, Saltash and Plymouth were the responsibility of the reeve or bailiff.[3]

Local Concerns

Although Edmund was a stranger in some of the country, his lordship was not always appreciated where he was a frequent resident. In London in 1288, a case was heard when Edmund's attorneys and the Rector of Ashridge argued that Ralph de North of Hemel Hempsted and seven others were born as Edmund's bondmen. The attorneys claimed that they had run away from their lands and asked that they be denied the freedom of the City.[4] This suggests that peasants in the Berkhamsted area were not content as unfree men on Edmund's estates and wished to take advantage of the opportunities offered by the growing capital city. This might have begun as a particular protest against the hardship of Edmund's administration but it was more likely an example of a national phenomenon whereby men were leaving the restricted life of the countryside for the promise of a freer life in a town.

But it was in Edmund's birthplace, Berkhamsted, that his most serious problems had their genesis. A royal writ, authorised at Berwick-on-Tweed on 4 June 1292, required the justices and jurors of of Middlesex, Buckingham, Hertford, Kent and Surrey to investigate

> 'touching the persons who attacked, by day and with drawn swords and knives, Roger de Drayton, treasurer of Edmund, Earl of Cornwall, and others of his household, specially sent by him to the Parliament lately held at Westminster, as they were passing through the streets of the City of London unarmed, while many people stood by in the adjoining streets who heard their cries before they were killed; and they are to enquire also touching the persons who by day and night supplied the malefactors with food and drink when they had taken refuge in a church and the persons who, on horseback and foot, conducted the said malefactors after their abjuration of the realm to the port of Dover, and who were the aiders and abettors in the said crime, and to do justice.'

The constable of Dover was also ordered to investigate what had happened there. The wording suggests that Roger was not the only servant of Edmund killed[5] and a pardon granted in 1298 identified two more servants.[6] It became clear that the murderers were three brothers from Berkhamsted enraged by Roger's alleged persecution of their mother. Roger was said to have maliciously contrived to have their mother put in the stocks at Berkhamsted and revenge was the motive for the attack. The guilty men succeeded in finding sanctuary and went into exile.[7] In October 1298 Robert Walerand was pardoned for Roger's murder as he was in the King's army in Flanders.[8] One wonders whether Edmund was content with this decision.

Sanctuary was involved again in the same year when Edmund's bailiff of Berkhamsted complained that Edmund Walerand, who had been convicted of novel disseisin at Berkhamsted, was rescued and placed in the sanctuary of the parish church, and, after keeping him for a day and a night, 'received him there from and let him go free'.[9] This was not all. A year earlier, Edmund's servants were accused of stopping the Rector of St Peter's, Berkhamsted, from the gathering in the tithes. The Bishop of Lincoln threatened excommunication against anyone who interfered with the collection.[10] These events might make a *prima facie* case for poor relationships in the vicinity of Edmund's main residence. But there were no reports on trespasses and attacks on the comital parks.

One long-standing grievance surfaced whilst complaints were made to those preparing the Hundred Rolls. This concerned Edmund's bailiff, Roger de Pridias, over the detention of oxen and animals in Colebrooke, Devon.[11] This almost certainly referred to the case brought by the Abbot of Forde which is dealt with in the next chapter.[12] Although some returns have not survived, considering the far-flung nature of his land holdings, it is striking that this was the only complaint made about Edmund or his officials in a wide-ranging inquisition.

Attacks on Edmund's Parks and Forests

A significant acreage of Edmund's holdings was set aside as parks and forests. There were at least twenty-five places where he had parks and, in some, there was more than one park. In addition he was the lord of the huge Dartmoor and the smaller Knaresborough forests. In Knaresborough he had two parks and a forest. From the existing records both forests suffered attacks as did eighteen parks. These figures rely on centrally-kept royal records and might underestimate the frequency or the amount of such trespasses. Some stewards might have been lax and unconcerned but others might have striven to exact as much as they could by using the landlord's rights. It is possible that not all the complaints made by Edmund or his officials were justified.

There are some patterns. The 1280s were the years of frequent attacks on forests, only two were mentioned in the 1290s and just one in the year of Edmund's death. Serious attacks occurred even when Edmund was Regent but the writs ordering investigation were granted soon after the King left for Gascony so the attacks might have occurred before Edmund became viceroy. When complaints were about more than one park, they were usually about Devon or Cornwall. However, in 1298, the parks affected included four in Cornwall, Dartmoor as well as two in Wiltshire. Dartmoor was the subject of six separate intrusions stretching from 1272 until 1296. There has to be a caveat; some of the complaints noted in the records might be a second entry. Knaresborough forest suffered four times.

Some parks were mentioned once whilst four were assailed four times, three in Cornwall and one, Corsham, in Wiltshire. Six parks namely Ashridge, Berkhamsted, Helston-in-Trigg, Henley, Princes Risborough and Sedgebrook, seemed to have remained peaceful. In some cases the number and names of the alleged attackers were noted. (See Table 16 in the Appendices.) In 1272, they were only noted as malefactors,[13] but in 1277, the list of suspects was headed by Master John de Curwenne and included John la Zouche, Nicholas Harpin and Richard le Pouere.[14]

Whilst sometimes the taking of deer was the motive for attacks,[15] in others the outcome was more serious. In 1276, Edmund's forester in Dartmoor was killed.[16] A year later, it was alleged that persons hunting in the park at Oakham had maltreated Edmund's keeper.[17] Then, in 1284, the justices were to investigate the fate of Hugh Langthwaite, killed in Knaresborough forest, for the transgression of hunting there.[18]

Other Assaults

When Edmund complained of widespread attacks on his parks in Devon and Cornwall after he succeeded to the earldom, he also accused malefactors of plundering a ship in the port of Topsham (Devon) of 400 marks belonging to him and his knight, John Wyger.[19] During 1288 and 1289, Edmund launched two actions citing nineteen men for transgressions in Lincolnshire.[20]

Cornwall

At the Atlantic end of Europe, Cornwall must have been one of the most difficult parts of England to govern. Distant from the centres of royal power, there must have been a tendency towards isolationism. Even the diocesan Bishop found Cornwall difficult to administer. An Anglo-Norman lord had the additional difficulty arising from language. Edmund's officials, needed a facility for English and would have had to communicate with the numerous Cornish speakers. As late as 1336, when John de Grandisson, Bishop of Exeter, preached he had to have the words translated into Cornish as well as French and English.[21] Cornwall could also be a violent, uncivilised place. At the 1284 Eyre, it was reported that the survivors of a wrecked ship from Shoreham had been murdered by men who carried away the cargo.[22] Had they caused the wreck?

Possibly fired by Arthurian enthusiasm, Edmund's father had built the castle at Tintagel and rebuilt most of Launceston Castle. Edmund himself remodelled the castles of Restormel and Trematon. He moved the centre of administration from Launceston on the Devon border to Lostwithiel on the river Fowey near Restormel castle. As part of the move he built a palace which contained the county hall, an exchequer and coinage hall, a 'blowing house' for the assaying and smelting of tin, a 'weighing house', the gaol for the Cornish stannaries, and limited living accommodation for officials.[23] Neither earl founded a religious house in Cornwall, giving preference to areas nearer their administrative headquarters and main residences. Both earls fostered the growth of boroughs in the county. Richard established one at Camelford and Edmund added Grampound built on the water pasture of Tybista manor.[24] Despite the amount of wealth generated by the county and the investment put into Restormel castle, the evidence for comital visits by Edmund is slight. He was at Launceston on 11 September 1275 when he issued a charter to the borough of Liskeard.[25] Making a grant to the bishopric of Exeter, Edmund was at his castle of Restormel on 12 May 1284.[26] Mark Page believed that Edmund was there on 30 December 1290[27] but he was actually at Ashridge with the King on that day. A charter for Roger de Inkpen was dated at Restormel that October.[28] Another charter, granted there, dated from May 1291.[29] Another possible presence was on 1 January 1292 when a grant was made to Oseney Abbey.[30] From Trematon castle, Edmund wrote to William Marsh on 20 November 1292.[31] This makes a total of only six visits, two more than those discovered by Page, but others might be unrecorded.

Relations with some Cornish men were not always good. In 1284, Edmund was accused of disseising Osmund de Talcarn of 200 acres but it is of interest that the second defendant was Edmund's steward, William de Monkton. There were eight other defendants.[32] This suggests that Edmund was not personally involved in the actions of which he was accused.

Lincolnshire

In 1289, Edmund accused three named men and others of taking his beasts.[33]

Nottinghamshire

During 1290, it was ordered that an assize should see if Edmund, Earl of Cornwall, Constance de Béarn (his sister-in-law), and thirteen others had unjustly distrained Robert Attekirke of Fyngele (probably Finningley) of 170 quarters, 10 acres of marsh and 10 acres of meadow. Edmund argued that it was part of the ancient demesne of Kirton in Lincolnshire. Sine die is recorded on the roll, suggesting that Robert lost.[34]

Yorkshire

Some fifty-two people led by baron Mauger le Vavasour were named in a Yorkshire action for trespass brought by Edmund in 1296. From the names of the places from which the men came, it related to West Yorkshire.[35] Also in Yorkshire, Edmund had problems with the powerful St Mary's Abbey, York, relating to his holding of Bishop Bek's manor of Howden. The Abbot complained to the King in 1298 that, although the abbey was quit by royal charters from the payment of toll throughout the whole realm, Edmund's bailiffs had distrained the Abbot and his men coming to Howden to pay a toll, having molested the Abbot's men 'in many ways'. The King ordered the bailiffs to desist from inflicting distraints and grievances and were also to release to the men 'any distress levied in this behalf'.[36]

Good Relations with the Local Community

One source of evidence as to whether good relations existing between Edmund and the local community can be ascertained from his charters. Benefactions to religious orders, especially to the friars who performed important services within urban areas, were welcome. The citizens of Chichester would have been grateful for his assistance to the Black Friars. The residents of Knaresborough, too, might have welcomed his support for the Red Friars as did those in Oxford.

Despite the potential for conflict, Edmund's relationship with other cities and towns over which he had some control was often co-operative. In Exeter he confirmed agreements made by the city with the Archdeacon of Totnes during 1299.[37] But relations were not always good with the

City. During the summer of 1286, at the urging of the King's daughters, Edmund reduced the sum of 250 marks by fifty owed from a bond by the Mayor and citizens and he remitted the rancour and indignation he felt against them. No details of the dispute have survived.[38] In this city, both the Black and Grey Friars also benefited.

Another city had problems with Edmund. He had granted privileges on the rivers flowing through York to St Mary's Abbey[39] and the Hospital of St Leonard.[40] However, in 1285, the citizens and the people living along the rivers Ouse and Ure between York and Boroughbridge asked the King to command that these rivers should not be in defence. They argued that Magna Carta was to be upheld including the provision that no river should be in defence, except for those that were so in the time of Henry II. However, these rivers had been put in defence, contrary to Magna Carta, by Richard of Cornwall, and this was continued by Edmund. The community of York, and the country of the rivers, had deraigned a franchise by an assize of twenty-six knights in the Yorkshire Eyre and were seised of this franchise for two years. But, two years later, Edmund had disseised them without a judgement, to their great impoverishment.[41]

One base for Edmund's Cornish interests was the borough of Liskeard and he issued two charters to benefit its townspeople, allowing them to commute the dues they owed to him to an annual £18 farm. Over a hundred years after Edmund's death, the townspeople had not forgotten the benefits that Edmund had brought them. In 1417, a commission set up to consider a complaint of the burgesses heard that Edmund had allowed them to settle their payments by free farm and the King had confirmed this right, but the tenants of the outlying towns had refused to render suit.[42]

Although Edmund's own cartulary is still extant, from other records it is clear that other charters once existed. Some would have oiled the wheels within his demesne holdings. From his accounts for 1296/7 it can be seen that he made grants to minor tenants. For example, Hugh Syward gained land at Risborough for 4s.6d. annually and Thomas de Weylete for a mere penny a year.[43] At Berkhamsted, Hugh the cook had lands for a penny a year.[44] People of Tybista and Helston in Trigg in Cornwall were all given their freedom from their villein status by charter. However, they paid for the release and, at Tyrwarnhaile, Lawrence Trevanwa bought his wife's freedom.[45] Other charter grants are disclosed in the *Inquisitions post mortem* of 1300. For example, Richard de la Garderobe gained 12 messuages, 200 acres of land, 30 of meadow, 60 of pasture and 100 of woods as well as 5 marks rent.[46]

A more unusual issue surfaced in 1295 when Edmund sent a writ to Simon Greenhill, his seneschal of the honour of St Valery, requiring him to investigate charges brought by St Frideswide's Priory, Oxford, against John Digby, Edmund's former seneschal, accusing him of forcing hospitality from the canons. Three years later, Greenhill was ordered not to oppress the Prior.[47]

One wonders whether records hide more friction between Edmund and his tenants. During a hearing about the liberty of Berkhamsted at the time of the Hertfordshire Eyre (1287), William, son of Jordan le Forester, accused William de Henman, Payn de Liskeard and William and Christina de Hartford of disseising him in Berkhamsted.[48] Liskeard was Edmund's clerk.[49] Were these defendants working for Edmund?

There is evidence that Edmund was a better landlord than his successors. Soon after his death, the men of Misson, Nottinghamshire, claimed that, during his time, they had the right to the wood in the vill, partly in Lincolnshire, but Countess Margaret, who now held it, had prevented them from taking or cutting wood.[50] In 1307, the Prior of Tydwardeath stated that Edmund had given the priory 4 marks a year to pay for a chaplain in the hermitage of Baldwin's Bridge but, during the new reign, he had been denied it.[51]

Did Edmund make conscious efforts to build up local support? Tilley argued that the foundation of the collegiate chapel of St Nicholas at Wallingford Castle was intended to assert the importance of the honour of Wallingford and to bind to him its knights as well as stressing his franchisal rights.[52] Tilley showed how seriously Edmund and his officials took these rights. In 1298, the King ordered the Sheriff of Berkshire to replevy thirteen men for goods or chattels which had been seized illegally. They had been imprisoned by Edmund and his officials, Simon de Greenhill and John de Hedsor. Edmund and his officials had declined to act, claiming that they held a ship belonging to the men on which they had harboured Simon de Cliveden who had murdered William le Rous of Aldermaston. The men had refused to surrender Simon who escaped by night.[53]

Conclusions

From this scant evidence it is possible to make the case that Edmund generally had good relations within the area where he was the lord of lands. The complaints about his officials seem to have been relatively few. The main doubt arises from the difficulties that he had with locals in his forests and parks but this might have been par for any such a landholder. If Edmund had been a bad neighbour and landlord, one would have expected more criticism in surviving records.

Chapter 17

Edmund at Law

L andlords in the thirteenth century pursued litigation almost as a sport; it was expected of them. From printed sources for such a wealthy landlord as Edmund, surprisingly little has been uncovered about land-related litigation in terms of numbers of cases, conducted by, or against, him. In all around twenty-nine actions can be found in Bishop's Registers and Rolls, one cartulary, Calendars of the Close and Patent Rolls, Feets of Fine, Oxfordshire Forest Eyres, Placita Quo Warranto and the Year Books of Edward I.[1]

This picture of relative inactivity seems to be confirmed by a search of the rolls of the courts of the King's Bench.[2] There are thirty cases spread over more than twenty-eight years but eight actions were already under way during the Trinity term of 1272. The King's Bench was the most senior of the four main law courts; those of the Common Pleas, the Exchequer and the Justices in Eyre, were the others. The King's Bench originally dealt with cases within the King's purview and was prohibited by chapter eleven of Magna Carta from hearing cases that should have been considered by the court of Common Pleas. This concession was valued as the Common Pleas court was required to meet in a fixed place and did not follow the royal court on its travels. However, the Commons Pleas court did sit in Shrewsbury in the Michaelmas term of 1282[3] and, around the turn of the century, York became the venue for several years.[4] During the period of Edmund's earldom, the King's Bench met as far away as Caernarvon, Berwick and Roxburgh.

In practice, the King's Bench concentrated on matters relating to the King's lands and rights, or a breach of his peace. It also acted as an appeal court considering mistakes made by other royal courts. Measured by the case numbers and the size of the rolls, its business was significantly less than that of the Common Pleas although business conducted by both courts grew rapidly during the reign of Edward I. In 1273 there were ten membranes in the roll for the Hilary term of the Common Pleas whilst by the Michaelmas of 1300 the number had grown to 399. Paul Brand prepared a table showing that the number of membranes for the Common Pleas increased from 415 in the 1280s to 1056 in the 1290s.[5]

Compared with the King's Bench, a very different picture emerges from a search for Edmund in the rolls of the Common Pleas.[6] The number of cases is more prolific and actions reach 147. In addition, nine cases have been found in the Eyre rolls and one in the Ancient Petitions. A total of 186 actions are found only in manuscript sources.

Overall it should be understood that not all cases were instigated by Edmund. Many stem from his alleged failure to allow widows to have their proper dower and others from unlawful detention which sounds as if he, or more likely, his officials were using their power to squeeze money or services from tenants. These rents and services might have been lawfully his but the frequency of such cases could substantiate the case for a rather harsh regime for his tenantry. In the early years of his earldom, Edmund was involved in litigation as an executor of his father's will.[7]

This chapter draws on the evidence uncovered and looks at the type of actions that Edmund was involved in and who were his opponents. It attempts to form conclusions as to Edmund's appetite for going to law and his success. The detail of the cases is included in the Appendix 2 and tables in Additional Appendices show the chronology, courts involved and the status of his opponents. The table below sets out the cases by type of litigation.

Table 17.1: Case Analysis.

Type of Litigation/Action	Number
Advowson	15
Bailiff's account	4
Chattels and debts	5
Concord/Convention	2
Darrien Presentment	1
Debt	21
Detention/distraint	17
Dower	35
Fair	1
Forest offences	2
Free Warren	2

Type of Litigation/Action	Number
Lands (including pasture)	40
Market	1
Mesne	1
Navigation	2
Novel Disseisin	2
Quo Warranto	15
Rent	2
Stallage	1
Transgression/Trespass	13
Utrum	2
View of Frankpledge	2
Villeinage	1
Wardship/Custody	15
Warranty	10
Wreckage	1
Unknown/Unclear	10
Total	223

It is no surprise that most actions were land-related. Some forty were listed only as actions over lands and relate to holdings from 100 to a few acres Others came under specific legal provisions. These included the assize of *novel disseisin* which was intended to be a quick way in which disputes over the control of land could be decided. Because of their efficacy they had become extremely popular but Edmund was involved in only two such cases.[8] Wardships and the custody of heirs enabled the guardian of an under-age heir to benefit from the income of an inheritance often for a significant time. For those guardians, this was of considerable importance. Rents due from lands which were unpaid were another source of contention in two suits. Actions for the recovery of chattels and debts were similar. Three involving Edmund were related to the effects of his late father disputed by Edmund and his widowed step-mother, Beatrix von Falkenburg. However, as they involved Richard of Cornwall's will, they were matters for the church and two of the actions mention church officials.

Dower was the right of a widow to a third of her late husband's lands for life and this applied to all tenants. As Alan Harding observed, actions to ensure that the widow received her full entitlement 'were complex and involved much warranty' the disputed lands often having been granted by the deceased husband's heir.[9] Most actions for dower were mainly brought by women who were otherwise under-represented in litigation. They open a window on the world of women, illustrating the only periods in their lifetimes when they had independence and wealth. When a wardship was granted, the rights of the widow to her dower could also create problems as the guardian had the other rights to the lands during the minority. As a major landholder, it is not surprising that Edmund was often involved in disputes over widow's entitlements; thirty-five dower actions have been discovered, although, interestingly, a full thirteen of these were claims made by his step-mother, Beatrix.

Another popular assize was that of *darrien presentment* which sought to establish who had the right to present a clerk to a living as the person who 'owned' the advowson. Although about spiritual matters, this was often a dispute over a financial benefit of the living which could be given to an official of a landlord in lieu of wages or to buy influence or favours from an influential man. The assize of *utrum* dealt with matters of contention between the laity and clergy. Edmund was involved in fifteen advowson actions, one of darrien presentment and two of utrum. In one instance both a manor and advowson were at stake.

Actions of warranty were brought by landholders whose right to the lands, rents or services was challenged by those who wanted to claim lands from others. A person called to warrant was a third party drawn into an action which did not usually have a direct impact on them. As a major landholder, Edmund must have been in a position to warrant for others about the true tenant, although sometimes he could have been seeking backing for his own position. Ten such cases have been noted. Similar to warranty is the action for mesne. This action followed a claim by a sub-tenant distrained by a lord for services owed by the sub-tenant's immediate lord, seeking acquittal by that mesne lord and damages for failure to acquit him.[10] One case involving the Abbot of Rewley has been discovered.[11]

Other rights could be disputed. The taking of the view of frankpledge brought a good annual income and its loss was worth contesting. River navigation was another source of income and possible contention (two claims). Coastal lordships could bring the profits from wrecks (one action). In towns, stallage, was a payment due for the exclusive right to occupy a portion of soil within a market and with markets as well as fairs.

These were also worth fighting for (one action each). Only one example of a challenge to the feudal status of tenants has been found. At stake in *villeinage* was whether a man was Edmund's villein or a free man.

Arising from unpaid loans, twenty-one actions for debt were pursued and Edmund, as a major lender, was plaintiff in twenty such cases.[12] Other cases arose from the failure of an official, usually a bailiff, to pay the full amount that he owed to his lord from the income due to the lord. Actions requiring the submission of proper accounts by a former steward or bailiff were also lodged. Four officials were sued in this way.

A special action involving the sovereign was that of *Quo Warranto*. Testing by what right a landlord exercised their feudal rights was one way in which English kings attempted to arrest the gradual erosion of their regal powers. The process of challenge by the King was termed *Quo Warranto* (by what right?). Whilst the process pre-dated the reign of Edward I, Edward was determined to halt the erosion of his rights.[13] On fifteen occasions the King questioned Edmund's rights.

Thirteen suits were described as trespass and transgression and Edmund was both accused and accuser. In some cases they stemmed from the actions of his officials whilst in others his lands had been attacked by his tenants or neighbours. Detention of animals and other distraining action was taken against persons for not paying rents or rendering services. The distraint of a tenant's possessions was usually to extract something from him or her. When challenged, these cases would also be listed as of detention. There were seventeen events in the rolls. Again these actions were likely to refer to officials acting on behalf of the landholder.

Despite the Charter of the Forest of 1225, the control of royal forests was strong and breaches could lead to severe penalties. Edmund was twice prosecuted but he was also granted extensive royal pardons for his illegal actions. However, as possibly the greatest private owner of forests and parks, he twice took action himself against those who infringed his right.

In some cases there is no clarity over the basis of a dispute. Often the only evidence of a case comes from the listing of an attorney on the court roll. In all, ten actions are uncategorisible.

A plea of convention brought by Martin de Trewalda from Cornwall in 1293 was listed in the following year: a dispute over one acre.[14] This may be similar to the concord reached with the Bishop of Rochester settling a disagreement over an advowson.[15]

Edmund's Opponents in Legal Cases

Of the 223 cases, more actions were brought against Edmund than by him. This should not be surprising. Only the King could initiate *Quo Warranto* inquiries and Edmund could not sue for dower. An analysis of opponents throws more light on Edmund's activities and attitudes. Three tables in Additional Appendices separate his opponents into those who were plaintiffs, those whom Edmund brought suits against and those people involved in a dispute where there is no certainty as to who initiated the action. Where known, their status in society has been added.

Some of the men who were against Edmund in legal disputes have already been discussed when his associates and fellow members of court were described in Chapter 8. Comital opponents included William de Beauchamp, Earl of Warwick; Gilbert de Clare, Edmund's brother-in-law; John de Warenne, Earl of Surrey; and Roger Bigod, Earl of Norfolk. Before he became Earl of Devon, Hugh de Courtenay also faced Edmund in court.

Litigation: Barons

Some actions reflected long-standing grievances. Amongst the barons, the challenges made by John de Stuteville for Knaresborough indicate a man chancing his arm. The Stutevilles had lost Knaresborough after a rebellion against King John.[16] Richard of Cornwall was given the honour as long ago as 1235.[17] The action by Robert de Brus about Boroughbridge might have been derived from his wife's inheritance as an heiress of the Irbys[18] and Baldwin Wake, another suitor, was the son of the eldest Stuteville heiress.[19] Baldwin's widow, Hawise, whose unsuccessful suits against Edmund lasted some years, was Baldwin's second wife. Her father was Roger de Quincy, the younger brother of the Earl of Winchester, whilst her mother was Helen, a daughter of Llywelyn Fawr, the greatest ruler of Wales.[20] Other baronial widows who brought actions against Edmund included Lora de Gant and Rose de Mowbray. Lora, the daughter of Henry de Balliol, had married Gilbert de Gant who held extensive lands in Lincolnshire and Yorkshire. For a while these were held by Edmund's brother, Henry of Almain, when Gilbert's father was captured at Northampton as a supporter of Montfort. Gilbert died childless and his heirs were his three sisters, one the wife of Peter III de Maulay. Peter IV de Maulay was Edmund's ward and thus he had control over a third of the Gant inheritance as well as his Maulay lands except for Lora's dower portion which she claimed.[21] Rose was the sister of Edmund's wife, Margaret, and she married Roger de Mowbray. When Roger died in 1297, his son, John, then 13, became another of Edmund's wards. The Mowbray lands were mainly in Yorkshire but also in seven other counties. Edmund and Rose quarrelled over dower.[22]

A far more formidable foe was Isabella de Fortibus, the Countess of Aumale and Lady of the Isle of White. She was the sister of Baldwin de Redvers, Earl of Devon and Lord of White. She married William de Fortibus, Count of Aumale, but the Earl's early death and that of her husband, transformed her position. Baldwin died childless and her own son and daughter died childless. These deaths left Isabella in charge of the Devon earldom, the Wight lordship and the Aumale estates including the honours of Holderness and Skipton in Yorkshire and Cockermouth in Cumberland. Through her grandmother, she also inherited the FitzGerold and Courcy estates and from these she disputed a wood near Harewood in Yorkshire with Edmund. Isabella was possibly the richest women of her time and she pursued her interests with vigour.[23] Barbara English has written that 'Isabella was much involved in litigation, pursuing dozens of civil and criminal cases through the royal courts; it is interesting that she appeared to have her own copy of statutes of the realm.'[24]

Amongst other Edmund's baronial opponents, were the relatives of Countess Isabella, the Insula (Lisle) family. Gerard of the Kingston Lisle branch and his wife, Alice, were in contention with Edmund the year before Gerard died.[25] Another Baron, William Latimer, had land holdings in Northamptonshire where his action against Edmund was recorded.[26] The beautiful church of Kilpeck in Herefordshire stands next to the castle home of Alan de Plukenet. He was involved in a case over debt with Edmund.[27]

Litigation: Clerics

Edmund had disputes with a wide range of clerics from archbishops to abbots, priors and even humble parsons as well as with the representatives of female orders. His legal disputes with Archbishop Pecham stemmed from their interests in Chichester. Edmund also contested Pecham's predecessor, Robert Kilwardby, but not his successor, Robert Winchelsea. Of the five Archbishops of York who held office during his earldom, Edmund disputed only with Walter Gifford. Law cases involved four bishops starting with the actions brought by Walter Bronescombe of Exeter which might have been triggered by events before Edmund succeeded as earl. The others involved his friends, Oliver Sutton of Lincoln and Thomas Cantilupe of Hereford, who was represented by his official in an advowson conflict. A possible conflict with Thomas Ingoldsthorpe of Rochester seems to have been settled amicably. Walter Scamel, who opposed Edmund in 1283 when a mere parson, later became Dean of Salisbury and then Bishop in the 1284.[28] The Dean and Chapter of York and the Dean of Arches were other senior clerical challengers to Edmund's rights. Archidiaconal opponents were found in the persons of Elias de Paston of Derby; Walter of Gloucester of York; Geoffrey St Martin of Richmond; and Robert de Radwell of Chester.

Amongst the religious houses with which Edmund had disagreements were his own foundations and those founded by his father including Oseney and Rewley Abbeys and the Trinitarian Friary of St Robert at Knaresborough. Other abbatial opponents were those of Bicester, Cirencester, Dore, Eynsham, Ford, Walden and St Mary's York. Priories with actions against Edmund included Bolton, Dunstable, Drax, Eye and St Frideswide's in Oxford. Of the female religious establishments there was a contention with Leighton Buzzard Priory. Hospital opponents included St John's, Northampton and St Leonard's, York. The two principal military orders in England, the Hospitallers and Templars were also in dispute with Edmund on occasion. Humble parsons who fell out with Edmund included those of Longborough, said to be in Herefordshire but probably in Gloucestershire, Mere, Wiltshire, Petham and Stonham Earl, Suffolk and Ripley, Yorkshire.

Litigation: Other Opponents

Of the *curial* opponents, John de Benstede was not just a King's clerk, he was a former controller of the King's wardrobe and future Keeper.[29] Of the knightly plaintiffs against Edmund, mention should be made of: Stephen de Chenduit, whose main estates were in Buckinghamshire and

Northamptonshire; shires where Edmund was powerful;[30] Robert de Coleville, a Yorkshire former Montfortian;[31] Walter de la Lynde who had extensive lands spread over four counties including Lincolnshire where Edmund was powerful although their dispute related to Dorset;[32] Peter de la Mare, who spent time as Constable of Bristol Castle and had lands in five counties including Lower Heyford in Oxfordshire;[33] and Hugh de Vautort, presumably a relative of Richard of Cornwall's mistress and a man with lands in Devon and Somerset.[34]

Defendants amongst the ranks of knights included Nicholas de Audley who was rich in lands in Staffordshire, Cheshire and Shropshire,[35] and John de St Elena, a fellow landholder in Buckinghamshire and Oxfordshire where he was Edmund's tenant,[36] as well as being a witness for one of Edmund's charters. Mauger le Vavasour of Hazlewood Castle and other Yorkshire lands, was a man whose family was on the verge of baronial rank.[37] The same was true of John de Umfraville who inherited lands in Devon from his brother in 1271 and whose relative Gilbert acquired the Scottish earldom of Angus.[38]

Timing of Litigation

Throughout Edmund's tenure of the earldom, the amount of litigation had peaks and troughs. There was a flurry when Edmund became Earl partly caused by the rash of actions taken by his step-mother over her dower. In the four years from 1280 until 1283 and from 1297 until 1300 there were no new actions before the King's Bench. The justices of the Common pleas had new actions from Edmund varying from 18 in 1275 to none in 1296 and 1299–1300. At times the only cases noted were re-hearings or references to old actions such as the long-running dispute with the Earl of Warwick which was not brought by Edmund. Many suits were pursued over many law terms and even years. The action to secure proper accounts and redress from his former bailiff, Henry de Raleigh, in parts of Devon began in 1277 but was still on the roll at Michaelmas term 1299, twenty-two years later.[39] The number of cases being pursued in the Common Pleas during one term could reach 15 in the Michaelmas terms of 1275 and 1277 but there were sessions when there were no references at all to Edmund. The largest number of actions in a term before the King's Bench twice reached eight.

Does the geographical distribution of cases throw light on where Edmund was most active or faced opposition? Considering his overwhelmingly powerful position in Cornwall, it is surprising that only fifteen actions relate to that county. There should have been far more scope for friction because of his large land holdings but the relative absence of action might be adjudged to show that his dealings with the county were marked by good relationships or maybe potential opponents were intimidated. In total, there was a single action in Bedfordshire, four in Berkshire, seventeen in Buckinghamshire and another shared between these two latter counties. Cambridgeshire featured only once with another case covering Suffolk as well. Another county with a single action was Derbyshire where Countess Beatrix was seeking her share of lands of Richard of Cornwall. There were ten Devon and two Dorset cases.

Some counties in which Edmund was not a landlord appear in the court rolls but this was because they usually related to his position as the guardian of a wardship granted to him by the King in return for the massive loans that he made to the Crown. Some of the four Leicestershire cases related to the Hastings wardship.[40] There is also evidence of a case involving John de Hastings before Parliament in 1283.[41] A wardship might involve lands stretching over a number of counties: Cambridgeshire, Essex, Norfolk and Suffolk were one example[42] and Lincolnshire, Rutland and Yorkshire another.[43] Essex was represented by three cases on its own and Gloucestershire by five. From Hampshire there were four actions, whilst from Herefordshire, where Edmund held no lands, there were three. Lancashire, another county where Edmund had no land, produced one case as did Huntingdonshire but Hertfordshire only eight which is surprising as Edmund had a major stake in the county. There were sixteen Lincolnshire cases although two were shared with other counties. London was mentioned twice but only because the Dean of Arches was based there. Two originated from Middlesex and six from Norfolk, one of which was shared with Suffolk. Nottinghamshire was another county where Edmund had no known lands but two actions were noted under the county with ten from Northamptonshire. The county with the largest number of actions was Oxfordshire with thirty-one, one linked to Berkshire. Rutland was one of Edmund's power bases but it was small so only five cases were listed under this county. Somerset was unusual as it only involved one case whilst three Staffordshire actions seem curious as Edmund held no lands there. Perhaps they related to lands controlled through wardships. Twelve single or shared cases related to Suffolk and two from Sussex. Finally there were nine Wiltshire actions and twenty-seven Yorkshire actions.

Other counties were mentioned in the records simply because a man indebted to Edmund had given sureties linked to his lands wherever they were. These mentions did not necessarily indicate poor relations between Edmund and men in a particular locality. John de Segrave's debt to Edmund was secured on John's lands in Warwickshire, Northampton-shire, Huntingdonshire and Derbyshire;[44] it did not follow that Edmund was involved in conflict in any of these counties.

Conclusions

For such a great landowner with interests stretching from Cornwall to Yorkshire, the amount of legal activity involving Edmund seems small. Unlike Eleanor of Castile, whose legal activities were part of a deliberate campaign of land acquisition and which brought her a bad reputation,[45] Edmund did not have her steely purpose in obtaining lands or keeping tight control of those he held. There is no evidence of continuing ruthlessness but this is not surprising. Eleanor had meagre landed estates and needed to build up her resources. Edmund was so wealthy that he could afford to be more relaxed. In addition, when it became clear that he was unlikely to have an heir, there was little point in pursuing claims for lands which would bring him only marginal extra benefits.

How successful was Edmund in his litigation? The records of court actions of the time are frustratingly inconclusive. Some cases are mentioned only once and no result is noted. Far more often, a suit was postponed and this could be repeated over law terms for years. Several cases went on for so long that one party died producing a result by default. Examples include the dower actions brought by Beatrix von Falkenberg and the dispute over the Wrandike hundred of Rutland with the Earl of Warwick, which lasted twelve years before the Earl died. Even when Edmund was successful, he might later make an agreement with his opponent as when he granted the advowson of Thorndon to Eye Priory.

It could be argued that Edmund was not avaricious by nature. Was he just well-meaning or was his attitude towards litigation influenced by his piety? Perhaps he simply left the decision as to how and when to litigate to his officials. They could have been inefficient or benevolent or they might have taken their tone from their master. Another possibility is that Edmund was not challenged as often as other magnates because complainants were well aware of his position as the King's cousin and, for several years when Regent, the greatest man in the land.

Chapter 18

Edmund, the Man and His Legacy

So what was Edmund of Cornwall like? H. Rothwell, editing the volume of *English Historical Documents* called him 'rather shadowy',[1] whilst C.S. Gilbert, the early nineteenth-century historian of Cornwall, airbrushed him out of history believing that Richard of Cornwall had only one son, Henry, who died childless.[2] Maurice Powicke called him 'a gentle and faithful man.'[3] Mary Midgley, who studied his life more closely than any other historian, wrote: 'What is surprising is that a man of his eminence, second only to members of the royal house in rank, should have made so little mark upon the affairs of the kingdom and so little impression upon contemporary chroniclers.'[4] Following Midgley, Eleanor Searle was savage about Edmund: 'His character seems to have been an unusual one in a man of his station' and he fulfilled his state duties 'if with little vigour'. She opined that: 'his regency of 1286–89, was, however, as far as he was primarily responsible, a fiasco'.[5] In his life time, Edmund was known as a very important man in English society. When the new Pope John XXI wrote to Edward I informing him of his election and exhorting him to 'rule his kingdom justly', he sent copies to several important people including the 26-year-old Edmund.[6]

Edmund died at just 50, not an unreasonable age for the time, but his male cousins who shared exactly the same gene pool, the King and Edmund of Lancaster, lived longer; the former for sixty-eight years and the latter fifty-six. Although he had fought in a tournament in 1278,[7] as early as 1278–79 there was evidence of Edmund's weak health. Summoned to a meeting in London, he was too ill to attend.[8] Towards the end of his life, he was unwell and there were writs preparing for his possible death in 1297.[9] His love of hunting, which he shared with the King,[10] show that he was not always physically frail. However, despite all Edward I's wars, Edmund served in person only twice including once as a military commander during the rebellion of Rhys ap Maredudd although it was unlikely that he fought during that time.

The Ashridge epitaph, quoted by the antiquarian Bishop of Peterborough, White Kennett runs:

> *Cornubiae comes et dominus mundusque beatus*
> *Dicitur Edmundus de regum germine natus.*
> *Virtutis titulum trahit a probitate parentum,*
> *Et decus addit ei comitiva modesta clientum.*
> *Dapsilis in mensa, frugalia pabula praestans,*
> *Sacratas domini leges in pectore gestans.*
> *Protervos domitans ne Wallia praedominetur,*
> *Regis et absentis regnum ratione tuetur.*
> *Dulcis in elloquio, justus, pius atque benignus,*
> *Prudens consilio, regni moderamine dignus,*
> *Fraxinei dorsi per eum novus ordo virescit,*
> *Summa coelicolae nova messis in aggere crescit.*
> *Sumptibus Edmundi comitis locus aedificatur,*
> *Regius Oxoniae, quo plebs studiosa moratur.'*[11]

Fraxinei dorsi is Ashridge and *Regius Oxoniae* is Rewley. Kennett gave his source as Dugdale in his Analecta manuscripts but the epitaph is from the Annals of Hailes.[12]

A possible translation reads:

> Edmund, born of the stock of kings, is called Earl and Lord of
> Cornwall, upright and blessed.
> He takes his designation of virtue and integrity from his parents,
> and is further enhanced through his reflection in the decency of his
> attendants and entourage.
> Lavish in his table, providing bountiful provisions/food/fare,
> bearing in his breast the hallowed laws of God. (i.e. the laws of
> hospitality – he was a generous host)
> Taming the arrogant lest Wales should take supremacy, he also
> watches over the kingdom by reason of its absent king.
> Sweet in utterance, just, pious and kind, prudent in counsel, worthy
> to manage the kingdom, through him flourishes the new order of

Ashridge, a new harvest grows for the Heaven-dweller (i.e. God)
on the high ridge.
A place/monastic place is built (being built?) at the expense of Earl
Edmund at Oxford, in which stay people who desire to learn.[13]

The Bury St Edmunds' chronicler, when referring to the death of Edmund, wrote that '*obiit pie memorie dominus Edmund Cornubie cuius pater fuit magnus Ricardus*'.[14] Maurice Powicke described him as the man 'who exceeded all other members in works of religious piety'.[15] There can be little doubt that the piety was real and this reputation lasted. In the 1660s, Anthony Wood wrote of Edmund as 'a great lover of religious orders'.[16] His father exercised a conventional piety and there is one piece of evidence that Sanchia had more than a normal religious commitment. A note in the handwriting of Matthew Paris on the flyleaf of a book containing a life of St Alban shows that she had borrowed a book that he had written on Thomas Becket and St Edmund.[17] This evidence proves that Edmund's mother was literate and, like his uncle, Montfort,[18] it can be assumed that Edmund himself was literate. Deidre Jackson, in the catalogue for the British Library's Royal Manuscripts exhibition of 2011–12, suggested that the Comestor Historia from Ashridge was commissioned for Edmund's personal use rather than as a gift to the Bonhommes.[19] Born in Champagne, Peter Comestor was attached for most of his life to Nôtre Dame de Paris where he died in 1178. His Historia was a popular sacred history starting with the Creation and covering the Bible up to and including the Acts of the Apostles. If it was owned and read by Edmund, it reinforces his reputation for personal piety and the evidence already set out demonstrates that his reputation for piety was well established.

Whilst Edmund's involvement with the Bonhommes shows a willingness to experiment with new forms of traditional Christianity, there is no indication that he was attracted to the Arthurian tradition which commended itself to his father and his cousin, Edward I.[20] Richard of Cornwall might have rebuilt the castle at Tintagel because of its traditional link with Arthur as fostered by Geoffrey of Monmouth. Richard even exchanged lands to obtain the site.[21] Although Edmund kept a constable and chaplain at Tintagel,[22] there is no record that Edmund ever visited it as Earl, although, as a boy, he might have been there with his father.

Was Edmund a man of courage? He was present during the rout of Lewes and had been imprisoned in at least three separate places but he had no choice as to his involvement. During this period he might have been threatened with murder on two occasions. He braved the uncertainty of a number of cross-Channel sailings and, above all, he joined the Lord Edward's crusade. As a crusader, he was prepared to face the dangers and rigours of an arduous campaign in a hostile environment. He might have witnessed the brutal murder of his half-brother and have been in danger himself. Edmund had experienced enough traumas to last a life-time before he became Earl. Although he took part in the first Welsh War, he did not take part in later Welsh or Scottish wars. This might be because he knew he could be more useful dealing with essential tasks back home. The only exception was when he led the royal armies into South Wales to put down the rebellion of Rhys ap Maredudd. With his overwhelmingly endowed forces, Edmund was in no personal danger but it should not be forgotten that Edward I was besieged in Conwy castle by Welsh rebels in the winter of 1294–95.

One biographer of Richard of Cornwall, Kieran S. Roche, was more sympathetic to Richard than others. He wrote: 'Never strong of physique, he (Richard) was centuries ahead of his time in preferring the art of mediation and diplomacy to the art of war.' He praised Richard's financial acumen and pointed out that 'despite his general aversion to conflict he could, when the need arose, take a swift decision and back it up with positive and daring action'. Richard was also 'seldom roused to the heights of Angevin anger which bedevilled his father and brother'.[23] Richard was not regarded as a soldier. Although these judgements appear too partial, there are echoes of his father's character in Edmund. Edmund seems to have been easy-going, although there were moments of anger over, for instance, the reaction to the Prior of Dunstable whose officials stopped his cart at Dunstable market and tried to levy a tax on Edmund's intended dinner. He was so wrathful that he persecuted the monks.[24] His anger with Bogo de Clare for his actions at Westminster Hall was clear. However, these seem to be isolated incidences although they might show that Edmund inherited the legendary Plantagenet temper.

As a boy, Edmund had travelled to the German imperial court. He would have been impressed by the ceremonial and the architecture and decoration of German cathedrals, churches, palaces and castles. But he must have known that it was never likely that he would become King of the Romans or Emperor himself. He would have been aware of the uncertainties and costs of an Imperial election. Even if his family had established a semi-hereditary claim on the throne, it would pass to his half-brother. By the time of his father's death, his young heir had no chance of retaining Richard's German status. Edmund possibly visited the French court, which was the epitome of artistic taste either as a young child or on his way to and from the crusade. His closeness to the King of England enabled him to see the latest styles in architecture and decoration in England. These experiences must have affected his aesthetic tastes, especially when he commissioned buildings. Although Ashridge was planned as a college for seven brethren, the building must have been far more substantial as Edmund lived there for long periods and it was large enough to accommodate a month's stay by the King including the feast of Christmas and a parliament. Edmund's continued commitment to the building and adornment of Hailes and Rewley Abbeys must also have been coloured by his architectural tastes.

Was Edmund a man influenced by splendour? His brother-in-law, Bogo, was, he had a gilt saddle covered with his embroidered arms.[25] Edmund's works at Hailes and Rewley were for the honour of God but Edmund had an interest in personal jewellery. He owned the bejewelled golden cross which he left to benefit religious orders and also a large ruby worth £1,000 which was given to Queen Margaret and an 'autre fermaille (a clasp) du doun Edmon Counte de Cornewaile a madame Isabelle, le seor, que poise quatre deniers'.[26]

Was Edmund a determined man? The evidence from his litigation is inconclusive. The prolonged dispute with Isabella de Fortibus might have stemmed from determination or stubbornness. However, the amount of legislation for a man with so many landed interests seems rather slight even though some cases were pursued for years. It is possible that he left his legal affairs to others and the long life of some actions was due to sheer inertia or the incompetence of his officials. However, there are two areas where firmness of purpose can be demonstrated. Edmund's continued religious patronage from an early age, shows a persistent commitment. The other area relates to his marriage. It is very clear that it was he who was keen to have a formal separation. He could have remained married to Margaret, living elsewhere on his extensive estates but he persisted in formalising their split. He was not seeking a divorce so that he could re-marry. Having been married for so long and Margaret having been pregnant, he would have had no legal case for an annulment. Edmund was adamant that the marriage should be known to have failed.

One characteristic not found in Edmund was a need to pursue grievances.[27] He was a man prepared to negotiate, to compromise. The negotiated final divorce settlement is one example whilst another was the agreement reached with his step-mother over her dower claims. He heeded urgings for leniency as seen in his willingness to settle his claims over the confrontation to him in Westminster Hall. At the bequest of the Bishops of Durham and Ely he settled[28] and his remittance of anger against the citizens of Exeter was at the request of the King's daughters.[29] Compliance with the wishes of the Queen and Chancellor led Edmund to settle the long running conflict with the Bishop of Exeter.

Completing a biography of Richard of Cornwall, Noel Denholm-Young felt able to write: 'Edmund ... seemed to have inherited his father's acquisitive habit.' He made this assessment based on Edmund's securing of a writ precluding the justices from proceeding with *Quo Warranto* cases in Oxfordshire in 1285.[30] This seems very thin justification for the assessment. Edmund might have been acquisitive but we cannot prove it.

One characteristic of Edmund that cannot be doubted was his loyalty. In nearly thirty years of service to Edward I, he never gave the King a moment of doubt as to his trustworthiness. One of Edward I's greatest assets was the constant support of his brother and cousin, the two Edmunds. Edmund of Cornwall did all that the King asked of him as well as being a major helper in raising money for regal activities. Throughout all the upheavals of the reign, Edmund had opportunities to take advantage of the King's weakness and become a focus for dissent. One might contrast his actions with those of Edward II's cousin, Thomas, Earl of Lancaster, who brought his King to his knees. One could question whether Edmund had anything to gain from fronting opposition to Edward I. He needed no more wealth, he had no long-standing grievances, and why should he have wanted to exert more control over, or even replace, the sovereign. But Thomas of Lancaster too was extremely rich and could have taken a back seat on political matters.

One reason for Edmund's apparent failure to use his wealth and position to achieve worldly success and fame might have stemmed from the fact that, until a few months before his father died, he had not expected to be his heir. Henry, his half-brother, was already a major player on the national scene and would have become one of the greatest men in the land. Edmund was not a knight and had no great prospects as a landholder or potential husband. He was not brought up to be a wealthy man. Unprepared for the greatness thrust upon him following Henry's murder, he might have found it difficult to adjust to his unexpected prominence. However, other people, who suddenly become powerful and wealthy, react in a different way both spending wildly and abusing their power. Edmund behaved in a more restrained way showing that he was sensible, level-headed and reliable.

There is no known description or depiction of Edmund's appearance. By his death, royal effigies such as those of Henry III and Eleanor of Castile could bear a resemblance to the persons they commemorated. Edmund's effigy might have been taken from his likeness but this is academic as it was destroyed. However, there is a later illustration of him. A version of the *Genealogical Chronicle of the English Kings* in the British Library shows the descendants of William I in roundels surrounded by coloured roundels with lines of descent shown in different colours. The roll has Edmund's head drawn on a gold background with a red bordure. His half-brother, Henry of Almain, faces him in a green circle and a blue background. Both men are shown with long curly hair and, unlike the King, they are clean shaven.[31]

Edmund shared exactly the same genes as Edward I. Their fathers were brothers and their mothers were sisters. It is likely that there was a pronounced resemblance between the two men. Huw Ridgeway wrote about Henry III: 'No contemporary description of Henry's appearance survives, suggesting that it was unremarkable.' Nicholas Trevet, son of a royal justice, recorded that Henry 'was of medium height and strong build, with a drooping eyelid covering part of the pupil'.[32] Can we assume that Edmund was as tall as his cousin, the King Edward I? Edward towered above other men and this was confirmed when his body was exhumed in 1774 and it was estimated that he must have been 6 foot, 2 inches tall.[33] Michael Prestwich emphasised the long length of Edward's arms and legs, hence his nickname 'Longshanks'.[34] Edmund's father, Richard, appeared to be shorter than Henry III but, according to Matthew Paris, 'his unwarlike nature was to be explained not by any specific physical infirmity but by a general lack of either martial spirit or good health'. Edmund was probably less striking than his cousin.[35] King Edward's brother, Edmund of Lancaster, known as 'Crouchback', also appears not to have had the impressive stature of his own brother. But one reading of 'Crouchback' as Cross Back indicated his entitlement to wear a cross as a crusader. Rhodes, in his 1895 article, stated that this epithet 'Crouchback' was not given to him by any contemporary. John of Gaunt's 1394 statement that Edmund of Lancaster was humpbacked, was strongly contradicted by the Earl of March, who said that it evidently appeared from the chronicles that Edmund was a handsome man and a noble knight.[36] However, Edmund of Cornwall and Edward I were likely to have had similar facial features and colouring. Marc Morris described Edward as being 'broad browed and broad chested, blond haired and handsome, despite having inherited a drooping eye lid from his father'.[37] Thus we might assume that Edmund himself was handsome and fair as a young man and might have inherited, like the famous Hapsburg lip, a drooping eye lid.

On the whole, Edmund's buildings have not fared well. Hailes Abbey is now a shell of itself. It was vast, having cloister walks, 12 feet wide around a 100 foot square garth. Edmund's tomb, said to be on the south side of the high altar, was swept away with most of Hailes Abbey following its surrender to Henry VIII in 1539,[38] but the destroyers found no use for the encaustic tiles which covered the floors. Some of these with their heraldic designs, celebrating Edmund, his mother and step-mother and his wife's family, are displayed at the abbey; others in Cheltenham Art Gallery.[39] A few carved bosses also remain at the abbey but these have been dated to the 1246–51 building.[40] David Verey, wrote: 'In the National Trust (actually English Heritage) Museum at Hailes, we can see some of the chapter house bosses close to and marvellously preserved they are. There is also part of the arm of Edmund of Cornwall's effigy, and elegant bits of the shrine, but compared with what must have been destroyed, they are almost as nothing.'[41] The latest English Heritage guidebook states: 'on view is part of a late thirteenth-century effigy of a knight, including portions of the forearm and three pieces of shield, the base of which has portions of the foot of a lion of Cornwall'. But this description of the shield pieces is not convincing. Indeed, it is difficult to believe that they were part of a shield. This book states that the pieces were found near the junction of the south transept and the presbytery aisle and 'it is not certain whether they belonged to Edmund, Earl of Cornwall or Sir Richard who died at Berwick'.[42]

Wall paintings in the parish church of Hailes were created two decades after Edmund's death but they feature the armorial bearings of Richard of Cornwall and his family. More encaustic tiles with possible connections to Edmund survive at Cleeve Abbey in Somerset. The refectory, built in the thirteenth century, has large areas of tiled floor. The heraldic designs on the tiles include the arms of England, the imperial arms of Richard of Cornwall and those of Edmund, or his father, as well as of the Clare family. It has been suggested that they commemorate the marriage of Edmund and Margaret de Clare.[43] But why they should be at Cleeve Abbey is not clear; there is no record of any connection between Edmund or the Clares and this house. They could have been bought from a tilery, possibly at Gloucester,[44] near the Clare mausoleum of Tewkesbury and have been available for whoever wanted tiled floors at the time.

Over 400 years after Edmund's death, the Portcullis Pursuivant, Richard Lee, recorded Edmund's arms in Ambrosden and Eynsham churches as well as in a house in Eynsham.[45] Those he noted in Dorchester Abbey are still there today; in the south-east window of the chancel being in the bottom right-hand corner above those of the Tyes family.[46]

High in the central tower of St Alban's Abbey, now the cathedral, there are four painted shields sited on the walls just under a painted ceiling. These depict the arms of Edmund as well as those of Edward I, Eleanor of Castile, and either Edward, Prince of Wales or Edmund, Earl of Lancaster. They might be intended commemorate the resting of the Queen's body on 13 December 1290 on its journey from her death place at Harby to Westminster.[47] The fourth shield assigned to Edward Prince of Wales by Rouse has a label of five points azure superimposed over the arms of England which are the arms born both by Edward of Caernarvon, Prince of Wales. and Edmund of Lancaster.[48] If the arms commemorate the death of Eleanor in 1290, it seems likely that Edmund of Lancaster would have been preferred to the 6-year old Edward.

Although Hailes Abbey is now a ruin, it should not be forgotten that Edmund's gift of the Holy Blood relic had an impact which lasted nearly three centuries. On 13 October 1247 Henry III led a procession from St Paul's Cathedral to Westminster Abbey where he presented a relic of the

Holy Blood to the monks. This had been given to him by the Patriarch of Jerusalem. Whilst it had royal support and certificates of verification and was given additional weight by episcopal indulgences, the Westminster relic never created a reputation to stimulate pilgrimages and subsequent wealth. By contrast, through careful nurturing, the Hailes relic implanted itself in the national consciousness and its reputation far outstripped that of Westminster. Vincent argued that this was partly because there was never any doubt about the provenance of the Hailes relic. It was unusual for relics to originate in Jerusalem which had been the scene of violent turmoil for centuries in contrast to the relics coming from Constantinople. There were historical facts supporting the provenance of the Hailes relic and its German origin.[49] Chaucer referred to the 'Blood of Christ that is Hailes' in the *Pardoner's Tale* and the shrine was wealthy enough to have been robbed of 1,000 marks in the fifteenth century. Bishop Latimer of Gloucester, writing in 1533, mentioned flocks of pilgrims traveling to the shrine and in 1535, the shrine still brought in at least £10 per year. But, three years later, it was attacked by the Bishop of Rochester who suggested that the blood was that of a duck. In the late 1540s its veracity was attacked again. Bishop Latimer reported that the blood was kept in a beryl which was garnished on every side with silver but, although it looked red, when it was taken out, it was found to be yellow. By then, the Dissolution had swept away the abbey.[50]

The coming of the railways led to the almost complete and final destruction of all that remained of Rewley Abbey. In 1851, it became the site of Oxford's Rewley Road station, the terminus for the Buckinghamshire Railway. It remained in use as a good's yard until 1984. Most of the site now lies under the Said Business School. However, in Rewley Road near the terminus of the Oxford Canal, there is still a small ancient gateway which once gave access to the abbey.

Ashridge College was swept away and replaced in 1813 by a building designed by James Wyatt for the Earl of Bridgewater. At the time, the Earl's chaplain recorded that in the Rectory or Convent Hall there was a series of arms in the glass windows. One was argent, a lion rampant gules within a bordure azure bezanty: the arms of Edmund. In the new building a series of sculptures were placed on the grand staircase where they still remain. One represents Edmund whilst two depict his father and mother.[51]

The Peter Comestor book from Ashridge, held by the British Library, is a 322 folio volume, beautifully written, with extensive use of red, blue and black ink as well as gold leaf. There are nineteen illuminated capitals or insets depicting amongst other subjects, Esther, and Church and Synagogue as well as extensive foliage-like decoration and vignettes of birds such as the chaffinch, magpie and stork. There are also real and imaginary animals. A rabbit blows a trumpet. Some monsters look like dragons and one appears to be a dinosaur with a dog's head. Humour is shown by a king with a bird's body. On one folio, at the start of the narrative on the New Testament, there are the heraldic arms of England, the Empire and Prince Edward, the future Edward II as well as those of Edmund himself.[52]

This page has been described as having a 'broad band with a most delicate pattern of blue and brown ground' which 'expands with cusped scrolls ending in ivy and oak leaves'. Animals and birds include a 'peacock with a grey-blue body, sapphire blue neck with an emerald neckband, dove-grey back and golden headpiece and tail'. This 'is so beautifully painted that the effect of soft texture and brilliant colour is achieved'.[53] Although, one critic thought that the style of the book was 'emphatically Frenchified'.[54] Briegel opined that it is a direct offspring of the bible of William of Devon. William, who may have worked at Oxford, was unusual as an English scribe who signed his work and showed the impact of the first wave of French, primarily Parisian, influence that played in the development of English art from the 1260s onwards. In the book, this influence showed 'itself both in terms of style (for example the adoption of so-called 'broad fold' draperies), and iconography: the Psalm initials in the present Bible are almost entirely dependent on French rather than English traditions'.[55] Briegel believed that 'the quality of the work is worthy of the most exacting patron.' He suggested that the painting of a banquet was similar to that shown in another British Library manuscript from the Cotton Collection, Vitellus A XII folio 3.[56]

Possibly at the same time as he gifted the book to Ashridge, Edmund might also have donated a *Mappa Mundi*, of which a fragment remains in the Duchy of Cornwall office. The curators of the *Magnificent Maps* exhibition at the British Library in 2010 asserted that the illustrations in the Comestor book and the map are in the same hand; but I am not convinced.[57]

Although there few traces of Edmund's religious buildings, Restormel castle, sited at the then lowest bridging point of the Fowey with its astonishing shell keep, is still a striking monument. It is now looked after by English Heritage. It was a sophisticated building, set in a large deer park and included an hydraulic system to supply water from a natural spring under pressure to the garderobes.[58] Nearby, at Lostwithiel, the palace built by Edmund was restored in 2012 by the Prince's Regeneration Trust in partnership with the Cornwall Buildings Preservation Trust.[59] Edmund's Trematon castle was let by the Duchy of Cornwall in 1961 to the eminent political family, the Foots. Lord Caradon (Sir Hugh Foot) lived there and it was where his son, the left-wing journalist, Paul Foot, spent his childhood. Sadly the castle is closed to the public.

An outstanding exhibit in the Medieval Galleries of the Victoria and Albert Museum is the Clare chasuble. A fine piece of *Opus Anglicanum*, the arms on the reverse are those of Edmund and Margaret de Clare which dates it to the period from their marriage until their separation, i.e. 1272 to 1294. Briegel believed that it was in the style of a lost frontal. It has a blue ground with thin and elastic foliated scrolls. These enclose lions and griffons 'as elegantly lively as the animals on the Westminster tiles'.[60] In the centre there is a broad orphrey embroidered in gold, silver and silk threads with four quatrefoils. In turn, the T contained four scenes: the Crucifixion, The Virgin and Child, St Paul and St Peter, and the Martyrdom of St Stephen. Briegel, quoting Christie, noted that the 'faces are worked in split stitch, in lines following the contour of the features, and the cheeks are stitched in indented spirals'. He then went on to write that 'This is the earliest example of such treatment in existing English medieval embroidery, and it continued in use throughout the "great period" until the decline set in towards the middle of the fourteenth century.'[61]

Conclusion

Wealthy, generous, loyal and pious, Edmund of Almain, Earl of Cornwall, was one of the most prominent men of his time. He did not push himself forward; he had no need to. He was of royal blood and maintained his dignity. His actions as a lender of money to the King and other great men helped to oil the wheels of state. He carried out his duties as the King's deputy and as his Regent with unspectacular dedication and, despite the criticisms of armchair historians of the last two centuries, managed to crush a potentially serious threat to the realm whilst the King and his well-trained logistical and administrative machine was abroad. With one brief exception during the rebellion of Rhys ap Maredudd, which was soon to be corrected, no royal criticism of him as an administrator or military commander has survived. His activities in the law courts do not show him as a grasping and aggressive man; the complaints of the monks of Dunstable are an isolated example. Edmund won golden opinions for his works at Hailes Abbey and for endowing it and his new foundation of Ashridge with the Holy Blood relic. His other new foundation, that of Rewley Abbey, was important to the development of scholarship at Oxford University. A man of taste and sensibility, Edmund of Cornwall was an ornament to his Plantagenet family and, despite Emily Holt's misplaced over-enthusiasm for him, he deserves a better historical reputation.

Genealogical Table A   Edmund of Almain, Earl of Cornwall's paternal family

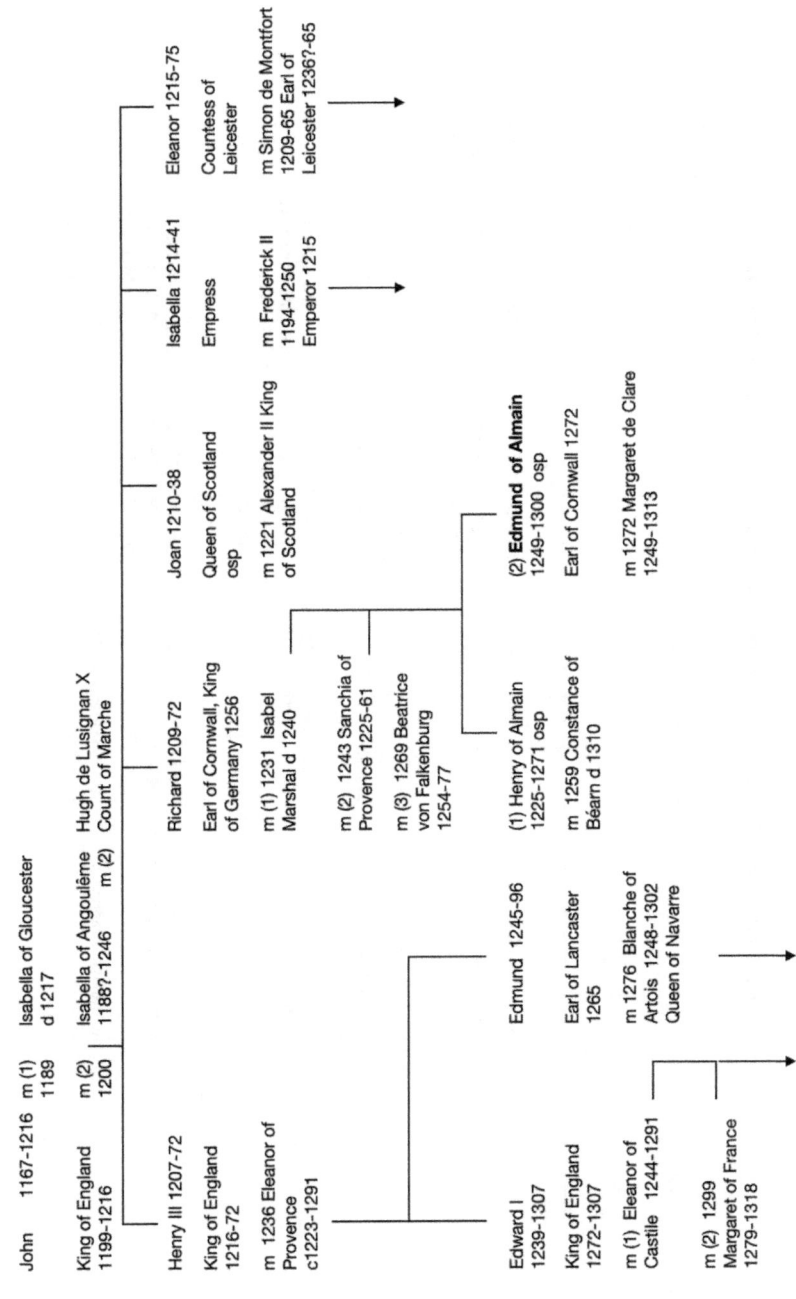

John   1167-1216   m (1)   Isabella of Gloucester
                    1189   d 1217

                    m (2)   Isabella of Angoulême   Hugh de Lusignan X
                    1200   11887-1246   m (2)   Count of Marche

King of England
1199-1216

Henry III 1207-72   Richard 1209-72   Joan 1210-38   Isabella 1214-41   Eleanor 1215-75

King of England   Earl of Cornwall, King   Queen of Scotland   Empress   Countess of
1216-72   of Germany 1256   osp   Leicester

m 1236 Eleanor of   m (1) 1231 Isabel   m 1221 Alexander II King   m Frederick II   m Simon de Montfort
Provence   Marshal d 1240   of Scotland   1194-1250   1209-65 Earl of
c1223-1291   Emperor 1215   Leicester 12367-65

                           m (2) 1243 Sanchia of
                           Provence 1225-61

                           m (3) 1269 Beatrice
                           von Falkenburg
                           1254-77

                           (1) Henry of Almain   (2) Edmund of Almain
                           1225-1271 osp   1249-1300 osp

Edmund 1245-96   m 1259 Constance of   Earl of Cornwall 1272
                           Béarn d 1310

Earl of Lancaster
1265   m 1272 Margaret de Clare
                                                                           1249-1313

m 1276 Blanche of
Artois 1248-1302
Queen of Navarre

Edward I
1239-1307

King of England
1272-1307

m (1) Eleanor of
Castile 1244-1291

m (2) 1299
Margaret of France
1279-1318

Genealogical Table B Edmund of Almain, Earl of Cornwall's maternal family

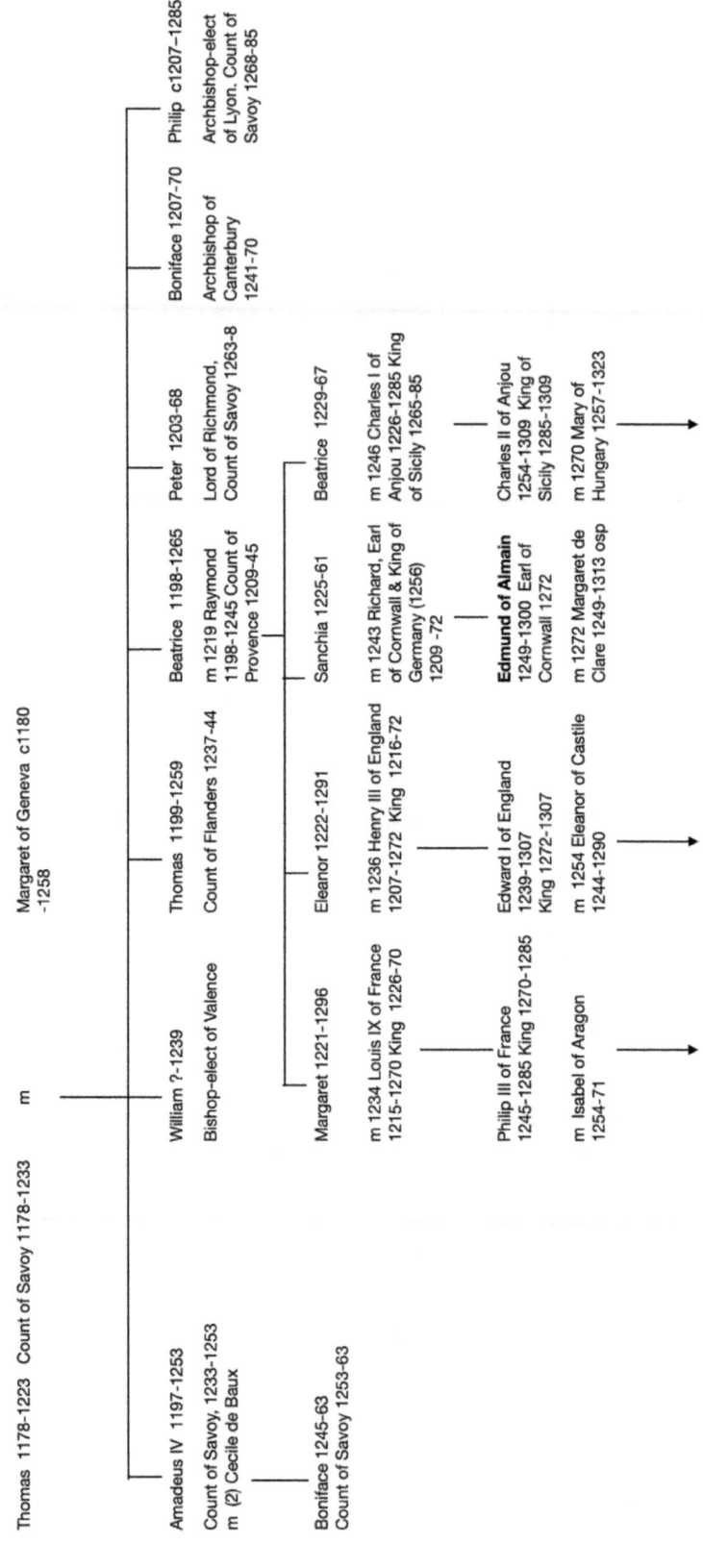

Notes

Preface
1. Barbara Brandon Schnorrenberg, 'Holt, Emily Sarah (1836–1893)', ODNB, online edn, May 2010.
2. Holt, *Not for Him, the Story of a Forgotten Hero*, especially pages 27, 50 and 139.
3. *CPR 1292–1301*, 63–5.

Chapter 1
1. Vincent, *Peter des Roches*, 510.
2. Michael of Northampton was the son of Simon de Houton, *CPR 1247–58*, 328: *CChR 1257–1300*, 181.
3. *Historia Minor*, iii, 68; *Chronica Majora*, v, 94; *Annals of Hailes*, 64.
4. *Complete Peerage*, iii, 431.
5. Midgley, 'Edmund of Cornwall', 7.
6. Cox, *The Eagles of Savoy;* Howell, *Eleanor of Provence.*
7. *Historia Minor*, iii, 68.
8. Westerhoff, *Death and the Noble Body in Medieval England*, 60.
9. Vincent, *The Holy Blood* , 9–10.
10. Denholm-Young, *Richard of Cornwall*, 62.
11. Denholm-Young, *Richard of Cornwall*, 80.
12. Denholm-Young, *Richard of Cornwall*, 3.
13. *ODNB*, 26, 567.
14. Maddicott, *Simon de Montfort*, 4 and 6; Bémont, *Simon de Montfort*, 2.
15. Morris, *A Great and Terrible King*, 6–7.
16. TNA:PRO E 101/349/12 m.2.
17. Wilkinson, *Eleanor de Montfort*, 9.
18. *Wykes,* 116; *Gervase of Canterbury*, 206.
19. *Chronica Majora*, vi, 735–6.
20. Denholm-Young, *Richard of Cornwall*, 153.
21. For the events of 1258 and their aftermath see D. Carpenter, 'What Happened in 1258?', *The Reign of Henry III*,183 – 197 and an excellent narrative of the whole period of Baronial Reform, Jobson, *The First English Revolution.*
22. Denholm-Young, *Richard of Cornwall*, 99.
23. Wilkinson, *Eleanor de Montfort*, 96 – 102.
24. Jobson, *The First English Revolution*, 51 – 2.
25. Denholm-Young, *Richard of Cornwall*, 104 – 5.
26. Denholm-Young, *Richard of Cornwall*, 112 – 3.
27. Howell, *Eleanor of Provence*, 195.
28. Jobson, *The First English Revolution*, 152.
29. For the battle see Carpenter, *The Battles of Lewes and Evesham 1264/5* and Blaauw, *The Barons' War*, 163–220.
30. *Flores Historiarum*, iii, 260.

31. *Annals of Hailes,* 69.
32. *Robert of Gloucester,* 751 – 2.
33. *Annals of Hailes,* 70.
34. Labarge, *Mistress, Maids and Men,* 135 and 161; *Manners and Household Expenses,* 13–14, 25–26 and 71.
35. *Metrical Chronicle,* 756 – 7.
36. BL MS Cleopatra D. III, fo.45; Maddicott, *Simon de Montfort,* 335.
37. *The Chronicle of William de Rishanger,* 50 – 1.
38. *Chronica de Mailros,*196; *ODNB,* 46, 710.
39. *Wykes,* 175.
40. *Annals of Hailes,* 72.
41. *CPR 1258–66,* 450 and 453. Also see 495.
42. Blaauw, *The Barons' War* (second edition, 1871), 331.
43. Jobson, *The First English Revolution,* 152 and 159.
44. *Merton Muniments Selected and Edited by P.S. Allen and H.W. Garrod,* 27.
45. The official guide book to Hailes Abbey states that Edmund bought the relic from the Count of Flanders in 1267, Coad, *Hailes Abbey, Gloucestershire,* 19.
46. Baddeley misread Bolanden as Holland and assumed that the relic had been obtained from Florence V, Count of Holland, St Clair Baddeley, 'The Holy Blood of Hayles', 277.
47. BL. MS Cotton Cleopatra D iii, fs. 46r-v (44 r-v); Vincent, *The Holy Blood,* 140 – 5 and 206–8.
48. TNA:PRO CP 40/6 ms. 71 and 91.
49. Denholm-Young, *Richard of Cornwall,* 140 – 1.
50. Huscroft, 'Robert Burnell and The Government of England 1270–74', 61 and 63.
51. Vincent, *The Holy Blood,* 150.
52. Tyerman, *England and the Crusades,* 128.
53. Denholm-Young, *Richard of Cornwall,* 150.
54. *Wykes,* 241.
55. Maddicott, *Simon de Montfort,* 370–1; Blaauw, *The Barons' War,* 342–5; *ODNB,* 26, 568–9; Montfort's head, feet, hands and testicles had been severed. His testicles were hung from his nose and the head was sent to Maud, the wife of Roger de Mortimer, *De Antiquis Legibus Liber,* 75; *Wykes,* 173–5.
56. Studd, 'The Marriage of Henry of Almain and Constance de Béarn', 169 – 70 and 177.
57. The viscera were buried in Viterbo cathedral, *ODNB,* 26, 568–9.
58. Dante, *The Divine Comedy,* 52.
59. *ODNB,* 26, 568–9.
60. *Annales Monastici,* iv, 244.
61. Denholm-Young, *Richard of Cornwall,* 152.
62. *CFR 1271–72,* 621–5; *CPR 1266 – 72,* 647.
63. TNA:PRO E 36/57 fo.38v.

Chapter 2

1. *Giffard Worcester Register,* 51.
2. *CPR 1266–72,* 668 – 9.
3. *CPR 1266–72,* 657.
4. *CChR 1257–1300,* 183.
5. Roth, *A History of the Jews in England,* 67; *CPR 1266 – 72,* 67.
6. *CPR 1266–72,* 654; Roth, *A History of the Jews in England,* 274.
7. *CPR 1266–72,* 654 – 5.

8. *De Antiquis Legibus Liber*, 154. The chapel was probably part of the castle/priory complex at Ruislip. For the marriage see Chapter 7. It is not clear why Ruislip was chosen. Edmund held the adjoining manor of Ickenham but it was sub-infeudated.
9. *Wykes*, 251.
10. Huscroft, 'Robert Burnell and the Government of England, 1270–1274', 59–70.
11. *CCR 1272–799*, 1.
12. Morris, *A Great and Terrible King*, 134.
13. Davies, *Domination and Conquest*, 308f.
14. Also the boundary between the dioceses of Hereford and St Asaph.
15. *Foedera*, i, 498; *CCR 1272–79*, 2.
16. *CCR 1272–79*, 7.
17. *CCR 1272–79*, 47.
18. *Bronescombe Register*, ii, 1429.
19. TNA:PRO E 159/47 m.5.
20. *CPR 1272–81*, 11.
21. TNA:PRO E 36/274 (Exchequer Liber A), fo.cciv.r.
22. LACCE, 22/40.
23. *ODNB*, 17, 771.
24. LACCE, 16/67.
25. *Itinerary*, i, 45.
26. *WL Edward I*, 4.
27. *PW*, i, part 2, 550.
28. *Itinerary*, i, 57.
29. *Itinerary*, i, 60.
30. *CCR 1272–79*, 303.
31. *PW*, i, part 2, 550; *Foedera*, i, 535.
32. *Itinerary*, i, 60.
33. *PW*, i, part 2, 550.
34. *PW*, i,198 and part 2, 550.
35. Morris, *The Welsh Wars of Edward I*, 60.
36. *CPR 1272–81*, 242.
37. *Complete Peerage*, iii, 432. The dispute over this will be dealt with in a later chapter.
38. LACCE, 10/26.
39. 1278–82, LACCE, 25/20A.
40. *CFR 1272–1307*, 90.
41. *Itinerary*, i, 81, 88 and 94.
42. Lloyd, *English Society and the Crusade*, 99 and note.
43. *CCR 1272–79*, 505; *PW*, i, part 2, 550.
44. *CPR 1272–81*, 309–10; *Foedera*, i, 568.
45. *Itinerary*, i, 98.
46. Kaeuper, *Bankers to the Crown*, 91 citing TNA:PRO E 101/352/15.
47. *CPR 1272–81*, 375.
48. *WL Edward I*, 23.
49. *Itinerary*, i, 110.
50. *Itinerary*, i, 117.
51. Morris, *A Great and Terrible King*, 161–2.
52. *Foedera*, i, 608, *PW*, i, part 2, 550.
53. *Welsh Rolls*, 217.
54. *Scutage Rolls*, 374.
55. *CPR 1281–92*, 19.

56. *CPR 1281–92*, 18.
57. *Foedera*, i, 608.
58. *CPR 1281–92*, 35; *CFR 1272–1307*, 168.
59. *CCR 1279–88*, 165.
60. *PW*, i, part 2, 550.
61. e.g. *CPR 1281–92*, 33.
62. *PW*, i, part 2, 550, *Registrum epistolarum fratris Johannis Peckham*, 501; Douie, *Pecham*, 255; Ramsay, *The Dawn of the Constitution*, 344–6.
63. *Welsh Rolls*, 269.
64. *CPR 1281–92*, 36.
65. *Scutage Rolls*, 365.
66. *CPR 1281–92*, 98.
67. *WL Edward I*, 49 and 50.
68. *CPR 1281–92*, 120.
69. *Quivel Register*, 361; TNA:PRO E 36/57 fo.14v.
70. *WL Edward I*, 57–8.
71. *Itinerary*, i, 181–206.
72. *WL Edward I*, 58–79.
73. *CPR 1281–92*, 248.

Chapter 3
1. Midgley, 'Edmund of Cornwall', 147.
2. Morris, *A Great and Terrible King*, 221.
3. Tout, *Chapters*, ii, 65–6.
4. Midgley, 'Edmund of Cornwall', 134–5.
5. TNA:PRO SC 1/25/ 43–60 provides some evidence for this. Tout noted that Edmund spent Christmas 1287 at Berkhamsted, Tout, *Chapters*, ii, 63.
6. TNA:PRO SC 1/25/59; *CFR 1272–1307*, 247.
7. TNA:PRO SC 1/25/55 and 56 and 1/12/147.
8. TNA:PRO SC 1/25/54–75.
9. For the rebellion see Morris, *The Welsh Wars of Edward I*, 204–19.
10. *CACW*, 168.
11. *Welsh Rolls*, 306.
12. *Foedera*, i, 675.
13. *Welsh Rolls*, 306–7.
14. *Welsh Rolls*, 311–2.
15. *Welsh Rolls*, 309–10.
16. *Welsh Rolls*, 312.
17. *Welsh Rolls*, 312–3.
18. *Welsh Rolls*, 312; *Giffard Worcester Register*, 313.
19. *Welsh Rolls*, 313–4.
20. *CFR 1272–1307*, 238.
21. *CFR 1272–1307*, 239.
22. *CACW*, 46–7; LACCE, 10/129; *Welsh Rolls*, 313.
23. CTNA:PRO SC 1/25/67 and 68.
24. Morris, 206–7.
25. *WL Edward I*, 27.
26. Griffiths, 'The Revolt of Rhys ap Maredudd 1287–8', 121–43, at 133; *Brut y Tywysogyon*, 121; Taylor, 'Who was "John Penardd, Leader of the Men of Gwynedd?"', 88.

27. *Welsh Rolls*, 311.
28. Morris, *The Welsh Wars of Edward I*, 214; *Welsh Rolls*, 315.
29. *Welsh Rolls*, 317.
30. Morris, *The Welsh Wars of Edward I*, 218.
31. Davies, *The Age of Conquest*, 381.
32. Prestwich, *Edward I* (1988), 219; Morris, *A Great and Terrible King*, 217.
33. Salzmann, *Edward I* (1968), 76.
34. Taylor, 'The King's Works in Wales 1277–1300', 398–9.
35. Kaeuper, *Bankers to the Crown*, 195–6.
36. *CACW*, 174–5; Prestwich, *Plantagenet England*, 137.
37. *Welsh Rolls*, 319–20.
38. *Welsh Rolls*, 319.
39. Owen de la Pole acknowledged the order and confirmed that he would comply, *CACW*, 166.
40. *Welsh Rolls*, 321–3.
41. *Welsh Rolls*, 323.
42. *Welsh Rolls*, 321.
43. *Welsh Rolls*, 306–7.
44. *Welsh Rolls*, 307.
45. *Welsh Rolls*, 308.
46. *Welsh Rolls*, 307.
47. *Welsh Rolls*, 307–8.
48. *Welsh Rolls*, 308.
49. *Welsh Rolls*, 312.
50. *Welsh Rolls*, 315.
51. *Welsh Rolls*, 317–8.
52. *Welsh Rolls*, 314.
53. *Welsh Rolls*, 314–5.
54. *Welsh Rolls*, 315.
55. *Welsh Rolls*, 318.
56. *Welsh Rolls*, 319.
57. *Welsh Rolls*, 232.
58. Kaeuper, *Bankers to the Crown*, 133.
59. *CLB London A*, 122.
60. *HBC*, 548; *CCR 1288–96*, 7.
61. *Registrum epistolarum fratris Johannis Peckham*, iii, 961.
62. *CPR 1281–92*, 392.

Chapter 4

1. *Itinerary*, ii, 73–77.
2. *Parliament Rolls*, 54.
3. e.g. *Foedera*, i, 822; *CCR 1288–96*, 461; *PW*, i, part 2, 551.
4. *PW*, i, part 2, 550.
5. *Itinerary*, ii, 92 and 110.
6. *CPR 1292–1301*, 71.
7. *PW*, i, part 2, 550.
8. *PW*, i, part 2, 551.
9. *CCR 1288–96*, 484.
10. *CCR 1296–1302*, 81; *PW*, i, part 2, 551.
11. For the background and the chronology of the crisis see Prestwich, *Documents Illustrating the Crisis of 1297–8 in England*, 1–37.

12. *CCR 1296–1302*, 47.
13. *PW*, i, part 2, 551.
14. Gemmill, 'The Ecclesiastical Patronage of the Earls during the Reign of Edward', 73.
15. *WL Edward I*,132.
16. *Foedera*, i, 914.
17. *Foedera*, i, 899.
18. *CCR 1296–1302*, 291; *PW*, i, part 1, 320.
19. *CCR 1296–1302*, 294–5; *PW*, i, part 2, 551.
20. *PW*, i, part 2, 551.
21. *CCR 1296–1302*, 306 and 313; *PW*, i, part 2, 551; *Foedera*, i, 908.
22. *CCR 1296–1302*, 265.
23. *CCR 1296–1302*, 373–4; *Foedera*, i, 916; *PW*, i, part 1, 327.
24. *CPR 1292–1301*, 510.
25. *Itinerary*, ii, 188.
26. *CCR 1296–1302*, 407; *Foedera*, i, 922.
27. TNA: PRO E 372/146 m.31d.
28. TNA: PRO E 372/144 m.8d.
29. White Kennett, *Parochial Antiquities*, i, 483.
30. Galbraith, 'The St Edmundsbury Chronicle 1296–1301', 75.
31. *Annales Monastici*, iv, 547.
32. *Annals of Hailes*, 114; Westerhoff, *Death and the Noble Body*, 79, 82 and 90; BL MS Harley 3725 (The Hailes Chronicle), f.19r.
33. *Annals of Hailes*, 114; White Kennett, *Parochial Antiquities*, i, 483.
34. Blaauw, 'The Visit of King Edward II to Battle', 50.
35. *CCR 1296–1302*, 480; White Kennett, *Parochial Antiquities*, i, 483.

Chapter 5
1. *WL Edward I*, 132.
2. *Foedera*, i, 914.
3. *WL Edward I*, 4–132 *passim*.
4. *WL Edward I*, xi-xvi.
5. *WL Edward I*, 35–6.
6. *CPR 1272–81*, 426.
7. *WL Edward I*, 4.
8. *WL Edward I*, 17 (10 and 12).
9. *WL Edward I*, x.
10. *WL Edward I*, 132 (9).
11. *WL Edward I*, 50 (1) and 89 (54).
12. Spencer, 'Royal Charters and Charter Witnessing under Edward I', paper given to the International Medieval Congress.
13. Prestwich, 'Royal Patronage under Edward I', 41–52.
14. *CCR 1272–79*, 303 and 468; *CCR 1279–88*, 95, 99 and 144; *CCR 1288–96*, 368.
15. *RWH 1286–89*, 1988.
16. *CPR 1281–92*, 35, 77, 288 and 364; *CCR 1279–88*, 396 and 509.
17. See later chapter.
18. Harcourt, 'The Amercement of Barons by their Peers', 738.
19. *CChW*, 25.
20. *CPR 1272–81*, 238.
21. Information from Professor Paul Brand.
22. *WL Edward I*, 17–21.

23. *CPR, 1281–92*, 70.
24. *CPR 1281–92*, 14.
25. *WL Edward I*, 22.
26. *CPR 1281–92*, 258.
27. e.g, TNA:PRO E 36/57 fo.66v.
28. *CPR 1291–1301*, 468.

Chapter 6

1. *Annales Monastici*, iv, xxx. The translation is from Vincent, *ODNB*, 46, 711.
2. *ODNB*, 46, 711.
3. 'Richard that thou be ever trichard, trichen shalt thou never more.' Wright, *Political Songs*, 69.
4. *ODNB*, 46, 711; Jobson, *The First English Revolution*, 51, 52, 71, 96, 103, 152 and 159.
5. *ODNB*, 46, 711.
6. Westerhoff, *Death and the Noble Body*, 60.
7. See chapter 11.
8. BL Ms Lansdowne 203 f.37v-38r; Medway Archives Office, D and C Rochester DRb/A2 f15v; Bodleian Rawlinson B 455 f.24r; *CChR 1300–26*, 490; *St Frideswide's Cartulary*, ii, no.1101.
9. *Monasticon*, v, part 1, 517; BL Ms Lansdowne 203 f.37v-38r; BL Ms Stowe 882; *Fountains Chartulary*, 689; *The Cartulary of St Michael's Mount*, no.4; Bodleian Ms Twyne 24, 647; *CPR 1377–81*, 114–5.
10. Todd, *Ashridge*, 4.
11. *CChR 1257–1300*, 209; *CPR 1307–13*, 448.
12. *Eye Cartulary*, no.109.
13. *CPR 1292–1301*, 608.
14. BL Harley charter 84 C11; *Oseney Cartulary*, v, no.869; TNA:PRO E 36/57 f.8r.
15. Howell, *Eleanor of Provence*, 2.
16. Cox, *The Eagles of Savoy*, 114–5.
17. Howell, *Eleanor of Provence*, 34.
18. Denholm-Young, *Richard of Cornwall*, 112.
19. Roche, *The King of Almayne*, 166–7.
20. Bazeley, 'The Abbey of St Mary, Hayles', 257–8.
21. TNA:PRO E 101/349/26 m.8; Howell, *Eleanor of Provence*, 185.
22. BL ms Lansdowne 203 f.37v-38r.
23. *VCH Oxfordshire*, ii, 103–4; *CChR 1257–1300*, 269.
24. Todd, *Ashridge*, 4.
25. Bodleian Ms Rawlinson B 455, f.24r; *CChR 1300–26*, 490; TNA:PRO E 36/57 f.14v; *CChR 1300–26*, 490.
26. Midgley, 'Edmund of Cornwall', 65.
27. *The Itinerary of John Leland*, 129. He is followed by Wood, *The Survey of the Antiquities of the City of Oxford*, 299.
28. Howell, *Eleanor of Provence*, 91–2.
29. Lewis, 'Beatrice of Falkenburg, the third wife of Richard of Cornwall', 281.
30. *Wykes*, 224–5.
31. Lewis, 'Beatrice of Falkenburg', 282. For Beatrix's charter safeguarding the interests of her new step-sons and more details of thee suits see chapter 14 and in *The Earliest English Law Reports, volume 1; Common Bench Reports to 1284*, 21–7.
32. TNA:PRO KB 26/208A m.18.
33. *Rotuli Gravesend*, 120.

34. TNA:PRO CP 40/5 m.17 and 40/6 ms. 71 and 91.

35. *Foedera*, i, 544.

36. *CCR 1272–79*, 268.

37. TNA:PRO CP 40/14 m.27.

38. *Giffard Worcester Register*, 91.

39. TNA:PRO E36/274 (Exchequer Liber A) f.269r.

40. *ODNB*, 26, 566–9.

41. TNA:PRO CP 40/11 m.62d.

42. Studd, 'The Marriage of Henry of Almain and Constance de Béarn', 160–79.

43. White Kennett, *Parochial Antiquities*, i, 486.

44. Lysons and Lysons, *Magna Britannia: volume 3: Cornwall*, cxxix.

45. *CPR 1272–81*, 395.

46. *CIPM*, iii, 482, 483, 487 and 488; Midgley, 'Edmund of Cornwall', xx.

47. *Ministers' Accounts*, 201.n.

48. *Annals of Hailes*, 102; BL MS Harley 3725 (The Hailes Chronicle), f.19r.

49. *Supplementary Close Rolls*, 67 and 72.

50. *CPR 1301–07*, 332.

51. *Sutton Rolls*, viii, 29, 163 and 167.

52. *CPR 1292–1301*, 499; Moor, *Knights*, i, 240.

53. Lysons and Lysons, *Magna Britannia*, cxxvii.

54. Medway Archives Office, D and C Rochester DRb/A2 f15v; *CChR 1257–1300*, 209.

55. Howell, *Eleanor of Provence*, 136.

56. *Foedera*, i, 922.

57. TNA:PRO E 36/57 f.14v; *CChR 1257–1300*, 209.

58. Tout, *Edward the First*, 77 and 79.

59. *ODNB*, 17, 757.

60. *Giffard Worcester Register*, 51; *CPR 1266–72*, 668–9.

61. *Wykes*, 243–4.

62. *WL Edward I*, 4–122 *passim*.

63. *CPR 1281–92*, 372–3.

64. LACCE, 30/39.

65. LACCE, 30/38.

66. *Ledger Book of Vale Royal*, 49.

67. *Welsh Rolls*, 313–4.

68. Parsons, *Eleanor of Castile*, 174.

69. TNA:PRO E329/191.

70. Parsons, *Eleanor of Castile*, 202, no.33.

71. Chaplais, *Piers Gaveston*, 126.

72. *The Chronicle of William de Rishanger*, 50–1.

73. Labarge, *Mistress, Maids and Men*, 135 and 161; *Manners and Household Expenses*, 13–14 and 23.

74. *Manners and Household Expenses of England*, 25–26.

75. Todd, *Ashridge*, 4.

76. *HMC, Exeter*, 3 no.XV.

Chapter 7

1. *CFR 1271–72*, 621.

2. Howell, *Eleanor of Provence*, 245–6.

3. Studd, 'The Marriage of Henry of Almain and Constance de Béarn', 161–79.

4. *WL Henry III*.

5. 'Twelve miles west of London', *De Antiquis Legibus Liber*, 154; *Annals of Hailes*, 80.
6. *Annals of Hailes*, 62.
7. *ODNB*, 46, 703.
8. *ODNB*, xi, 746–50.
9. *Complete Peerage*, v, 700–02.
10. *ODNB*, xi, 768–9.
11. *ODNB*, xi, 742–3.
12. *Complete Peerage*, v, 701.
13. Parsons, ed. *Medieval Queenship*, 66–8.
14. Wilkinson, *Eleanor de Montfort*, 24 and 58.
15. *CIPM*, v, no. 363.
16. Altschul, *A Baronial Family in Medieval England*, 51.
17. *VCH Buckinghamshire*, iv, 289; *Feudal Aids, 1*, 83.
18. *Pontissara Register*, 300.
19. TNA:PRO PRO 66/3/1, ps. 584 and 685.
20. *Complete Peerage*, ii, 127.
21. *Sutton Rolls*, iii, lxxii.
22. *ODNB*, 11, 750.
23. *Complete Peerage*, v, 702.
24. *Registrum Peckham*, 995–6.
25. *Giffard Worcester Register*, 360, *Pecham Register*, ii, 246.
26. *Sutton Rolls*, iii, 54.
27. *Pontissara Register*, 378.
28. *Sutton Rolls*, iii, 33–36; Douie, *John Pecham*, 226.
29. *Registrum epistolarum fratris Johannis Peckham*, 982.
30. *Sutton Rolls*, iii, 33–36; *Rotuli Parliamentorum*), 17a; *Reg Epist Peckham*, iii, 969.
31. *CPR 1281–92*, 420.
32. *ODNB*, xi, 734; *Parliamentary Rolls*, 174–6.
33. *ODNB*, xi, 734.
34. *CPR 1292–1301*, 63–5; The translation of Margaret's document is from *EHD*, iii, no.202.
35. *WL Edward I*, 119.
36. He had only a few months to live but he died suddenly in December, *ODNB*, xi, 743.
37. Greenway, *Fasti Ecclesiae Anglicanae 1066–1300: volume 1: St. Paul's, London*, 8.
38. Schofield, *Medieval London Houses*, 231.
39. *VCH Surrey*, ii, 75.
40. *CIPM*, v, no.363.
41. *CIPM*, iii, no. 604, 482–89.
42. TNA:PRO CP 40/110 m.229d.
43. *CPL*, ii, 11. She also successfully intervened with the Pope to obtain permission for her 20-year old nephew, Richard who was the son of Thomas de Clare, to hold benefices in Ireland and York worth £200 and not to be ordained as he was studying, *ibid*, 12.
44. *Complete Peerage*, iii, 433.
45. White Kennett, *Parochial Antiquities*, i, 463.
46. thepeerage.com/p10684.htm citing A. Weir, *Britain's Royal Family*, 69.
47. *Complete Peerage*, v, 707.
48. Wilkinson, *Eleanor de Montfort*, 32.
49. BL Ms Cotton Cleopatra A vii fos. 70–106.
50. *The Chartulary of St John of Pontefract*.
51. *The Percy Chartulary*, Surtees Society, cxvii (1911), 318.

52. *Cartularium Abbathiae de Rievalle*, 273.
53. *The Chartulary of the Priory of Lewes*, i, 52; *The Surrey Portion of the Chartulary of St Pancras of Lewes*, 105.
54. *The Chartulary of the Register of the Abbey of St Werburgh, Chester*, no.18; *The Chartulary of Dieulacres Abbey*, 311 passim.
55. *CPR 1313–17*, 459.
56. *CPL*, ii, 11; *Parliament Rolls of Medieval England*, Edward I, Roll 12, 255 (245); *CPR 1313 17*, 159.
57. Woodcock and Robinson, *The Oxford Guide to Heraldry*, 118.
58. ODNB, xi, 746–50; Altschul, *Baronial Family in Medieval England,* especially chapters III and IV.
59. 'Hic rubens canis vorabit nos hodie.' *The Chronicles of the Reigns of Stephen, Henry II and Richard I*, ii, 547; Maddicott, *Simon de Montfort*, 341.
60. *CCR 1272–79*, 9.
61. *WL Edward I*, 4–94 *passim*; *Foedera*, i, 914.
62. *Registrum epistolarum fratris Johannis Peckham*, 961.
63. *Wykes*, 318.
64. Powicke, *King Henry III and the Lord Edward*, 497–8; *Metrical Chronicle*, 756–7; Blaauw, *Barons' War*, 262–4.
65. *London Eyre 1276*, 481.
66. BL Add.28206 (Scrope cartulary.) fo.11v.
67. *ODNB*, xi, 768–9.
68. *ODNB*, xi, 742–3.
69. In his career he amassed thirty-one livings, eight canonries and prebends and six other dignitaries, Altschul, *Baronial Family in Medieval England*, 488–90, *The Wardrobe and Household Accounts of Bogo de Clare, 1284–6*, 1–2.
70. TNA:PRO C 49/44/8 and 49/44/9; SC 1/14/15.
71. See above.
72. *Select Cases Kings Bench*, ii, 24.

Chapter 8

1. e.g. Those men who were his fellow witnesses on 2 December 1280 were frequent colleagues, *CPR 1272–81*, 426.
2. *ODNB*, 8, 898–901.
3. *ODNB*, 4, 265–6.
4. Christopher Harper-Bill, 'Middleton, William (d. 1288)', *ODNB*, (2008).
5. Susan J. Davies, 'Giffard, Godfrey (1235?–1302)', *ODNB*, (2004).
6. *ODNB*, 36, 604–5.
7. See above.
8. *WL Edward I*, vii-viii.
9. TNA:PRO CP 40/103 m.168; 40/105 m.168d; 40/110 m.24d.
10. TNA:PRO CP 40/131 m.242d; *ODNB*, 32, 523–5.
11. His brother and uncle were Bishops of Bath and Wells and another relative was Archbishop of York. Nicholas Orme, 'Bitton, Thomas (d.1307)', *ODNB*, (2008); TNA:PRO CP 40/131 m.242d.
12. *Complete Peerage*, iv, 322–4.
13. *Complete Peerage*, xii/2, 173–177.
14. *Complete Peerage*, ii, 375.
15. *Complete Peerage*, x, 377–82.
16. *Complete Peerage*, xi, 384–5.

17. *Complete Peerage*, i, 240–1.
18. *Complete Peerage*, xii/2, 368–72.
19. *Complete Peerage*, vi, 459–67.
20. TNA:PRO CP 40/131 m.242d.
21. *WL Edward I*, 4, 67 (55) and 72 (16–17).
22. *WL Edward I*, 58 (136), 63 (101) and 64 (95).
23. *Complete Peerage*, vii, 681–7.
24. *CFR 1271–72*, 621–5.
25. *Foedera*, i, 568.
26. *CCR 1279–88*, 67–8; *Foedera*, i, 914.
27. *Welsh Rolls*, 319.
28. *CPR 1292–1301*, 535.
29. *Complete Peerage*, xii/1, 503–7.
30. LACCE, 17/93.
31. LACCE, 25/4 and 31/37, *CACW*, 137 and 134–5; Blaauw, 'Warenniana', 117 citing Tower Mss no.1136; LACCE, 29/183.
32. *Welsh Rolls*, 319.
33. TNA:PRO CP 40/66 m.84d; 40/67 m.25d and 81d; TNA:PRO CP 40/66 m.84d; 40/67 m.25d and 81d.
34. TNA:PRO CP 40/9 ms. 60; 40/11 ms.76 and 137; 40/23 m.63; 40/27 ms.41 and 122.
35. Prestwich, *The Three Edwards*, 148.
36. *ODNB*, xxiii, 269–70;'M.G.I. Ray, The Savoyard Cousins', 148–178; Clifford, *A Knight of Great Renown*.
37. *CPR 1281–92*, 372–3; *CChR 1257–1300*, 366.
38. Ray,'The Savoyard Cousins', 148–78.
39. Moor, *Knights*, ii, 49.
40. Moor, *Knights*, ii, 44–5.
41. Moor, *Knights*, i, 74–5.
42. Moor, *Knights*, i, 114.
43. Tout, *Chapters*, ii, 168.
44. Moor, *Knights*, ii, 253–4.
45. Moor, *Knights*, i, 200.
46. Moor, *Knights*, v, 96–7; *CPR 1272–81*, 462.
47. A.J. Musson, 'Hamilton, William (d. 1307)', *ODNB* (2004).
48. *CACW*, 134–5; LACCE, 25/48.
49. *Recueil de letters anglo-francaises*, 57.
50. *ODNB*, lvi, 387–8; *Complete Peerage*, XII/II, 278–80.
51. W.E. Rhodes, 'Tiptoft, Robert, Lord Tiptoft (1228?–1298)', rev. R.R. Davies, *ODNB*, 2005.
52. Prestwich, *The Three Edwards*, 148.
53. *CPR 1281–92*, 372–3.
54. TNA:PRO CP 40/55 m.15.
55. *Complete Peerage*, vi, 171–3.
56. LACCE, 17/93.
57. *Welsh Rolls*, 319.
58. *ODNB*, xxxix, 391–4; *Complete Peerage*, ix, 276–80.
59. TNA:PRO CP 40/6 m.66; 40/10 m.50d; 40/11 m.48d; 40/13 m.18d; 40/21 m.20; 40/29 m.21d.
60. TNA:PRO CP 40/9 m.60.
61. *WL Edward I*, 75–77.

62. *Complete Peerage*, iii, 290.
63. TNA:PRO CP17 m.77; *Complete Peerage*, v, 472–4.
64. See chapter 11.
65. *Complete Peerage*, v, 472–5.
66. *Complete Peerage*, vii, 634–7.
67. *Complete Peerage*, vi, 387–9.
68. *ODNB*, 7, 136–7.
69. *ODNB*, 28, 99–100.
70. *ODNB*, 37, 973–4.
71. *ODNB*, 58, 336–7.
72. *ODNB*, 26, 350–1.
73. TNA:PRO CP 40/131 m.242d; *Bronescombe* ii, 1119, *Romeyn Register*, 26.
74. *ODNB*, 54, 630–1.
75. *ODNB*, 26, 259; Moor, *Knights*, ii, 216–7.
76. TNA:PRO CP 40/131 m.242d.
77. *ODNB*, 51, 441.
78. TNA:PRO CP 40/131 m.242d.
79. *Documents Illustrating the Rule of Walter de Wenlock*, 7, 25, 27, 36, 169 and 38.
80. See chapter 14.

Chapter 9

1. Crouch, *William Marshal*, appendix I, 195–204.
2. Crouch, *William Marshal*, appendix I, 137–40.
3. Crouch, *William Marshal*, appendix I, 142–7.
4. Maddicott, *Simon de Montfort*, 69, citing G.G. Simpson, 'The Familia of Roger de Quency, Earl of Winchester and Constable of Scotland', *Essays on the Nobility of Medieval Scotland*, ed. K.J. Stringer, 107.
5. Maddicott, *Simon de Montfort*, 61 and 69.
6. Morris, 'The Bigod Earls of Norfolk in the Thirteenth Century', 74 and 163.
7. Prestwich, *Edward I*, 91.
8. Page, 'Royal and Comital Government', 91.
9. Coss, *The Origins of the English Gentry*, 140f, and *The Knight in Medieval England*, chapter 4.
10. Morris, 'The Bigod Earls of Norfolk in the Thirteenth Century', 151.
11. Denholm-Young, *Seigneurial Administration in England*, 27–8.
12. Morris, 'The Bigod Earls of Norfolk in the Thirteenth Century', 73.
13. Keen, *England in the Later Middle Ages* (1973), 15f; McFarlane, 'Bastard Feudalism', 161–180.
14. Coss, *The Origins of the English Gentry*, 208. but see Coss, 'Bastard Feudalism Revised', 27–64. and Crouch and Carpenter, 'Debate: Bastard Feudalism Revised', 165–89, Carpenter, 'The Second Century of English Feudalism', 30–71.
15. Polden, 'The Social Networks of the Buckinghamshire Gentry in the Thirteenth Century', 378–85.
16. Polden, 'The Social Networks of the Buckinghamshire Gentry', 384–5.
17. Coss, *The Origins of the English Gentry*, 134 citing Fernandes, 'The Role of Midland Knights in the Period of Reform and Rebellion 1258–67', 331.
18. A. Jobson, 'The Knights of Oxfordshire during the Barons' War', paper given to the Late Medieval Seminar, Institute of Historical Research, 26 November 1999.
19. Ray, 'Living with Father's Reputation', 171.
20. Denholm-Young, *Richard of Cornwall*, 90–1.

21. *WL Edward I*, 4–122.
22. *CPR 1292–1301*, 574–5; Denholm-Young, *Richard of Cornwall*, 90.
23. *CPR 1292–1301*, 574–5; Denholm-Young, *Richard of Cornwall*, 91.
24. Denholm-Young, *Richard of Cornwall*, 90; TNA:PRO CP 40/54 m.67d.
25. Moor, *Knights*, i, 292.
26. Page, 'Royal and Comital Government', 91.
27. *PW*, i, 198. They were William de Alleman, Robert de Amory, Henry de Appleby, Ralph Basset, Richard Belet, Peter de Chalun, Richard de Cornwall, Robert de Dinham, Thomas le Erkedene, William de Eynford, Robert Malet, Walter de la Poyle, William de Punchardon and Henry de Ralegh.
28. *CPR 1272–81*, 211, 215 and 221.
29. *PW*, i, part 2, 550.
30. *CPR 1291–92*, 273–4.
31. *CIPM*, iii, 476 and 532.
32. Moor, *Knights*, iv, 105.
33. Moor, *Knights*, iv, 72–3; *Aspilogia*, 345.
34. St Philibert of Jumieges was a Norman saint and St Philibert-des-champs is near Honfleur.
35. Moor, *Knights*, iv, 194.
36. Moor, *Knights*, ii, 252–3; *Aspilogia*, 234.
37. *CIPM*, iv, nos. 149 and 237.
38. Moor, *Knights*, i, 52; *Aspilogia*, 33; *CIPM*, iii, 604, p. 480.
39. *CIPM*, ii, no. 78, iii, nos. 249–50.
40. *CIPM*, iii, 395; Moor, *Knights*, iv, 29.
41. Cambridge University Library ms. Mm.2.20, f.17v; TNA:PRO 36/57f.41r.
42. Moor, *Knights*, 241.
43. Page, 'Royal and Comital Government', 91.
44. Moor, *Knights*, iv, 251–2.
45. TNA:PRO E 36/57 f8v; *HMC Hastings*, i, 277.
46. *CPREJ*, vi, no 579; *CPR 1272–81*, 375; *Oxfords FF 1198–1291*, 218; TNA PRO E 36/57 f.59v.
47. *CPR 1281–92*, 70 and 91.
48. TNA:PRO E 159/61 m. 21d.
49. *Eye Priory Cartulary and Charters*, 33.
50. Ray, 'Living with Father's Reputation', 167–82.
51. *Feudal Aids*, iv, 158.
52. *CIPM*, iii, 534.
53. *PW*, i, 198.
54. *CCR 1272–79*, 511.
55. *CCR 1272–79*, 398.
56. *CChR 1257–1300*, 208 and 240.
57. *Ministers' Accounts*, 159.
58. *List of Sheriffs*, 112.
59. *CCR 1296–1302*, 268.
60. *Aspilogia*, 133; Moor, *Knights*, i, 10–11; *PW*, i, 198.
61. *CIPM*, iii, 604, p. 479.
62. *CIPM*, iii, 276.
63. *PW*, i, 198.
64. *CPR 1281–92*, 515.
65. Moor, *Knights*, i, 124; *CChR 1257–1300*, 24–5.

66. *CIPM*, iii, 604, p. 475.
67. Moor, *Knights*, i, 124; *CIPM*, iv, 95.
68. *Aspilogia*, 13; Moor, *Knights*, i, 15.
69. Page said that there were two.
70. TNA:PRO E 36/57 f.31v.
71. *List of Sheriffs*, 21.
72. *PW*, i, p. 198.
73. Prestwich, *Edward I*, 175.
74. TNA:PRO E 36/57 f.3v.
75. *CAD*, D 1129; TNA:PRO E/210/1129; TNA:PRO E 159/88 m.147.
76. *CIPM*, iii, 604, pp. 476 and 483.
77. *CChR 1300–26*, 479.
78. BL Stowe 882 fs.1r-2r.
79. Page, 'Royal and Comital Government', 95.
80. Moor, *Knights*, iii, 15–16.
81. *Ministers' Accounts*, 238–9.
82. Moor, *Knights*, v, 45.
83. Moor, *Knights*, i, 192.
84. Lysons and Lysons, *Magna Britannia*, cxxvii.
85. Moor, *Knights*, i, 99–100.
86. Page thought that were three but Page had none in Edmund's favour although that of John Redbyle exists.
87. He was remitted distraint of knighthood as a servant of the Bishop of London in 1260 but it was thought important that the Sheriff of Cornwall be notified. *CCR 1259–61, 131*. He was going overseas with the Bishop in 1261, *CPR 1258–66*, 187.
88. Page put it at four.
89. *CIPM*, iii, 604, p. 467.
90. *CIPM*, iii, no. 413; TNA:PRO E 36/57 f.20r, 25r. and 63r; *St Michael's Cartulary*, no.4; Moor, *Knights*, ii, 216–7.
91. *Feudal Aids*, i, 198 and 204.
92. *CIPM*, iii, no. 413; *CCR 1279–88*, 319 and 356.
93. *The Cartulary of St Michael's Mount*, no. 26.
94. TNA:PRO CP 40/18 m.26.
95. TNA:PRO CP 40/18 m.26.
96. *CPR 1272–81*, 29; Maddicott, 'Edward I and the Lessons of Baronial Reform', 7–8.
97. Moor, *Knights*, i, 63.
98. Moor, *Knights*, i, 81; *Aspilogia*, 46; *CIPM*, iii, n. 604, 480.
99. *CPR 1281–92*, 515.
100. *CPR 1292–1301*, 574–5.
101. *CChR 1257–1300*, 383–6; TNA:PRO E 36/57 fs. 8v., 27r., 49v. and 65v.
102. Moor, *Knights*, i, 127.
103. Moor, *Knights*, iii, 265–6; *Aspilogia*, 317.
104. Moor, *Knights*, ii, 99; *CIPM*, iii, 20.
105. *CChR 1257–1300*, 383–6; TNA:PRO E 36/57 fos. 8v., 27r., 49v. and 65v.
106. Moor, *Knights*, iv, 55; , *CIPM* iii, 339, 426 and 513.
107. TNA:PRO E 36/57 fs.25r. and 63r.
108. Moor, *Knights*, iii, 117.
109. Moor, *Knights*, iii, 160; *Aspilogia*, 294; *CIPM*, iv, 345.
110. Moor, *Knights*, iv, 289.
111. *CPR 1272–81*, 395.

112. Moor, *Knights*, ii, 269–70.
113. TNA:PRO E 36/57 fo.20r.
114. *List of Sheriffs*, 21.
115. Philipps, *Aymer de Valence,* 256, 258 and 296.
116. Moor, *Knights*, i, 114, but see chapter 8; *Feudal Aids,* ii, 6, 9 and 35 and iii, 113.
117. *CIPM*, iii, no. 31, 27.
118. Sheriff of Oxfordshire, Moor, *Knights*, i, 269.
119. *Book of Fees*, 940.
120. Also served as Sheriff of Surrey and Hampshire, Moor, *Knights*, iii, 246; *Aspilogia,* 232.
121. Moor, *Knights*, iii, 112–3. Including Cherrington (Gloucestershire) of Edmund, *CIPM*, iii, 33–4.
122. John de la Penne witnessed for Richard of Cornwall. Moor, *Knights*, iv, 35.
123. *CIPM*, iv, 79.
124. *List of Sheriffs*, 112. He drowned himself, Moor, *Knights*, v, 205.
125. *List of Sheriffs*, 21.
126. *List of Sheriffs*, 21; *St Frideswide's Cartulary*, 310; TNA:PRO 36/57 f.32r.
127. *Ministers' Accounts*, 186; *CIPM*, iii, 604 (p. 473).
128. Moor, *Knights*, iv, 90.
129. Moor, *Knights*, i, 170.
130. Moor, *Knights*, ii, 135.
131. Moor, *Knights*, v, 125.
132. *VCH Buckinghamshire*, iv, 89.
133. *FA*, i, 76 and iv, 3; *CIPM*, ii, 67.
134. *PW*, i, 198.
135. Moor, *Knights*, i, 9; *Aspilogia,* 9.
136. Moor, *Knights*, i, 102.
137. Moor, *Knights*, v, 148.
138. *CCR 1296–1302*, 69. He died in 1297 having been Coroner for the county.
139. *CAD*, B 4135; *CPR 1272–81*, 340.
140. Moor, *Knights*, i, 261.
141. TNA:PRO E 36/57 fo.61r.
142. TNA:PRO E 36/57 fo.43v.
143. Moor, *Knights*, i, 138.
144. Moor, *Knights*, v, 79.
145. *CIPM*, iii, 606 (p. 467).
146. *CCR 1296–1302*, 69.
147. Moor, *Knights*, ii, 257.
148. *CPR 1266–72*, 705–6.
149. TNA:PRO KB 27/18 m.6d.
150. He was later used by the King in the Channel Islands, *CPR 1272–91*, 46 and 73.
151. *CPR 1272–91*, 198; *List of Sheriffs*, 34.
152. *CIPM*, ii, nos. 265 and 505. His principal overlord was Henry de Pomeroy.
153. Moor, *Knights*, ii, 60, *Aspilogia,* 172.
154. *Feudal Aids*, i, 83; TNA:PRO E 36/57 fo.31v.

Chapter 10

1. *Sutton Rolls*, viii, 173 and 201.
2. *CLB London A*, 170.
3. *Ministers' Accounts*, 125.

4. *Ministers' Accounts*, 1; *CPR 1292–1301*, 608.
5. Documents illustrating the rule of Walter de Wenlock, 25n.
6. TNA:PRO CP 40/131 m.242d.
7. *Bronescombe*, ii, no. 1119; *Romeyn Register*, 26.
8. E.Gemmill, 'The Ecclesiastical Patronage of the Earls during the Reign of Edward I', 69.
9. *CPR 1247–58*, 328.
10. *CPR 1259–66*, 505.
11. Denholm-Young, *Richard of Cornwall*, 92, 120 and 153; *Registrum Peckham*, i, 169.
12. *CChR 1257–1300*, 169.
13. Braiboeuf witnessed a charter in favour of Edmund and had lands in Hampshire and Wiltshire, Moor, *Knights*, i, 137; *CIPM*, ii, no. 522.
14. *CPR 1281–92*, 14.
15. *CPR 1272–81*, 375.
16. Emden, *Biographical Register of the University of Oxford to AD 1500*, 1368; *CPR 1272–81*, 418; *List of Sheriffs*, 201.
17. *Sutton Rolls*, viii, 2.
18. *Sutton Rolls*, viii, 4.
19. TNA:PRO CP 40/58 m.8d.
20. *Oseney Cartulary*, iv, 346.
21. *Sutton Rolls*, viii, 5. He was mainperned by the *curiales*, Hugh fitzOtto and Walter de Helion, *CCR 1272–79*, 474.
22. *CCR 1272–79*, 508.
23. *VCH Northampton*, iv, 252–9.
24. TNA:PRO CP 40/126 m.177d.
25. *Documents Illustrating the Rule of Walter de Wenlock*, 7 and 28.
26. *CPL*, i, 485.
27. *CPR 1272–81*, 395.
28. *CCR 1288–96*, 203.
29. *Pontissara Register*, xxi, 16 and 40.
30. *Bronescombe Register*, ii, nos. 487 and 1172.
31. *Bronescombe Register*, ii, no. 1351.
32. *Annals of Hailes*, 109.
33. TNA:PRO CP 40/26 m.18.
34. *Sutton Rolls*, viii, 172 and 179.
35. *CCR 1279–88*, 357; TNA:PRO E 159/60 m.16 (x3).
36. *CPR 1292–1301*, 367.
37. *Sutton Rolls*, viii, 19 and 21; *CPR 1327–30*, 255.
38. *Feudal Aids*, iv, 220; *CChR 1257–1300*, 319; Moor, *Knights*, i, 29.
39. *CPR 1292–1301*, 509.
40. *List of Sheriffs*, 21.
41. *Sutton Rolls*, ii, 102 and 137.
42. *CPR 1292–1301*, 603.
43. *CCR 1302–07*, 230.
44. Tout, *Chapters*, i, 3–4.
45. Tout, *Chapters*, vi, 116.
46. Denholm-Young, *Seigneurial Administration*, 13, note 3.
47. *Ministers' Accounts*, 251.
48. Little, *The Grey Friars of Oxford*, 218; Bodleian Library MS Digby 154 f 38.
49. Midgley, 'Edmund of Cornwall', 162; *CIPM*, iii, 604 (p. 461).

50. Paul Brand thought that he might have been related to the judge, Roger of Seaton, who came from Seaton in Rutland. Personal information 29 June 2010 and P. Brand, 'Seaton, Roger of', *ODNB*, 49, 633.
51. See above.
52. Page, 'Royal and Comital Government', 116.
53. *List of Sheriffs*, 21.
54. Midgley, 'Edmund of Cornwall', 88; *CCR 1272–79*, p. 524.
55. *CPR 1281–92*, 176 and 263.
56. Page, 'Royal and Comital Government', 116.
57. He was in mercy.
58. *Ministers' Accounts*, 223, 231, 247 and 250.
59. *CPR 1272–81*, 220. and *1281–92*, 411 and 451.
60. *Registrum Peckham*, 379.
61. *CPR 1292–1301*, 145.
62. *Thornton's History of Nottinghamshire*, ii, 275.
63. *A Calendar of the Feet of Fines for London and Middlesex*, 218–21.
64. TNA:PRO CP 40/21 m.101; 40/22 m.23d.
65. *PW*, i, 198.
66. *CPR 1272–81*, 153; *CPR 1281–92*, 145, 202, 454, 466 and 513.
67. *CCR 1288–96*, 22; *CPR 1291–1302*, 257.
68. TNA:PRO CP 40/26 ms.18 and 42d.
69. TNA:PRO CP 40/26 ms.22d and 128d.
70. TNA:PRO CP 40/36 m.121d and 40/41 m.24d.
71. For the origin and development of attorneys see P. Brand, *The Origins of the English Legal Profession*, 33–4, 43, 45, 72–5, 77, and 86–9 plus the relevant footnotes.
72. *CCR 1279–88*, 357; TNA:PRO CP 40/72 m.94 etc; *CPR 1281–92*, 267.
73. *CPR 1272–81*, 375.
74. *CPR 1281–92*, 14.
75. *CPR 1272–81*, 375; TNA:PRO E 36/57, f.159v.
76. TNA:PRO KB 27/96 m.14.
77. Brand, *Origins of the English Legal Profession*, 77 and footnote 32 on page 192.
78. TNA:PRO CP 40/126 m.177d.
79. *Rotuli Parliamentum Anglie Hactenus Inediti MCCLXXIX–MCCCLXXIII*, no. 21.

Chapter 11

1. Vincent, *ODNB*, 46, 711.
2. Robert was never formally canonised. He died in 1218 and had received patronage from King John. Brian Golding, 'Robert of Knaresborough (d. 1218?)', *ODNB* (2004).
3. Vincent, *ODNB*, 26, 568–9.
4. Prestwich, *Edward I*, 111–2.
5. Maddicott, *Simon de Montfort*, 103.
6. Westerhoff, *Death and the Noble Body in Medieval England*, 59.
7. Carpenter, *The Struggle for Mastery*, 447.
8. Vincent, *The Holy Blood*, 140–5 and 150; *Annals of Hailes*, 75–9.
9. *Annals of Hailes*, 64; *Chronica Majora*, v, 262.
10. Vincent, *The Holy Blood*, 137–40.
11. Briegel, *English Art 1216–1307*, 198–9.
12. *Annals of Hailes*, 82 and 92.
13. *CChR 1257–1300*, 208; TNA:PRO C56/39 m.2 (C).
14. *CChR 1300–26*, 490; TNA:PRO C56/39 m.2 (D).

15. *CChR 1300–26*, 490; TNA:PRO C56/39 m.2 (E).
16. *CChR 1257–1300*, 349; TNA:PRO C56/39 ms.1–2 (A).
17. *CChR 1300–26*, 490; TNA:PRO C56/39 m.2 (F).
18. *Annals of Hailes*, 100.
19. *CChR 1300–26*, 2.
20. *Giffard Worcester Register*, 537.
21. *CChR 1300–26*, 490; TNA:PRO C56/39 m.2 (B).
22. *CChR 1300–26*, 490; TNA:PRO C56/39 m.2 (G), After Edmund's death, Countess Margaret sought her dower for these lands, *CIPM*, iii, 604 (p. 484).
23. *CChR 1300–26*, 490; TNA:PRO C56/39 m.2 (H).
24. Martene, *Thesaurus Novus Anecdotum*, iv, 1476.
25. *VCH Oxfordshire*, ii, 81.
26. *VCH Oxfordshire*, ii, 81–3.
27. *The Ledger Book of Vale Royal*, 5.
28. Prestwich, *Edward I*, 113; Davies, *The Age of Conquest*, 355.
29. BL Harley Charter 84 C II.
30. Oxford, Queen's College, ms. 88, f. 219v.
31. *Victoria County History of Warwickshire*, ii, 78.
32. John Rylands ms. 224, fo.238 (r–v (sic).
33. *CPR 1324–27*, 109, Bod ms. Top.Devon d.5, fo.27r.
34. *CChR 1327–41*, 169.
35. *CPR 1377–81*, 114–5.
36. *Launceston Cartulary*, no.265.
37. TNA:PRO E 36/57, fo.49r–v.
38. TNA:PRO CP 40/60 m.50.
39. *Oseney Cartulary*, v, 398.
40. *Bolton Cartulary*, CB 436, Bodleian Library ms Dodsworth 144 fs.75v–76r. The latter gives the date as 1288.
41. *CChR 1327–41*, 125.
42. *Sutton Rolls*, viii, 197.
43. *VCH Oxfordshire*, 103.
44. *Reports on Manuscripts in Various Collections*, i, 382.
45. Vincent, *The Holy Blood*, 138–9.
46. Todd, *The History of the College of Bonhommes*, 2.
47. Newcome, *The History of the Abbey of St Alban*, 301–2.
48. Coult, *A Prospect of Ashridge*, 31–3; Newcome, *The History of the Abbey of St Alban*, 302.
49. Chettle, 'The Boni Hommes of Ashridge and Edington', 40–4 and 'The Friars of the Sack in England', 239–251.
50. Knowles, *The Religious Orders in England* (Cambridge, 1948), 202.
51. Chettle, 'The Boni Hommes', 41 and 48.
52. Emden, *Biographical Register of the University of Oxford to AD 1500*.
53. Searle, 'The Calendar, Martyrology and Customal of the Boni Homines of Ashridge', 263 quoting *The Black Prince's Register*, iv, 105.
54. *Dunstable*, 305.
55. Westminster Abbey ms. Domesday f.601r.
56. *VCH Suffolk*, ii, 72.
57. *Eye Cartulary*, no.109.
58. *CCR 1288–96*, 479.
59. Medway Area Archives D. and C.Rochester DRb/Ar2, fo.15r.
60. *Grandisson Register*, i, 86–7.

61. *VCH Oxfordshire*, xvi (2011), 160; *VCH Cornwall*, ii, 32 and 164.
62. *St Michael's Mount Cartulary*, no.4.
63. Bodl.ms.Twyne, 24, p.647; *VCH Oxfordshire*, ii, 77 and v, 122.
64. *CPR 1422–29*, 132.
65. *VCH Somerset*, ii, 123.
66. TNA:PRO C 143/8/7.
67. *CChR 1257–1300*, 330.
68. Midgley, 'Edmund of Cornwall', 177.
69. *CChR 1257–1300*, 285.
70. TNA:PRO SC 8/249/12411.
71. *HMC Exeter*, 401.
72. Exeter City Archives ECA Misc. Roll 66.
73. *CPR 1377–81*, 518–9.
74. *The Itinerary of John Leland*, 180; *Monasticon*, vi, 1510; *VCH Cornwall*, ii, 155. Also Wood, *The Survey of the Antiquities of the City of Oxford*, 300.
75. Midgley, 'Edmund of Cornwall', 178–9. Professor Johnstone had noted that Queen Margaret had wanted to have the cross for herself, TNA:PRO E 101/361/3 m.1.
76. Midgley, 'Edmund of Cornwall', 177–8.
77. *CChR 1257–1300*, 240.
78. John Rylands ms. 224, fo.238 (r-v (sic).
79. *CChR 1257–1300*, 209.
80. *VCH Berkshire*, ii, 104.
81. *The Itinerary of John Leland*, i-iii, 118.
82. Midgley, 'Edmund of Cornwall', 65.
83. *Reports on Manuscripts in Various Collections*, i, 370; TNA:PRO C 143/22 no.2.
84. *Quivel Register*, 361.
85. *Reports on Manuscripts in Various Collections*, iv, 72–3.
86. *CChR 1257–1300*, 443; Bodleian Library ms.Rawlinson B455, fo.24r.
87. *Bolton Cartulary*, CB 436, Bodleian Library ms.Dodsworth 144 fos. 75v-76r, The latter gives the date as 1288.
88. TNA:PRO KB 27/37 m.24d.
89. *St John, Oxford Cartulary*, 437.
90. *VCH Oxfordshire*, ii, 150.
91. *CPR 1327–30*, 255.
92. *The Itinerary of John Leland*, i-iii, 33.
93. *CCR 1296–1302*, 448; *VCH Cornwall*, ii, 304.
94. TNA:PRO SC 8/202/10088.
95. *Ministers' Accounts*, 79.
96. *Dunstable*, 407.
97. TNA:PRO CP 40/11 m.1.
98. *CR 1272–77*, 487; *CPR 1272–81*, 240–1; TNA:PRO CP 40/20 ms.20d and 31d. In the last entry, the Archdeacon is also sued.
99. TNA:PRO CP 40/17 m.115, 40/21 m.50d; 40/22 m.54 (two cases); 40/23 m.58d. Lincolnshire, Master of the Temple (1) v Edmund re. pasture in Swinhope for 50 sheep and (2) v Edmund re. suit of Court and distraint value of 20 shillings, 40/22 m.54, (AALT Image 7568).
100. TNA:PRO KB 27/29 m.1d, 27/30 m.4d.
101. TNA:PRO CP 40/21 m.110.
102. TNA:PRO CP 40/72 m.9d; 40/91 m.91.
103. *Wykes*, 318.

104. Lincoln Record Office, ms.D. and C.Lincoln Di/20/2 m.2.
105. Preston, *The Church and Parish of St Nicholas, Abingdon*, 12; *VCH Berkshire*, ii, 54.
106. *Annales Monastici*, iv, 499.
107. Jancey, 'A Servant Speaks of His Master: Hugh le Barber's Evidence in 1307', *St Thomas Cantilupe*, 200.
108. *CPR 1272–81*, 309–10; *Foedera*, i, 568.
109. *Acta Sanctorum*, 705.
110. Flint, 'The Hereford Map: Its Author(s), Two Scenes and a Border', 35; Another witness said that there were forty birds *Acta Sanctorum*, 705.
111. *St Thomas Cantilupe*,13.
112. *ODNB*, 17, 773.
113. *Sutton Rolls*, v, 143.
114. *Sutton Rolls*, v, 176.
115. *CPL*, i, 570.
116. *Sutton Rolls*, v, 212.
117. *VCH Kent*, ii, 205.
118. *CPR 1292–1301*, 608.
119. Vincent, *ODNB* , 46, 772.
120. *CPL*, ii, 11.
121. Vincent, *ODNB*, 17, 772.
122. The possible sixth benefaction is for the Charterhouse of Witham.

Chapter 12
1. Dyer, *Standards of Living in the Later Middle Ages*, 29.
2. Vincent, *ODNB*, 17, 772.
3. Using the TNA currency convertor.
4. Dyer, *Standards of Living in the Later Middle Ages*, 29.
5. Morris, 'The Bigod Earls of Norfolk in the Thirteenth Century', 74.
6. Holmes, *Estates of the Higher Nobility in Fourteenth-century England*, 109.
7. They consisted of Leicester, Hinkley, Shilton, Deresford, Thornton and Bagworth plus rents at Gunthorpe. In addition there were the great court, view of frank pledge and other things belonging to the barony of Leicester in the counties of Leicester, Northampton, Warwick, Nottingham and Rutland together with the farms of Godmanchester and Huntingdon with the cellars and fair of St. Ives, *CPR 1266–72*, 668–9.
8. *CPR 1292–1301*, 145.
9. *CIPM*, iii, no. 604.
10. *CCR 1279–88*, 367.
11. *CIPM*, i, 719.
12. *CCR 1279–88*, 212.
13. *Complete Peerage*, xii, 2, 301; *CIPM*, iii, 439.
14. *CPR 1281–92*, 35.
15. *CIPM*, iii, 439. pages 259–60.
16. *CFR 1272–1307*,168; *CPR 1281–92*, 163.
17. *CPR 1292–1301*, 326.
18. TNA:PRO E 372/149 m. 27 and 27d.
19. The sub-totals on the Pipe Roll appear to add up to £7826 .2s.11^{1}/2d.
20. Waugh.'The Fiscal Uses of royal wardships in the Reign of Edward I', 59. Waugh used TNA:PRO E 101/506/8 to make this assessment.
21. *Sutton Rolls*, viii, 116.

22. *CIPM*, ii, no. 74.
23. TNA:PRO CP 40/13 m.14.
24. *CIPM*, ii, nos. 528 and 820.
25. *CIPM*, ii, nos. 470 and 388.
26. *CIPM*, ii, nos. 154, 98, 524 and 528.
27. TNA:PRO CP 40/20 ms.13 and 1d.
28. *Rotuli Gravesend*, 160.
29. TNA:PRO CP 40/31 m.116d; 40/31 ms.16 and 2d.
30. TNA:PRO CP 40/43 m.89d.

Chapter 13

1. *Ministers' Accounts*.
2. *Ministers' Accounts*, 69.
3. *Ministers' Accounts*, 247.
4. *Ministers' Accounts*, 222, 234, 237–8, 241 and 247–8.
5. *CIPM*, iii, 604, (p. 456).
6. *Minister's Accounts*, 243–5.
7. *Ministers' Accounts*, 55.
8. *Ministers' Accounts*, 12.
9. *Ministers' Accounts*, 1.
10. Letters, *Gazetteer of Markets and Fairs*, 91 and 241.
11. *Ministers' Accounts*, 49, 91, 218 and 241.
12. Bennett, *Life on the English Manor*, 331.
13. *Ministers' Accounts*, 102.
14. Farr, *Accounts and Surveys of the Wiltshire Lands of Adam de Stratton*.
15. *Ministers' Accounts*, 204 and 31–2.
16. *Ministers' Accounts*, 213.
17. *Ministers' Accounts*, 217.
18. In table 14.3 appendix, *Ministers' Accounts*, 6.
19. *Ministers' Accounts*, 13.
20. *Ministers' Accounts*, 31.
21. *Ministers' Accounts*, 92.
22. *Ministers' Accounts*, 31.
23. *Ministers' Accounts*, 92.
24. *Ministers' Accounts*, 85.
25. *Ministers' Accounts*, 2; *Wiltshire Lands of Adam de Stratton*, 171.
26. *Ministers' Accounts*, 188.
27. *Ministers' Accounts*, 27.
28. *Ministers' Accounts*, 174.
29. *Ministers' Accounts*, 110.
30. *Ministers' Accounts*, 12; *Wiltshire Lands of Adam de Stratton*, 61.
31. *Ministers' Accounts*, 40.
32. *Ministers' Accounts*, 69.
33. *Ministers' Accounts*, 12–3.
34. *Ministers' Accounts*, 12 and 31.
35. *Ministers' Accounts*, 55.
36. *Ministers' Accounts*, 212.
37. *Ministers' Accounts*, 12.
38. *Ministers' Accounts*, 91.
39. *Ministers' Accounts*, 95.

40. *Ministers' Accounts*, 31 and 56.
41. *Ministers' Accounts*, 155 and 233.
42. *Ministers' Accounts*, 2.
43. *Wiltshire Lands of Adam de Stratton*, 39 and 50.
44. Bennett, *Life on the English Manor*, 147–50.
45. *Ministers' Accounts*, 164.
46. *Ministers' Accounts*, 2.
47. Bennett, *Life on the English Manor*, 210ff.
48. *Ministers' Accounts*, 197.
49. *Ministers' Accounts*, 240.
50. *Ministers' Accounts*, 70.
51. *Ministers' Accounts*, 224.
52. *Ministers' Accounts*, 225.
53. *Ministers' Accounts*, 31.
54. TNA:PRO SC 6/863/4; *Ministers' Accounts*, 12–3.
55. TNA:PRO SC 6/863/5; *Ministers' Accounts*, 1–2.
56. TNA:PRO SC 6/863/5.
57. TNA:PRO SC 6/863/5; *Ministers' Accounts*, 12–3.
58. TNA:PRO SC 6/1055/21.
59. TNA:PRO SC 6/1055/21; *Ministers' Accounts*, 55.
60. TNA:PRO SC 6/1055/21 dorse; *Ministers' Accounts*, 62.
61. TNA:PRO SC 6/1089/12; *Ministers' Accounts*, 73.
62. TNA:PRO SC 6/1089/12; *Ministers' Accounts*, 74–5.
63. TNA:PRO SC 6/1089/12; *Ministers' Accounts*, 78.
64. TNA:PRO SC 6/1089/12; *Ministers' Accounts*, 82.
65. TNA:PRO SC 6/1089/12; *Ministers' Accounts*, 82.
66. TNA:PRO SC 6/1055/21; *Ministers' Accounts*, 56.
67. *The Buckinghamshire Eyre of 1286*, 461–7.
68. *Ministers' Accounts*, 15–7.
69. *Ministers' Accounts*, 161.
70. *Ministers' Accounts*, 175.
71. *Ministers' Accounts*, 234.
72. *Ministers' Accounts*, 164 and 168.
73. *Ministers' Accounts*, 166.
74. *Ministers' Accounts*, 166. His relative, Roger, had lands in Oxfordshire and Buckinghamshire, Moor, *Knights*, i, 70.
75. *Ministers' Accounts*, 115–6.
76. *Ministers' Accounts*, 195.
77. *Ministers' Accounts*, 176 and 180.
78. *Ministers' Accounts*, 170.
79. *Ministers' Accounts*, 172.
80. *Ministers' Accounts*, 242.
81. *Ministers' Accounts*, 225.
82. *Ministers' Accounts*, 172.
83. Bennett, *Life on the English Manor*, 245–6.
84. *Ministers' Accounts*, 162 and 227.
85. *Ministers' Accounts*, 167.
86. *Ministers' Accounts*, 254, 263 and 265.
87. This section draws heavily on 'The Havener's Accounts of the Earldom & Duchy of Cornwall, 1287–1356', ed. M. Kowaleski, Devon and Cornwall Record Society, new series, xliv (2001).

88. *Havener's Accounts*, xii.
89. The seigneurial ports were Plymouth, Saltash, Lostwithiel and Tintagel.
90. TNA:PRO E372/146 m.31 and 31d; *Havener's Accounts*, table 2.
91. *Havener's Accounts*, 3–4 and 23.
92. *CPR 1317–21*, 605–6.
93. *Havener's Accounts*, 24–5.
94. TNA:PRO SC6/816/9 m.2.
95. *Ministers' Accounts*, 248.
96. *Havener's Accounts*, 25.
97. *Havener's Accounts*, 87–8.
98. *Havener's Accounts*, 27.
99. *Havener's Accounts*, 136 and 151.
100. *Havener's Accounts*, 82 and 202.
101. *Havener's Accounts*, 36–40.
102. *Ministers' Accounts*, 87.
103. *Havener's Accounts*, 45–6.
104. *Rotuli Hundredorum*, i, 76–7.
105. *Havener's Accounts*, 57.
106. *Havener's Accounts*, 59.
107. Page, 'Royal and Comital Government', chapter 2; TNA:PRO SC.6/816/9; PRO SC.6/811/1; TNA:PRO E.372/146.
108. PRO SC.6/811/1, ms.2–2d.
109. PRO SC.6/811/1, ms.2–2d.
110. Page, 'Royal and Comital Government', 55.
111. Hatcher, *Rural Economy*, 188–90; *Ministers' Accounts*, ii, 224, 226, 229, 236, 249; PRO SC.6/811/1, mm.1–2; PRO E.372/146, ms.30d-31.
112. Hatcher, *Rural Economy*, 69.
113. PRO E.372/146, m.31d.
114. Huscroft, *Expulsion: England's Jewish Solution*, 76.
115. Mundill, *England's Jewish Solution*, 60–1.
116. Mundill, *England's Jewish Solution*, 107.
117. *CPR 1266–72*, 654.
118. TNA:PRO SC 1 30/39 and 45/37.

Chapter 14

1. *Ministers' Accounts*.
2. *Ministers' Accounts* 193.
3. *Ministers' Accounts* 162.
4. *Ministers' Accounts* 163.
5. *Ministers' Accounts* 162; *CIPM*, iii, 604 (p. 461).
6. *Ministers' Accounts* 21, 224, 239 and 241.
7. *Ministers' Accounts* 65.
8. *CCR 1279–88*, 463–4.
9. *Ministers' Accounts* 21, 224 and 241; Denholm-Young, *Seigneurial Administration*, 35.
10. *Ministers' Accounts* 129.
11. *CIPM*, iii, 604, (p. 463).
12. These calculations were made by Dr Andrew Spencer from *Ministers' Accounts* .
13. Vincent, *ODNB*, 46, 711.
14. N. Vincent, *ODNB*, 46, 711.
15. Roth, *A History of the Jews in England*, 67.

16. TNA:PRO C 62/69 m.2.
17. TNA:PRO SC 1/17/40. This document is difficult to read because of its condition.
18. Table 14.3A is sorted by date. Table 14.3B is another version sorted by name of borrower.
19. In table where a debt was owed by more than one person, it has been apportioned equally amongst the debtors.
20. *CPR 1266–72*, 683.
21. TNA:PRO CP 40/30 m.31.
22. TNA:PRO CP 40/60 m.52.
23. Holmes, *Estates of the Higher Nobility in Fourteenth-century England*, 112.
24. It is not clear whether he spent any significant sums on his birthplace, Berkhamsted castle, but, as his father had, perhaps this was not necessary and he did have a residence at nearby Ashridge.
25. TNA:PRO SC 6/863/8.
26. *Ministers' Accounts*, 64–5, 133–4, 224 and 250.
27. Campbell, 'Measuring the Commercialisation of Weigneurial Agriculture', 188.

Chapter 15

1. *VCH Shropshire*, x, 138.
2. *Waverley*, 303.
3. *CChR 1226–57*, 139; *Foedera*, i, part ii, 651.
4. *Close Rolls 1231–4*, 385.
5. *CChR 1226–57*, 191; Denholm-Young, *Richard of Cornwall*, 30.
6. *CChR 1226–57*, 193.
7. *CChR 1226–57*, 247.
8. Denholm-Young, *Richard of Cornwall*, 167.
9. *CChR 1226–57*, 280; *VCH Oxfordshire*, xvi, 73–4.
10. *CChR 1226–57*, 276.
11. *CChR 1226–57*, 281.
12. *CChR 1226–57*, 392; *Foedera*, i, 88.
13. TNA:PRO E36/57 f.38v-39r., cxxxvii.
14. Denholm-Young, *Richard of Cornwall*, 167; *Ministers' Accounts*, xix.
15. Denholm-Young, *Richard of Cornwall*, 167 and 169; *Foedera*, i, 88.
16. *CAD*, v, A 10842–3.
17. Ralegh Radford, *Restormel Castle, Cornwall*, 1.
18. Denholm-Young, *Richard of Cornwall*, 167; *Foedera*, i, 88.
19. There are no entries for Cornwall before 1303 but some of these entries, as well as those for 1306, are helpful.
20. *Boarstall Cartulary*, 295–327.
21. TNA:PRO E36/57.
22. *CIPM*, iii, 439, pages 259–61.
23. *CIPM*, iii, 615; *Complete Peerage*, ix, 376–7.
24. Cam, *The Hundred and the Hundred Rolls*, 262.
25. *CIPM*, iii, 604 (p. 458).
26. Cam, *The Hundred and the Hundred Rolls*, 262.
27. Cam, *The Hundred and the Hundred Rolls*, 264, 276–7 and 283.
28. *CCR 1296–1302*, 426.
29. *CIPM*, i, 719.
30. *Complete Peerage*, vi, 345; *CPR 1258–66*, 540.
31. *Rotuli Gravesend*, 160.

32. *CIPM*, iii, 439, pp. 259–61.
33. *CIPM*, iii, 439, p. 262.
34. *CIPM*, iii, 439, p. 258.
35. *Ministers' Accounts*, 212.
36. Pounds, *The Medieval Castles in England and Wales: A Social and Political History*, 82.
37. *CIPM*, iii, 50.
38. The English Heritage web site at www.pastscape.org/hob.aspx?hob_id=425399.
39. At the time of Edmund's death, Lydford was described as ruinous, *CIPM*, iii, 604 (p. 456).
40. Coss, *The Origins of the English Gentry*, 40–1.
41. Carpenter, 'The Second Century of English Feudalism', 30–71.
42. BL Harley Charter 84 C II; TNA:PRO CP 40/21 m.59; CP 40/31 m.25d; CP 40/42 m.137d; CP 40/42 m.44; CP 40/55 m.36d; CP 40/68 m.10; KB 27/114 m.9d; *Oseney Cartulary*, v, 398; *CCR 1296–1302*, 55; TNA:PRO CP 40/121 m.212; CP 40/121 m.115; *Ministers' Accounts*, 2, 14, 32, 40, 75, 86, 92, 96, 100, 116 passim, 138, 140, 144, 165 passim, 175,189,195, and 204.
43. Brand, *The Origins of the English Legal Profession*, 5–6 and 18.
44. TNA:PRO CP 40/118 m.143d.
45. Jobson, 'The Knights of Oxfordshire During the Barons' War', paper given to the Late Medieval Seminar, Institute of Historical Research, 26 November 1999.
46. Prestwich, *Documents Illustrating the Crisis of 1297–8*, 31 and no. 126.

Chapter 16

1. *CPR 1216–25*, 468.
2. *Havener's Accounts*, 317–8.
3. *Havener's Accounts*, 49.
4. *CLB London A*, 170. North's case was also brought to the King's Bench in the same year when Ralph was noted as Ralph Bynorthe, TNA:PRO KB 27/114 m.51d.
5. *CPR 1281–92*, 489, 517 and 520; *Annales Londoniense de Tempore Edwardi Primo: Chronicles of the Reigns of Edward I and Edward II*, 100.
6. *CPR 1292–1301*, 367.
7. Prestwich, *Edward I*, p. 281.
8. *CPR 1292–1301*, 367.
9. *CPR 1281–92*, 515.
10. *Sutton Rolls*, ii, 140.
11. *Rotuli Hundredorum*, i, 67.
12. TNA:PRO CP 40/11 m.1. The county is missing on the first mention but later records show that it is Devon, 40/15 m.3d; 40/16 m.19; 40/17 m.105; 40/18 m.26; 40/19 m.38d; 40/21 m.70; 40/22 m.34; 40/24 m.57; 40/27 m.106; 40/29 m.43d.
13. *CPR 1266–72*, 705–6.
14. *CPR 1272–81*, 178.
15. *CPR 1272–81*, 284, 287, 292 and 473; *CPR 1281–92*, 14, 41, 70, 91, 92 , 258, 271 and 298; *CPR 1292–1301*, 215, 218 and 553; *CCR 1272–79*, 466.
16. *CPR 1272–81*, 153.
17. *CPR 1272–81*, 238.
18. TNA:PRO SC 8/304/15196.
19. *CPR 1266–72*, 705–6.
20. TNA:PRO KB/27/114 m.11d; 27/116 m.20; 27/118 m.28d; TNA:PRO KB/27/120 m.30d.
21. *The Registers of John de Grandison, Bishop of Exeter*, 820.

22. TNA:PRO JUST 1/112 m.3.
23. Saunders, 'Administrative Buildings and Prisons in the Earldom of Cornwall', 208.
24. Beresford, *New Towns of the Middle Ages: Town Plantation in England, Wales and Gascony*, 403–5.
25. *CPR 1327–30*, 333 and *1399–1401*, 322–3.
26. *Quivel Register*, 361.
27. Citing *St Michael's Mount Cartulary*, no. 4.
28. TNA:PRO E 36/57 fo.202.
29. *CPR 1377–81*, 114–5.
30. *Oseney Cartulary*, v, 398.
31. *Recueil de letters anglo-francaises*, 67.
32. TNA:PRO JUST/111 m.16d.
33. TNA:PRO KB 27/121 m.23d.
34. KB 27/125 m.66; (AALT image 7937).
35. TNA:PRO KB 27/149 m.11.
36. *CCR 1296–1302*, 219.
37. Devon Record Office ms.ED/M/181.
38. *HMC, Exeter*, 3 no.XV.
39. TNA:PRO KB 26/208B m.6; CP 40/11 m.84d; 40/23 m.28; 40/26 m.117; 40/27 ms.128 and 145; 40/50 m.26d; 40/51 m.48d.
40. TNA:PRO KB/27/37 m.24d, 27/38 m.11d, 27/39 ms.20d and 25d; CP 40/48 m.43; 40/53 m.17.
41. TNA:PRO SC8/7/314. 1317.
42. *CPR 1416–22*, 84; BL Egerton Charter 7232.
43. *Ministers' Accounts*, 1.
44. *Ministers' Accounts*, 12.
45. *Ministers' Accounts*, 231, 234 and 236.
46. *CIPM*, iii, 604 (pp. 483–4).
47. *St Frideswide's Cartulary*, 310, White Kennett, *Parochial Antiquities*, i, 475.
48. TNA:PRO JUST 1/325 m.17.
49. *Bronescombe Register*, ii, 1172.
50. TNA:PRO SC 1/8/E593.
51. TNA:PRO SC 8/202/10088.
52. Tilley,'The Honour of Wallingford 1066–1300', 281–2.
53. Tilley,'The Honour of Wallingford, 205–6.

Chapter 17
1. *Bronescombe Register*, ii; *CCR*; *CPR*; *Eye Cartulary*, ii; *FF Cornwall*; *FF Devon*; *FF Yorkshire*; *Oxfordshire Forests*; *Placita Coram Rege*; *PQW*; *Rotuli Gravesend*; *Sutton rolls*, ii, iii and viii; *Year Books 21–22 Edward* I and the Parliamentary Rolls.
2. TNA:PRO KB 26/207-208B and KB 27/1 to 162 (1273–1300).
3. TNA:PRO CP 40/46 ms.47 and 22d; 40/47 m.1.
4. See TNA:PRO CP 40/124–133.
5. Brand, *The Origins of the English Legal Profession*, table 2.2 which has some inaccurate dates in the first column.
6. TNA:PRO CP 40/1 to 26, 1273–1278.
7. TNA:PRO CP 40/60 m.50.
8. Hudson, *The Formation of the English Common Law: Law and Society in England from the Norman Conquest to Magna Carta*, 131f.
9. Harding, *The Roll of the Shropshire Eyre of 1256*, xxix.

10. I am grateful to Professor Paul Brand for explaining this case.
11. TNA:PRO CP40/91 m.91.
12. It is possible that some of these actions were for unpaid rent.
13. Plucknett, *Legislation of Edward I*, 35f.
14. TNA:PRO CP 40/102 m.141; 40/104 m.24.
15. TNA:PRO CP 40/66 m.38d.
16. Holt, *The Northerners: A Study in the Reign of King John*, 230–1.
17. Denholm-Young, *Richard of Cornwall*, 168.
18. *Complete Peerage*, ii, 358–9.
19. *Complete Peerage*, xii/ii, 299.
20. *Complete Peerage*, xii/ii, 300.
21. *Complete Peerage*, v, 625–8.
22. *Complete Peerage*, v, 701, ix, 377.
23. *Complete Peerage*, i, 355–6, iv, 318–23.
24. *ODNB*, 20, 480–1.
25. *Complete Peerage*, viii, 48; Moor, *Knights*, iii, 43.
26. *Complete Peerage*, vii, 461–2.
27. *Complete Peerage*, x, 552–4.
28. TNA:PRO CP 40/48 m.20; TNA:PRO CP 40/20 ms.13 and 1d.
29. Tout, *Chapters*, ii, 18–20, 192–3 and vi, 6.
30. Moor, *Knights*, i, 204.
31. Moor, *Knights*, i, 224.
32. Moor, *Knights*, iii, 90.
33. Moor, *Knights*, iii, 112–3.
34. Moor, *Knights*, v, 92.
35. Moor, *Knights*, i, 26–7.
36. Moor, *Knights*, iv, 173; *CIPM*, iii, 267.
37. Moor, *Knights*, v, 99–100; *Complete Peerage*, xii/2, 230–2.
38. Moor, *Knights*, v, 76; *Complete Peerage*, i, 146–8.
39. TNA:PRO CP 40/21 m.101 and 40/130 m.168.
40. TNA:PRO CP 40/2A m.33.
41. *Rotuli Parliamentum Anglie Hactenus Inediti*, no.18.
42. TNA:PRO KB 27/104 m.35d.
43. TNA:PRO CP 40/125 m.306.
44. TNA:PRO CP 40/103 m.9.
45. Parsons, *Eleanor of Castile*, 150; *ODNB*, 18, 26.

Chapter 18

1. Rothwell, *English Historical Documents, iii 1189–1327*, 832.
2. Gilbert, *Historical Survey of the County of Cornwall* (1817), 9.
3. Powicke, *King Henry III and the Lord Edward: The Community of the Realm in the Thirteenth Century*, 734.
4. *Ministers' Accounts*, viii.
5. Searle, 'The Calendar, Martyrology and Customal of the Boni Homines of Ashridge', 262–3.
6. Sayers, *Original Papal Documents in England and Wales from the Accession of Pope Innocent III to the Death of Pope Benedict XI (1198–1304)*, no. 785.
7. Lloyd, *English Society and the Crusade 1216–1307*.
8. LACCE, 10/26.
9. *CPR 1292–1301*, 300.

10. Prestwich, *Edward I*, 115.
11. White Kennett, *Parochial Antiquities*, i, 484.
12. He cites as his source, Dugdale, Analecta Mss vol. L, fo.17, *Annals of Hailes*, 116.
13. I am very grateful to Drs Lesley Boatwright and Hazel Gray for their help with this translation.
14. Galbraith, 'The St Edmundsbury Chronicle 1296–1301', 75.
15. Powicke, *King Henry III and the Lord Edward*, 734.
16. Wood, *The Survey of the Antiquities of the City of Oxford*, i, 103.
17. Howell, *Eleanor of Provence*, 91.
18. Bémont, *Simon de Montfort*, 2.
19. McKendrick, Lowden, Doyle, Fronska and Jackson, *Royal Manuscripts: The Genius of Illumination*,128.
20. Morris, *A Great and Terrible King*, 162–6.
21. *ODNB*, 46, 711; O.H. Creighton, *Castles and Landscapes*, 72; Ralegh Radford, *Tintagel Castle*, 9–10.
22. *Ministers' Accounts*, 224.
23. Roche, *The King of Almayne*, 217.
24. *Dunstable*, 407.
25. *The Wardrobe and Household Accounts of Bogo de Clare*, 10.
26. Chaplais, *Piers Gaveston: Edward II's Adoptive Brother*, 95 and 126.
27. Maddicott, *Simon de Montfort*, 359.
28. *ODNB*, xi, 734; *Parliamentary Rolls*, 174–6.
29. *HMC, Exeter*, 3 no.XV.
30. Denholm-Young, *The Country Gentry in the Fourteenth Century with Special Reference to the Heraldic Rolls of Arms*, 121 footnote 4; *CChW*, 25.
31. BL Ms Royal 14B V. This was on display during the Royal Manuscripts exhibition at the British Library in 2011–2. McKendrick et al, *Royal Manuscripts*, 344–6.
32. Ridgeway, in *ODNB*, 26, 469.
33. Morris, *A Great and Terrible King*, 22; Prestwich, *Edward I*, 566–7.
34. Prestwich, *Edward I*, 108.
35. Vincent in *ODNB* , 46, 711.
36. Rhodes, 'Edmund of Lancaster', 235.
37. Morris, *A Great and Terrible King*, 22.
38. Bazeley, 'The Abbey of St Mary, Hayles', 261 and 268.
39. Alexander and Binski, *Age of Chivalry*, 182 and 245 (illustration; catalogue number 131).
40. Alexander and Binski, *Age of Chivalry*, 320 with illustration.
41. Verey, *The Diary of a Cotswold Parson: Reverend F.E. Witts 1783–1854*, 144.
42. Coad, *Hailes Abbey, Gloucestershire*, 23.
43. Harrison, *Cleve Abbey*, 13.
44. Harrison, *Cleve Abbey*, 13.
45. 'The Visitation of the County of Oxford Taken in the Years 1566, 1574 and 1634', 106–8.
46. In two separate windows, Sherwood and Pevsner, *The Buildings of England: Oxfordshire*, 582–3.
47. E. Clive Rouse, *Paintings on the Walls and Timber Ceiling of the Central Tower of St. Albans Cathedral. St Albans & Hertfordshire Architectural & Archaeological Society* (1953).
48. This was drawn to my attention by the kindness of Christine Bain. *Aspilogia*, vol iii, ii, 152–3.
49. Vincent, *The Holy Blood*, 1–3 and 140–50.

50. Vincent, *The Holy Blood*, 196–9; St Clair Baddeley, 'The Holy Blood of Hayles', 283.
51. Todd, *Ashbridge,* 58 and 71. See also the plates following page 70.
52. BL Add Royal 3 Dvi, fo.243r. For a description of the book see G.E. Hutchinson, 'Attitudes towards Nature',13–14.
53. Briegel, *English Art 1216–1307*, 218. See plate 82b for Church and Synagogue.
54. Sharpley, 'English Manuscripts at the British Museum', iii, no. 2, 21.
55. British Library on-line catalogue.
56. Briegel, *English Art 1216–1307*, 218.
57. Barber and Harper, *Magnificent Maps: Power, Propaganda and Art*, 79.
58. Creighton, *Castles and Landscapes*, 54; C.A. Ralegh Radford, *Restormel Castle, Cornwall*, 1–6.
59. www.bbc.co.uk/news/uk-england-cornwall-18704503.
60. Briegel, *English Art 1216–1307*, 210–11.
61. Briegel, *English Art 1216–1307*, 210–11 quoting Christie, *English Medieval Embroidery*, 78.

Bibliography

The place of publication is London unless otherwise indicated

Manuscripts

Berkeley Castle
BC A2/58/2
BCM/A/2/60/7

Bibliothèque Nationale, Paris
BN ms. Latin 10072

British Library, London
Add 28206 (Scrope Cartulary)
Add 34792A (Dinham Chartulary)
Add Royal 3 Dvi (*Historia Scholastica*)
MS Cotton Cleopatra A VII, folios 70–106; Tewkesbury Abbey Cartulary
MS Cotton Cleopatra D. III (The Chronicle of Hailes)
MS Cotton Galba E II (St Benet of Hulme Cartulary)
MS Harley 3725 (Hailes Chronicle)
Egerton Charter 7232
Harley Charter 84CII
Lansdowne 203
Royal 14B V (Genealogical Chronicle of the English Kings)
Stowe 882 (Blaunchard Cartulary)

Cambridge University Library
ms.Mm.2.20 (Bromholm Cartulary)

College of Arms, London
London, College of Arms ms.Vincent 7

Cornwall Record Office
AR/1/185

Devon County Record Office, Exeter
ED/M/181
Exeter City Archives ECA Misc.Roll 66
Exeter City Charters ECA

Dijon
Archives Départmentales ms.11H22

East Sussex Record Office, Lewes now The Keep
ms.Glynde GLY/1/5/1139 (Waleys family Cartulary; the Gaunt Roll)

John Ryland's Library, Manchester
John Rylands ms.224 (Fountains Cartulary)

Lincoln Record Office
ms.D. and C. Lincoln Di/20/2 m.2, s.xiii ex

Medway Area Archives Office, Strood
ms.D. and C. Rochester DRb/Ar2

The National Archives: Public Record Office
TNA:PRO, C 49, Chancery and Exchequer: King's Remembrancer Parliamentary and Council Proceedings
TNA:PRO, C 56/60, Confirmation Rolls
TNA:PRO, C 62, Liberate Rolls
TNA:PRO, C 143/22, *Inquisitions post mortem*
TNA:PRO, C 143/32, *Inquisitions ad quod damnum*
TNA:PRO, CP 40, Court of Common Pleas
TNA:PRO, C 241, Chancery: Certificates of Statute Merchant and Statute Staple
TNA:PRO, CP 40, Court of Common Pleas: Plea Rolls
TNA:PRO, E 13/83, Exchequer Plea Roll
TNA:PRO, E 36/57, Cartulary of the charters of Edmund, Earl of Cornwall
TNA:PRO, E 36/274, Exchequer Miscellaneous Books, *Liber*
TNA:PRO, E 101/349/12
TNA:PRO, E 101/349/26 King's Rembrancer, accounts various; Roll of Alexander de Brodeham relating to rings, 41–47 Henry III
TNA:PRO, E 101/ 361/3 Records of the Exchequer and its related bodies with those of the Office of First Fruits and Tenths, and the Court of Augmentations 1300–1303
TNA:PRO, E 101/506/8 King's Remembrancer, accounts various; Account of the executors of Edmund, Earl of Cornwall, of certain custodies granted to them
TNA:PRO, E 159 Memoranda Roll
TNA:PRO, E 210/11283 Exchequer: King's Remembrancer, Ancient Deeds, Series D
TNA:PRO, E 211/338 Exchequer: King's Remembrancer, Ancient Deeds, Series DD
TNA:PRO, E 329/191 Exchequer Augmentation Office, Ancient Deeds: Confirmation by Edmund of Cornwall of William Chenduit's conveyance of Langley to Queen Eleanor of Castile
TNA:PRO, E 372 Pipe Rolls
TNA:PRO, JUST 1 Justices in Eyre, of Assize, of Oyer and Terminer, and of the Peace, etc: Rolls and Files
TNA:PRO, KB 26 Court of Common Pleas and King's Bench, and Justices Itinerant: Early Plea and Essoin Rolls, formerly known as the *Curia Regis* Rolls
TNA:PRO, KB 27 Rolls of the King's Bench
TNA:PRO, PRO 66/3 Transcripts of Records and Scholars' Notes, G. H. de M. Plantagenet Harrison; Notes on the Public Records
TNA:PRO, PRO 31/8/140 Transcripts of Records and Scholars' Notes, Public Record Office: Record Commission Transcripts, Series II, '*Cartulaire de la Basse Normandie, ou Copie des chartes et autres actes concernant les biens et privilèges concédé*s en Angleterre à *diverses maisons religieuses de cette province; accompagnee des sceaux et contresceaux*

Anglo-Normands, qui etoi Par Le Chaude d'Anisy, membre de plusieurs sociétes savantes et correspondant de la Commission des Archives d'Angleterre.' Caen, mdcccxxxv-vi.
Vol II contains a catalogue of the MSS in the library at Avranches
TNA:PRO, SC 1 Special Collections: Ancient Correspondence of the Chancery and the Exchequer
TNA:PRO, SC 6 Special Collections, Ministers' and Receivers' Accounts
TNA:PRO, SC 9/1 Parliamentary Rolls

Oxford, Bodleian Library
ms.Dodsworth 144
ms.Digby 154 f 38
ms.Dugdale 17
ms.Rawlinson B455 (Cartulary of St Leonard's Hospital, York)
ms.Top.Devon (Newenham Cartulary)
ms.Twyne 24 (Excerpts from lost cartulary of Studley Priory)

Oxford, Queen's College
ms.88

Westminster Abbey
ms.Domesday

Windsor, St George's Chapel
Windsor, St George's Chapel muniments, ms.IV.B1 (Arundel White Book)

Primary Sources

An Abstract of Feet of Fines for the County of Sussex, ii, ed. L.F. Salzmann, Sussex Record Society, vii (1908)

Abstract of Feet of Fines relating to Gloucestershire 1199–1299, ed. C.R. Elrington, Bristol and Gloucestershire Archaeological Society, Gloucestershire Record Series, xvi, (2003)

Abstract of Feet of Fines relating to Wiltshire for the Reigns of Edward I - Edward II, ed. R.B. Pugh, Wiltshire Archaeological and Natural History Society, Records Branch, i, (1939)

Abstracts of the Charters and other Documents contained in the Chartulary of Fountains Abbey, ed. W.T. Lancaster (1915)

Accounts and Surveys of the Wiltshire Lands of Adam de Stratton, ed. M.W. Farr, Wiltshire Archaeological and Natural History Society, Records Branch, xiv for 1958 (1959)

Acta Sanctourm Octobris, tomus primus (Brussels, 1970)

Annales Londoniense de Tempore Edwardi Primo, Chronicles of the Reigns of Edward I and Edward II, Roll Series, lxxvi, ed. W.S tubbs, i (1882)

Annales Monasterii de Waverleia in *Annales Monastici,* ii, Rolls Series, xxxvi, ed. H.R. Luard (1866)

Annales Prioratus de Dunstaplia, Annales Monastici, Roll Series, xxxvi, ed. H.R. Luard, iii (1866)

Annales Prioratus de Wigornia in *Annales Monastici,* Roll Series, xxxvi, ed. H.R. Luard, iv (1869)

Antient Kalendars and Inventories of the Treasury of His Majesty's Exchequer, ed. F. Palgrave (1836)

The Boarstall Cartulary, ed. H.E. Salter, Oxford Historical Society, lxxxviii (1930)

Brut y Tywysogwon or the Chronicle of the Princes, Peniarth ms. 20 Version, ed. T.J ones (Cardiff, 1952)

The Buckinghamshire Eyre of 1286, ed. L. Boatwright, Buckinghamshire Record Society, xxxiv (2006)

Calendar of Ancient Correspondence Concerning Wales, ed. J.G. Edwards, (Cardiff, 1935)

Calendar of Chancery Warrants 1244–1326 (1927)

Calendar of the Charter Rolls (1903–)

Calendar of the Close Rolls (1892–)

Calendar of Documents Relating to Ireland, ed. H.S. Sweetman (1877–86)

Calendar of Documents Relating to Scotland, ed. J. Bain (1881–8)

Calendar of Entries in the Papal Registers Relating to Great Britain and Ireland; Papal Letters, i, 1198–1304, ed. W.H. Bliss (1893)

A Calendar of the Feet of Fines for Buckinghamshire 1259–1307, ed. A. Travers, Buckinghamshire Record Society, xxv (1989)

A Calendar of the Feet of Fines for London and Middlesex, volume i, Richard–Richard III, ed. W.J. Hardy and W. Page (1892)

Calendar of the Fine Rolls (1911–62)

Calendar of Inquisitions Miscellaneous (Chancery), i-iii (1916–37)

Calendar of the Inquisitions Post Mortem Henry III–Henry V, i-xx (1904–1995)

Calendar of the Letter Books Preserved among the Archives of the Corporation of the City of London at the Guildhall, A to E, ed. R.A. Sharpe (1899–1903)

Calendar of the Liberate Rolls (1916–1964)

Calendar of the Patent Rolls (1906–)

Calendar of the Plea Rolls of the Exchequer of the Jews Preserved in the Public Record Office, ii, Edward I 1273–1275, ed. J.M. Rigg, Jewish Historical Society of England (1910)

Calendar of the Plea Rolls of the Exchequer of the Jews Preserved in the Public Record Office, iii, Edward I 1275–1277, ed. H. Jenkinson, Jewish Historical Society of England (1929)

Calendar of the Plea Rolls of the Exchequer of the Jews Preserved in the Public Record Office, iv, Edward I 1275–1277, ed. H.Jenkinson, Jewish Historical Society of England (1972)

Calendar of the Plea Rolls of the Exchequer of the Jews Preserved in the National Archives (formerly the Public Record Office), vi, Edward I 1279–1281, ed. P. Brand, Jewish Historical Society of England (2005)

Calendar of Various Chancery Rolls; Supplementary Close Rolls, Welsh Rolls and Scutage Rolls A.D.1277–1316 (1912)

Cartularium Abbathiae de Rievalle, Surtees Society, lxiii (1889)

The Cartulary of Byland Abbey, ed. J.Burton, Surtees Society, ccviii (2004)

The Cartulary of Canonsleigh Abbey, ed. V.C.M. London, Devon and Cornwall Record Society, new series, viii, 1962 (1965)

Cartulary of Cirencester Abbey, Gloucestershire, ii, ed. C. Ross, (Oxford 1964) and iii, ed. M. Devine (Oxford, 1977)

The Cartulary of Eynsham Abbey, ed. H.E. Salter, Oxford Historical Society, xlix and li (1906–8)

The Cartulary of Oseney Abbey, ed. H.E. Salter, i-vi, Oxford Historical Society, lxxxix-xic, xcvii-viii and ci (1929–36)

The Cartulary of the Hospital of St John the Baptist, Oxford, ed. H.E. Salter, Oxford Historical Society, lxvi and lxviii-ix (1914–7)

The Cartulary of the Monastery of St Frideswide, ed. S.R.Wigram, *Oxford Historical Society*, xxviii and xxxxi (1895–6)

The Chartulary of St John of Pontefract, ed. R. Holmes, Yorkshire Archaeological Society Record Series, xxv and xxx, 1898 and 1901 (1899 and 1902)

The Cartulary of St Michael's Mount, ed. P.L. Hull, Devon and Cornwall Record Society, new series, v (1962)

The Chartulary of Dieulacres Abbey, Collections for the History of Staffordshire; William Salt Society, new series, ix (1906)

The Chartulary of the Priory of Lewes, i, 52: *The Surrey Portion of the Chartulary of St Pancras of Lewes*, ed. D Harrison, *Surrey Archaeological Collections*, xliii (1938)

The Chartulary of the Register of the Abbey of St Werburgh, Chester ed. J. Tait, Chetham Society, parts 1 and 2, new series, lxxix and lxxxii (1920–3)

The Chartulary of St John of Pontefract, ed. R. Holmes, Yorkshire Archaeological Society Record Series, xxv and xxx, 1898 and 1901 (1899 and 1902)

Chronica de Mailros e codice unico a bibliotheca Cottoniana servato, ed. J.Stevenson (Edinburgh, 1835)

The Chronicles of the reigns of Stephen, Henry II and Richard I, ii, ed. R. Howlett, Rolls Series, lxxxii, (1885) (*The Furness Chronicle*)

The Chronicle of William de Rishanger of the Barons' War and the Miracles of Simon de Montfort, ed. J.O. Halwell, Camden Society, series, i, xv (1840)

Chronicon Vulgo Dictum Chronicon Thomae Wykes A.D.1066–1289, *Annales Monasticii*, Roll Series, xxxvi, iv, ed. H.R. Luard (1869)

Close Rolls of the Reign of Henry III (1902–75)

Devon Feet of Fines, ii 1272–1369, ed. O.J. Reichel, F.B. Prideux and H. Tapley-Smith, xccc (1939)

Documents Illustrating the crisis of 1297–8 in England, ed. M. Prestwich, Camden Society, fourth series, xxiv (1980)

Documents illustrating the rule of Walter de Wenlock, Abbot of Westminster 1283–1307, ed. B.F. Harvey, Camden Society, fourth series, ii (1965)

Dugdale, W., *Monasticon Anglicanum*, i–vi, ed. J. Caley, H. Ellis and B. Bandinel (1817–30)

The Earliest English Law Reports, volume 1; Common Bench Reports to 1284, ed. P. Brand, Selden Society, cxi (1996)

English Historical Documents, iii, 1189–1327, ed. H. Rothwell (1975)

Episcopal Registers, Diocese of Worcester; Register of Geoffrey Giffard 1268–1307, ed. J. Willis-Bund, Worcestershire Historical Society (1902)

Eye Priory Cartulary and Charters, ed. V. Brown, Suffolk Record Society, xii–iii (1992 and 1994)

Fasti Ecclesiae Anglicanae 1066–1300: volume i, St. Paul's, London, ed. D.E. Greenway (1968)

Fasti Ecclesiae Anglicanae 1066–1300: volume x, Exeter, ed. D.E. Greenway (2005)

Feet of Fines for Cornwall, i, 1195–1377, ed. J.H. Rowe, Devon and Cornwall Record Society (1914)

The Feet of Fines for Oxfordshire 1195–1291, ed. H.E. Salter, Oxford Record Society, xii (1930)

Feet of Fines for the County of York 1272–1300, ed. F.H. Slingsby, Yorkshire Archaeological Society, Record Series, cxxi (1956)

Foedera, Conventiones, Litterae et cujuscunque generis Acta Publica, ed. T. Rymer (1816)

'*The Havener's accounts of the Earldom and Duchy of Cornwall, 1287–1356*', ed. M. Kowaleski, Devon and Cornwall Record Society, new series, xliv (2001)

Historic Manuscripts Commission, *Reports on Manuscripts in Various Collections*, i and iv (1901–1907)

Historic Manuscripts Commission, *Report on the Records of the City of Exeter* (1916)

Historic Manuscripts Commission, *Report on the manuscripts of the late Reginald Rawdon Hastings of the Manor House, Ashby de la Zouche*, i (1928)

The Historical Works of Gervase of Canterbury, ed. W. Stubbs, Rolls Series, lxxiii (1879–80)

The Itinerary of John Leland 1535–1543, i–v, ed. L. Toulmin Smith (1907–1910)

The Ledger Book of Vale Royal, ed. J. Brownbill, The Record Society of Lancashire and Cheshire, lxviii (1914)

De Antiquis Legibus Liber; Chronica Maiorum et Vicecomitum Londoniarum, ed. T. Stapleton, Camden Society (1846)

Liber Quotidianus Contrarotularis Garderobae Anno Regni Regis Edward Primus Vicesimo Octavo (1787)

List of Ancient Correspondence of the Chancery and Exchequer, Lists and Indexes, 15 (revised edition, 1968)

List of Original Ministers' Accounts preserved in the Public Record Office, part one (1894)

The London Eyre of 1276, ed. M. Weinbaum, London Record Society, xii (1976)

The Lost Cartulary of Bolton Priory, ed. K.J. Legg, Yorkshire Archaeological Society, clx, 2008 (2009)

Manners and Household Expenses of England in the Thirteenth and Fifteenth Centuries Illustrated by Original Records, ed. B. Botfield (1841)

Martene, E., *Thesaurus Novus Anecdotum*, (Paris, 1717)

Matthaei Parisiensis Chronica Majora, ed. H.R. Luard, ii -vii, Roll Series, lvii (1875–89)

Matthaei Parisiensis, monachi Sancti Albani: Historia Anglorum, sive, ut vulgo dicitur, Historia minor. Item, ejusdem Abbreviatio chronicorum Angliæ, Rolls Series, xliv, ed. F.Madden (1866–69)

Memorials of London and London Life, ed. H.T. Riley (1868)

Merton Muniments Selected and Edited by P.S. Allen and H.W. Garrod (Oxford, 1928)

The Metrical Chronicle of Robert of Gloucester, ed. W.A. Wright, RS, lxxxvi (1887)

Ministers' Accounts of the Earldom of Cornwall 1296–7, ed. L.M. Midgley, Camden Society, third series, lxvi and lxviii (1942–5)

Original Papal Documents in England and Wales from the Accession of Pope Innocent III to the Death of Pope Benedict XI (1198–1304), ed. J.E. Sayers (Oxford, 1999)

Oxfordshire Forests 1246–1609, ed. B. Schumer, Oxfordshire Record Society, lxiv (2004)

Patent Rolls of the Reign of Henry III (1901–3)

Parliament Rolls of Medieval England, ed. C. Given-Wilson, P. Brand, S. Phillips, M.Ormrod, G.Martin, A. Curry and R. Horrox (2004)

The Parliamentary Writs and Writs of Military Summons, ed. F. Palgrave, i-ii (1827–34)

The Percy Chartulary, Surtees Society, cxvii (1911)

Placita coram domino rege apud Westmonasterium de termino Sancte Trinitatis anno regni regis Edwardi, filii regis Henrici, vicesimo quinto. The Pleas of the Court of King's Bench, Trinity term, 25 Edward I, 1927, ed. W.P.W. Phillimore (1898)

Placita de Quo Warranto temporibus E I, II and III in Curia Receptae Scaccarii Westm. asservata (1818)

The Records of Antony Bek, Bishop and Patriarch, ed. C.M. Fraser, Surtees Society, clxii (1947)

Records of the Wardrobe and Household 1286–1289, ed. B.F. Byerly and C.R. Byerly (1986)

Recueil de letters anglo-francaises, ed. F.J. Tanquerey (Paris, 1916)

The Registers of John de Grandison, Bishop of Exeter, ed. F.C. Hingeston-Randolph (1894–9)

The Register of John Le Romeyn, Lord Archbishop of York, 1286–1296, Surtees Society cxxiii and cxxviii (1913)

The Register of John Pecham, Archbishop of Canterbury 1279–1292, i, ed. F.N. Davies, ii, ed. D. Douie, Canterbury and York Society, lxv and lxiv (1967–8)

The Registers of Walter Bronescombe (A.D. 1257–1280) and Peter Quivil (A.D. 1280–1291), Bishops of Exeter: With some Records of the Episcopate (1889)

The Register of Walter Giffard, Lord Archbishop of York 1266–1279, Surtees Society, cix (1904)

Registrum epistolarum fratris Johannis Peckham: archiepiscopi cantuariensis, ed. C.T. Martin, Rolls Series, xxxxcv (1882–5)

Registrum Johannis de Pontissara Diocesis Wintoniensis 1282–1304, ed. C. Deedes, Canterbury and York Society, xix and xx (1915–24)

Registrum Ricardi Swinfield Episcopi Herefordensis 1283–1317, ed. W. Capes, Canterbury and York Society, vi (1909)

Registrum Roberti de Winchelsey, Cantuariensis Archiepiscopi 1294–1313, ed. R. Graham, Canterbury and York Society, li and lii (1952 and 1956)

The Rolls and Register of Bishop Oliver Sutton 1280–1299, ii, iii, viii, ed. R.M.T. Hill, Lincoln Record Society, xlIII, xlviII, lx, lxxvi (1950–81)

The Roll of the Shropshire Eyre of 1256, ed. A. Harding, Selden Society, xcvi (1980)

Rotuli Hundredorum (1812–8)

Rotuli Parliamentorum ut et petitiones et placita in parliamento tempore Edward I (1767)

Rotuli Parliamentum Anglie Hactenus Inediti MCCLXXIX-MCCCLXXIII, ed. H.G. Richardson and G.O. Sayles, Camden Society, third series, li (1935)

Rotuli Ricardi Gravesend Diocesis Lincolniensis, ed. F.N. Davies, Canterbury and York Society, xxxi (1925)

The Royal Charter Witness Lists of Edward I (1272–1307) from the Charter Rolls in the Public Record Office Transcribed and Edited with an Introduction by Richard Huscroft, List and Index Society, no. 279 (1999)

The Royal Charter Witness Lists of Henry III (1226–1272), edited with an introduction by Marc Morris, List and Index Society, nos. 291 and 292 (2001)

The Scrope and Grosvenor Controversy, ed. N. Nicholas (1832)

Select Cases in the Exchequer of Pleas, ed. H. Jenkinson and B.E.R. Formoy, Selden Society, xlviii, 1931 (1932)

Select Cases in the Court of King's Bench, ii, ed. G.O. Sayles, Selden Society, lvii (1938)

The Survey of the Antiquities of the City of Oxford composed in 1661–6 by Anthony Wood, i-iii, ed. A. Clark (Oxford, 1889, 1890 and 1898)

The Thame Cartulary, ed. H.E. Salter, Oxford Record Society, xxv-vi (1947)

Treaty Rolls, i, 1234–1325, ed. P. Chaplais (1983)

'The Visitation of the County of Oxford Taken in the Years 1566, 1574 and 1634 together with the Gatherings of Oxfordshire Collected by Richard Lee, Portcullis, Marshal to Robert Cooke, Clarenceux King of Arms', ed.W.H. Turner, *Harleian Society*, v (1871)

'The Wardrobe and household accounts of Bogo de Clare, 1284–6', ed. M.S. Giuseppi, *Archaeolgia*, lxx (1920), 1–56

Year Books of Edward I, 21 and 22, ed. A.J. Horwood, Roll Series, xxxi (1873)

Year Books of Edward I, 30 and 31, ed. A.J. Horwood, Roll Series, xxxi (1863)

Secondary sources

Alexander, J. and Binski, P., ed. *Age of Chivalry; Art in Plantagenet England 1200–1400* (1987)

Altschul, M., *A Baronial Family in Medieval England: The Clares 1217–1314* (Baltimore, 1965)

Barber, P. and Harper, T., *Magnificent Maps: Power, Propaganda and Art* (2010)

Bazeley, W., 'The Abbey of St Mary, Hayles', *Transactions of the Bristol and Gloucestershire Archaeological Society*, xxii (1899), 257–71

Bémont, C., *Simon de Montfort, Earl of Leicester*, translated by E.F. Jacob (Oxford, 1930)

Bennett, A., 'The Windmill Psalter: The Historiated Letter E of Psalm One', *Journal of the Warburg and Courtauld institutes*, xliii (1986), 52–67

Bennett, H.S., *Life on the English Manor* (Cambridge, 1937)

Beresford, M., *New Towns of the Middle Ages: Town Plantation in England, Wales and Gascony* (1967)

Blaauw, W.H., *The Barons' War* (second edition, 1871)

Blaauw, W.H., 'The Visit of King Edward II to Battle', *Sussex Archaeological Society Collections*, vi, (1853), 41–53

Blaauw,W.H., 'Warenniana, Ancient Letters and Notices Relating to the Earls of Warenne, partly from original MS', *Sussex Archaeological Society Collections*, vi, (1853), 107–128

Bolton, J.L., *The Medieval English Economy 1150–1500* (1980)

Briegel, P., *English Art 1216–1307* (Oxford, 1957)

Brand, P., *The Origins of the English Legal Profession* (Oxford, 1992)

Brown, R.A., Colvin, H.M. and Taylor, A.J., *The History of the King's Works*, i-ii, *The Middle Ages* (1963)

Cam, H.M., *The Hundred and the Hundred Rolls: An Outline of Local Government in Medieval England* (1930)

Campbell, B.M.S., 'Measuring the Commercialisation of Seigneurial Agriculture', in R.H. Britnell and B.M.S. Campbell, ed., *A Commercialising Economy: England 1086 to c. 1300* (Manchester, 1995), 132–193

Carpenter, D., *The Battles of Lewes and Evesham 1264/5* (Keele, 1987)

Carpenter, D., *The Reign of Henry III* (1996)

Carpenter, D., 'The Second Century of English Feudalism', *Past and Present*, 168 (2000), 30–71

Carpenter, D., *The Struggle for Mastery, Britain 1066–1284* (2009)

Chaplais, P., *Piers Gaveston: Edward II's Adoptive Brother* (Oxford, 1994)

Chettle, H.F., 'The Boni Hommes of Ashridge and Edington', *Downside Review*, lxii (1944), 40–55

Chettle, H.F., 'The Friars of the Sack in England', *Downside Review*, (1945), 239–251

Clifford, E.R., *A Knight of Great Renown: The Life and Times of Othon de Grandson* (Chicago, 1961)

Coad, J.C., *Hailes Abbey, Gloucestershire* (revised reprint 2011)

Cokyane, G.E.C., *The Complete Peerage*, revised by V. Gibbs, H.E. Doubleday and Lord Howard de Walden (1910–57)

Coss, P., 'Bastard Feudalism Revised', *Past and Present*, 125 (1989), 27–64

Coss, P., *The Knight in Medieval England 1000–1400* (Stroud, 1993)

Coss, P., *The Origins of the English Gentry* (Cambridge, 2003)

Coult, D., *A Prospect of Ashridge* (1980)

Cox, E.L., *The Eagles of Savoy: The House of Savoy in Thirteenth-Century Europe* (Princeton, 1974)

Creighton, O.H., *Castles and Landscapes: Power, Community and Fortification in Medieval England* (2005 edition)

Crouch, D., *William Marshal; Court, Career and Chivalry in the Angevin Empire 1147–1219* (1990)

Crouch, D., and Carpenter, D., 'Debate: Bastard Feudalism Revised', *Past and Present*, 131 (1991), 165–189

Dante, *The Divine Comedy*, ed. E. Gardner (1908)

Davies, R.R., *The Age of Conquest: Wales 1063–1415* (Oxford, 1991)

Davies, R.R., *Domination and Conquest: The Experience of Ireland, Scotland and Wales* (Cambridge, 1990)

Denholm-Young, N., *The Country Gentry in the Fourteenth Century with Special Reference to the Heraldic Rolls of Arms* (Oxford, 1969)

Denholm-Young, N., *Richard of Cornwall* (Oxford, 1947)

Denholm-Young, N., *Seigneurial Administration in England* (Oxford, 1937)

Dyer, C., *Standards of Living in the Later Middle Ages: Social Change in England c.1200–1520* (Cambridge,1989)

Ekwall, E., *The Concise Oxford Dictionary of English Place Names* (fourth edition, Oxford, 1960)

Emden, A.B., *Biographical Register of the University of Oxford to A.D. 1500*, i-iii (Oxford, 1957–9)

Flint, V.I.J., 'The Hereford Map: Its Author(s), Two Scenes and a Border', *TRHS*, 6th series, viii (1998), 19–44

Galbraith, V.H., 'The St Edmundsbury Chronicle 1296–1301', *EHR*, lviii (1943), 51–78

Gemmill, E., 'The Ecclesiastical Patronage of the Earls during the Reign of Edward I', *Thirteenth-Century England, iii, Proceedings of the Newcastle upon Tyne Conference 1989*, eds. P.R. Coss and S. Lloyd (Woodbridge, 1991), 65–74

Gough, H., *The Itinerary of King Edward the First throughout His Reign*, 2 vols (1900)

Griffiths, R.A., 'The Revolt of Rhys ap Maredudd 1287–8', *Welsh History Review*, iii (1966–7), 121–143

The Handbook of British Chronology, 3rd edition, eds. E.B. Fryde, D.E. Greenway, S. Porter and I. Roy (1986)

Harcourt, L.W.V., 'The amercement of Barons by their peers', *EHR*, xxii (1907), 732–40

Harrison, S., *Cleve Abbey* (2000)

The Heads of Religious Houses in England and Wales, ii, 1216–1377, eds. D.M. Smith and V.C.M. London (Cambridge, 2001)

Holmes, G.A., *Estates of the Higher Nobility in Fourteenth-century England* (Cambridge, 1957)

Holt, E.S., *Not for Him: The story of a Forgotten Hero* (1883)

Holt, J.C., *The Northerners: A Study in the reign of King John* (Oxford, 1961)

Howell, M., *Eleanor of Provence: Queenship in Thirteenth-Century England* (Oxford, 1998)

Hudson, J., *The Formation of English Common Law: Law and Society in England from the Norman Conquest to Magna Carta* (Cambridge, 1996)

Hutchinson. G.E., 'Attitudes towards Nature in Medieval England: the Alphonso and Bird Psalters', *Isis*, vol. 65, no.1 (1974), 5–37

Huscroft, R., *Robert Burnell and the government of England, 1270–1274, Thirteenth-Century England viii, Proceedings of the Durham Conference 1999*, eds. M. Prestwich, R. Britnell and R. Frame (Woodbridge, 2001), 59–70

Huscroft, R., *Expulsion: England's Jewish Solution* (Stroud, 2006)

Jancey, M., *St Thomas de Cantilupe, Bishop of Hereford: Essays in his Honour* (Hereford, 1982)

Jobson, A., *The First English Revolution: Simon de Montfort and the Barons' War* (2012)

Kaeuper, R.W., *Bankers to the Crown: The Ricardi and Edward I* (Princeton, 1973)

Keen, M.H., *England in the Later Middle Ages* (1973)

Kennett, White, *Parochial Antiquities Attempted in the History of Ambrosden, Burcester and other adjacent Parts of the Counties of Oxford and Buckingham*, i (Oxford, 1818)

Kingsford, C.L. *Additional Material for the History of the Grey Friars, London* (Manchester, 1922)

Knowles, D., *The Religious Orders in England* (Cambridge, 1948)

Labarge, M.W., *Mistress, Maids and Men: Baronial Life in the Thirteenth Century* (2003) (originally published as *A Baronial Household in the Thirteenth Century*, 1965)

Letters, S., *Gazetteer of Markets and Fairs in England and Wales to 1516*, List and Index Society (2003)

Lewis, F.R., 'Beatrice of Falkenburg: The Third Wife of Richard of Cornwall', *EHR*, lii (1937), 279–282

Little, A.G., *The Grey Friars of Oxford*, Oxford Historical Society, xx (1892)

Lloyd, S., *English Society and the Crusade 1216–1307* (Oxford, 1988)

Loyd, L.C., *The Origins of Some Anglo-Norman Families*, Harleian Society, ciii (Leeds, 1951)

Lysons, D. and Lysons, S., *Magna Brittania*: volume 3: *Cornwall* (1814)

Maddicott, J.R., *Simon de Montfort* (Cambridge, 1994)

McFarlane, K.B., 'Bastard Feudalism', *BIHR*, xx (1945), 161–180

McKendrick, S., Lowden, J., Doyle, K. with Fronska, J. and Jackson, D., *Royal Manuscripts; The Genius of Illumination* (2011)

Meisel, J., *Barons of the Welsh Frontier: The Corbet, Pantulf and FitzWarin families 1066–1272* (Lincoln, Nebraska, 1980)

Moor, C., *The Knights of Edward I*, i-v, Harleian Society, lxxx-lxxxiv (1929–32)

Morris, J.E., *The Welsh Wars of Edward I* (Oxford, 1901)

Morris, M., *A Great and Terrible King: Edward I and the Forging of Britain* (2008)

Morris, W.A., *The Mediaeval English Sheriff to 1300* (Manchester, 1927)

Mundill, P.R., *England's Jewish Solution: Experiment and Expulsion 1262–1290* (Cambridge, 1998)

Newcome, P., *The History of the Abbey of St Alban from the founding thereof in 793 to its dissolution in 1539* (1793)

Oxford Dictionary of National Biography (Oxford 2001–2004 and on-line)

Parsons, J.C., *Eleanor of Castile, Queen and Society in Thirteenth Century England* (New York, 1995)

Parsons, J.C., ed., *Medieval Queenship* (Stroud, 1998)

Philipps, J.R.S., *Aymer de Valence, Earl of Pembroke, 1307–1324: Baronial Politics in the Reign of Edward II* (Oxford, 1972)

Pluknett, T.F.T., *Legislation of Edward I* (Oxford, 1949)

Polden, A., 'The Social Networks of the Buckinghamshire Gentry in the Thirteenth Century', *Journal of Medieval History*, xxxii (2006), 371–394

Pounds, N.J.G., *The Medieval Castles in England and Wales: A Social and Political History* (Cambridge, 1990)

Powicke, F.M., *King Henry III and the Lord Edward; The Community of the Realm in the Thirteenth Century* (Oxford, 1947)

Preston, A.E., The *Church and Parish of St Nicholas, Abingdon*, Oxford Historical Society, xcix (1935)

Prestwich, M., *Edward I* (1988)

Prestwich, M., *Plantagenet England 1225–1360* (Oxford, 2005)

Prestwich, M., 'Royal Patronage under Edward I', *Thirteenth-Century England, i, Proceedings of the Newcastle upon Tyne Conference 1985*, ed. P. Coss and S.D. Lloyd (Woodbridge, 1986), 41–52

Prestwich, M., *The Three Edwards; War and State in England 1272–1377* (1980)

Radford, C.A., Ralegh, *Restormel Castle, Cornwall* (1947)

Radford, C.A., Ralegh, *Tintagel Castle* (1939)

Ramsay, J.H., *The Dawn of the Constitution* (Oxford, 1908)

Ray, M.G.I., 'Living with Father's Reputation: The Career of Two Thirteenth-century Oxfordshire Knights of Alien Origin, Thomas de Bréauté and Hugh de Plessis', *Thirteenth-Century England, xii, Proceedings of the Gregynog Conference 2008*, eds. J. Burton, P. Schofield and B. Weiler (Woodbridge, 2009), 167–182

Ray, M.G.I., 'The Savoyard Cousins: A Comparison of the Careers and Relative Success of the Grandson (Grandison) and Champvent (Chavent) Families in England', *Antiquaries Journal*, Volume 86, (2006), 148–178

Ray, M.G.I., 'Three Alien Royal Stewards in Thirteenth-Century England: The Careers and Legacy of Matthias Bezill, Imbert Pugeys and Peter de Champvent', *Thirteenth-Century England, x, Proceedings of the Durham Conference 2003*, eds. M. Prestwich, R. Britnell and R. Frame (Woodbridge, 2004), 51–67

Rhodes, W.E., 'Edmund of Lancaster,' *EHR*, x, no.38 (1895), 208–237

Roche, T.W.E., *The King of Almayne* (1966)

Roth, C., *A History of the Jews in England* (third edition, Oxford, 1964)

Rouse, Clive E. *Paintings on the Walls and Timber Ceiling of the Central Tower of St. Albans Cathedral. St Albans & Hertfordshire Architectural & Archaeological Society* (1953)

St Clair Baddeley, W., 'The Holy Blood of Hayles,' *Transactions of the Bristol and Gloucestershire Archaeological Society*, xxiii (1900), 276–84

Salzman, L.F., *Edward I* (1968)

Sanecki, K.N., *Ashridge; A Living History* (Chichester, 1996)

Saunders, A.D., 'Administrative Buildings and Prisons in the Earldom of Cornwall', in *Warriors and Churchmen in the High Middle Ages: Essays _resented to Karl Leyser*, ed. Timothy Reuter (1992)

Schofield J., *Medieval London Houses* (second printing with corrections, 2003)

Searle, E., 'The Calendar, Martyrology and Customal of the Boni Homines of Ashridge', *Medieval Studies*, xxiii (1961), 260–293

Sharpley, J., 'English Manuscripts at the British Museum', *Parnassus*, vol.3, no.2 (1931), 18–23

Sherwood, J. and Pevsner, N., *The Buildings of England: Oxfordshire* (Harmondsworth, 1974).

Simpson, G.G., 'The *familia* of Roger de Quency, Earl of Winchester and Constable of Scotland', in *Essays on the Nobility of Medieval Scotland*, ed. K.J. Stringer (Edinburgh, 1985)

Studd, R., 'The Marriage of Henry of Almain and Constance de Béarn', *Thirteenth-Century England, iii, Proceedings of the Newcastle upon Tyne Conference 1989*, ed. P.R. Coss and S. Lloyd (Woodbridge, 1991), 161–79

Taylor, A.J., 'Who was "John Penardd, Leader of the Men of Gwynedd"?', *EHR*, xci (1976), 79–97

Thoroton's History of Nottinghamshire, ii, (1790)

Todd, H.J., *The History of the College of Bonhommes at Ashridge in the County of Buckingham, Founded in the year 1286 by Edmund, Earl of Cornwall* (1823)

Tout, T.F., *Chapters in Medieval Administrative History*, i-vi (Manchester, 1920–33)

Tout, T.F., *Edward the First* (1896)

Tyerman, C., *England and the Crusades 1095–1588* (Chicago 1988)

Verey, D., ed. *The Diary of a Cotswold Parson: Reverend F.E.Witts 1783–1854* (Stroud, 1998)

Victoria County History of Bedfordshire, ii, ed. W. Page (1908)

Victoria County History of Berkshire, ii, ed. P.H. Ditchfield and W. Page (1907)

Victoria County History of Buckinghamshire, iii, ed. W. Page (1925)

Victoria County History of Buckinghamshire, iv, ed. W. Page (1927)

Victoria County History of Cornwall, ii, ed. N. Orme (Woodbridge, 2010)

Victoria County History of Hertfordshire, iv, ed. W. Page (1914)

Victoria County History of Kent, ii, ed. W. Page (1926)

Victoria County History of Middlesex, iii, ed. S. Reynolds (1962)

Victoria County History of Northampton, iv, ed. L.F. Salzman (1937)

Victoria County History of Oxfordshire, ii, ed. W. Page (1907)

Victoria County History of Oxfordshire, v, ed. R. Pugh (1957)

Victoria County History of Oxfordshire, vi, ed. M. Lobel (1959)

Victoria County History of Oxfordshire, viii, ed. M. Lobel (1964)

Victoria County History of Oxfordshire, xvi, ed. S. Townley (Woodbridge, 2011)

Victoria County History of Shropshire, x, ed. C.R.J. Currie (1998)

Victoria County History of Somerset, ii, ed. W. Page (1911)

Victoria County History of Surrey, ii, ed. H.E. Malden (1905)

Victoria County History of Surrey, iv, ed. H.E. Malden (1912)
Victoria County History of Sussex, iv, ed. L.F. Salzman (1953)
Victoria County History of Warwickshire, ii, ed. W. Page (1908)
Victoria County History of Warwickshire, iii, ed. P. Styles (1945)
Victoria County History of Warwickshire, iv, ed. L.F. Salzman (1947)
Vincent, N., *The Holy Blood: King Henry III and the Westminster Blood Relic* (Cambridge, 2001)
Vincent, N., *Peter des Roches; An alien in English Politics 1205–1238* (Cambridge, 1996)
Waugh, S.L., 'The fiscal uses of royal wardships in the reign of Edward I', *Thirteenth-Century England, i, Proceedings of the Newcastle upon Tyne Conference 1985*, ed. P. Coss and S.D. Lloyd (Woodbridge, 1986), 53–60
Waugh, S.L., *The Lordship of England; Royal Wardships and Marriages in English Society and Politics 1217–1327* (Princeton, 1988)
Westerhoff, D., *Death and the Noble Body in Medieval England* (Woodbridge, 2008)
Wilkinson, L.J., *Eleanor de Montfort: A Rebel Countess in Medieval England* (2012)
Woodcock, T. and J.M. Robinson, *The Oxford Guide to Heraldry* (*Oxford*, 1988)

Unpublished Sources
Blount, M.N., 'A Critical Edition of the Annals of Hailes: (Ms Cotton Cleopatra D iii), f35–59v with an Axamination of their Sources', MA thesis, University of Manchester (1974)
Fernandes, M.J., 'The Role of Midland Knights in the Period of Reform and Rebellion 1258–67', PhD thesis, University of London (2000)
'The Itinerary of King Edward I', typescript kept in the Map Room of The National Archives
Jobson, A., 'The Knights of Oxfordshire during the Barons' War', paper given to the Late Medieval Seminar, Institute of Historical Research, 26 November 1999
Midgley, L.M., 'Edmund, Earl of Cornwall, and his place in history', MA thesis, University of Manchester (1930)
Morris, M., 'The Bigod Earls of Norfolk in the Thirteenth Century', D.Phil thesis, Oxford University (2003)
Page, M., 'Royal and Comital Government and the Local Community in Thirteenth-Century Cornwall', D.Phil. thesis, Oxford University (1995)
Spencer, A.M., 'Royal Charters and Charter Witnessing under Edward I', paper given to the International Medieval Congress, Leeds 13 July 2010
Tilley, C.D., 'The Honour of Wallingford 1066–1300', PhD thesis, King's College, London (2012)

Index